Smart Phone Film Making

Andrew Parry

Published by Andrew Parry, 2024.

While every precaution has been taken in the preparation of this book, the publisher assumes no responsibility for errors or omissions, or for damages resulting from the use of the information contained herein.

SMART PHONE FILM MAKING

First edition. November 1, 2024.

Copyright © 2024 Andrew Parry.

ISBN: 979-8227077240

Written by Andrew Parry.

Table of Contents

The Power in Your Pocket: Why Smartphone Filmmaking Works

Smartphone filmmaking is an exciting, accessible revolution in the world of cinema. In the past, making a film required access to expensive cameras, editing software, and an entire crew of professionals. Today, thanks to the advanced technology packed into modern smartphones, the power to create a movie is literally at your fingertips. What makes smartphone filmmaking work so well isn't just the technical capabilities of the device—it's the combination of accessibility, portability, and versatility that opens the door to filmmakers of all levels, allowing them to turn ideas into cinematic experiences without the traditional barriers.

The first thing to understand is that smartphones are no longer just communication devices; they've evolved into all-in-one filmmaking tools. With high-resolution cameras, intuitive editing apps, and the ability to upload your content instantly, smartphones empower creators to shoot, edit, and share their films in ways that weren't imaginable just a decade ago. This has democratized the process of filmmaking, allowing people who wouldn't otherwise have access to film production equipment to dive into storytelling. You no longer need to rent or buy expensive cameras, lighting, or sound equipment to make a movie. The device you carry every day in your pocket is capable of doing it all.

Another key factor that makes smartphone filmmaking so effective is its portability. Traditional filmmaking equipment is bulky, requires setup time, and often limits where you can shoot. Smartphones, on the other hand, are lightweight, discreet, and can be taken anywhere. Want to film in a crowded market, on a quiet beach, or inside a busy café? Your smartphone allows you to blend into the environment without drawing much attention. You can shoot guerrilla-style in places that would normally require permits or cause a scene if you were using large cameras. This flexibility allows for a more spontaneous and creative approach to filmmaking. It encourages filmmakers to experiment with locations, angles, and situations that might not be possible with traditional equipment.

The accessibility of smartphone filmmaking also extends to the software and apps available. Apps like Filmic Pro, LumaFusion, and Adobe Premiere Rush are designed specifically for mobile devices, providing powerful tools for both shooting and editing. These apps give filmmakers complete control over their footage, with manual settings for focus, exposure, and frame rates. You can shoot in 4K, adjust your frame rate, and even apply professional-level color grading all from your phone. This means that not only is the hardware in your pocket ready for filmmaking, but the software you need is just a few taps away.

One of the biggest advantages of smartphone filmmaking is the ability to shoot quickly and efficiently. With traditional filmmaking, setting up a shot can take hours, as lights, cameras, and sound equipment need to be arranged just right. But with a smartphone, you can simply pull it out of your pocket and start shooting. This speed allows for more improvisation on set and gives filmmakers the freedom to capture moments as they happen, without needing to plan every detail in advance. This spontaneous style of shooting can lead to more authentic performances and creative breakthroughs that wouldn't occur in a more controlled, traditional filmmaking environment.

Another benefit of using a smartphone is that it makes filmmaking more personal. Because smartphones are so ubiquitous, the sight of one doesn't put people on edge the way a professional camera might. Actors and non-actors alike feel more at ease in front of a phone camera, leading to more natural, relaxed performances. This is particularly useful in documentary filmmaking, where capturing real, unguarded moments is essential. The personal nature of the smartphone as a device that people use every day helps filmmakers build a closer connection to their subjects, creating a sense of intimacy in the footage.

Let's not forget the cost factor. Traditional filmmaking can be an expensive endeavor. From renting equipment to hiring a crew, the expenses add up quickly. But with smartphone filmmaking, most of what you need is already in your hand. The cost savings here are significant. Instead of investing in costly cameras, lenses, and other gear, you can allocate your budget to other important areas like props, costumes, or even marketing your finished film. It's possible to create a professional-quality film on a shoestring budget when the majority of the production is done with a smartphone.

Smartphone filmmaking also allows for instant feedback. Unlike traditional film cameras where you may not know if a shot worked until you review it later, with a smartphone, you can immediately watch your footage and make adjustments on the spot. This reduces the need for reshoots and helps you fine-tune your film as you go. Plus, with the ability to edit directly on your phone, you can piece together rough cuts right on set, giving you a real-time sense of how your film is coming together.

The instant connectivity of smartphones is another advantage. You can upload your film to social media, YouTube, or Vimeo directly from your device. This has huge implications for filmmakers looking to build an audience. You no longer have to wait for film festivals or distribution deals to get your work seen. With a smartphone, you can share your film with the world the moment it's finished, bypassing the traditional gatekeepers of the industry.

However, as powerful as smartphones are, they do have limitations, and understanding these is essential to making them work to your advantage. Battery life can be an issue, especially during long shoots, so having portable chargers or backup batteries is crucial. Storage space can also fill up quickly when shooting in high-resolution formats like 4K, so it's important to manage your files efficiently and consider cloud storage solutions or portable hard drives. Sound is another area where smartphones fall short, so investing in external microphones can significantly improve your audio quality.

In conclusion, smartphone filmmaking works because it removes the traditional barriers to entry in the world of cinema. It makes filmmaking accessible, portable, and affordable. With the right apps and a little creativity, anyone can tell a compelling story with the device in their pocket. The future of filmmaking is in your hands—literally. Whether you're a seasoned filmmaker looking for a new challenge or a beginner eager to dive into the world of cinema, your smartphone is the perfect tool to bring your vision to life.

From Idea to Concept: Finding Your Film's Core

The process of creating a film always starts with an idea, a spark of inspiration that excites you. But how do you turn that initial thought into a full-fledged film concept? This chapter is about discovering the essence of your idea and transforming it into the foundation for your film. Finding your film's core is a critical step that will guide every decision you make moving forward, from writing the screenplay to shooting the final scene.

At the heart of every film is an idea, but not all ideas are created equal. Some are small and personal, while others are expansive and grand. The first task is identifying which ideas have the potential to be developed into a film. Not every random thought is film-worthy, and it's important to filter through your ideas and find the ones that resonate with you on a deeper level. A good starting point is to ask yourself, "What excites me about this idea? Why do I want to tell this story?" If you can identify a sense of passion or intrigue, you're on the right track.

Your idea might start as a single image, a character, or a "what if" scenario. It could be a moment that you saw in real life or a question you've been wrestling with internally. Whatever it is, your next step is to expand that idea into a concept. A concept is more developed than an idea—it's the foundation upon which your story will be built. It's where you begin to flesh out the world of your film, its characters, and its central conflict.

To move from an idea to a concept, it's helpful to brainstorm. Write down everything that comes to mind when you think about your idea. Let's say you've been inspired by the idea of a person waking up in a different city every day without knowing how they got there. What questions does that raise? Who is this person? Why is this happening to them? Is this a dream, or is there some kind of external force at play? As you start to ask these questions, your idea begins to transform into something more substantial.

At this stage, don't worry about whether your idea is fully formed or "good enough." Let your creativity run wild. Some of your initial thoughts might be discarded later, but they're still valuable because they help you explore the boundaries of your idea. This is the time to play with possibilities and see what excites you. It's important to be open to new directions your idea might take as you brainstorm and develop it into a concept.

Once you've brainstormed a range of possibilities, you can start refining your idea into a more coherent concept. This is where you focus on the core elements of your story. What's the central conflict? Who is your main character, and what is their goal? What are the stakes? For example, in our earlier scenario of the person waking up in different cities, the central conflict might be the protagonist's quest to regain control of their life. Their goal could be to discover who—or what—is behind this strange phenomenon. The stakes are high because, without answers, they'll continue to lose themselves and their identity.

A film's concept can often be boiled down to a simple premise, something you can describe in one or two sentences. Think of your favorite films—most of them can be summarized this way. For example, "A young farm boy must join a rebellion to defeat an evil empire," is the basic concept of *Star Wars: A New Hope*. Similarly, "A detective with short-term memory loss hunts for his wife's killer," is the concept behind *Memento*. These concise descriptions aren't just loglines—they reveal the core of the film. This is where you want to get with your own idea.

Now that you have a working concept, it's important to evaluate it critically. Does it have the potential to sustain a feature-length film, or is it more suited to a short film? This is where you begin to think about scope. Some ideas are best explored in a short, punchy narrative, while others have layers that can unfold over the course of a full-length movie. Ask yourself if there's enough depth in your concept to sustain a full narrative arc. Does the character have room for growth? Are there enough twists and turns to keep the audience engaged? If the answer is yes, then you've found the core of your film.

Another essential aspect of your concept is its emotional core. Every successful film connects with its audience on an emotional level. Whether it's laughter, fear, suspense, or empathy, your film needs to provoke some kind of emotional response. As you develop your concept, think about how it will make the audience feel. What emotions do you want to evoke? If your film is about a character's struggle for identity, you might want the audience to feel a sense of frustration, confusion, or even hope. By considering the emotional core of your film, you can ensure that your story resonates with viewers on a deeper level.

It's also helpful to think about the theme of your film at this stage. What is your story really about? Beneath the surface plot, what are the larger ideas or messages you're exploring? For example, a film about a character trying to survive in a post-apocalyptic world might also be about the resilience of the human spirit. A romantic comedy could have a theme about the importance of honesty in relationships. Identifying your theme will help guide your story as it develops, ensuring that all the elements of your film work together to reinforce your central message.

By this point, your idea has evolved into a well-rounded concept with a central conflict, characters, emotional depth, and a theme. You've found the core of your film, and now it's time to move forward with confidence. Remember, your concept is the foundation for everything that comes next. The screenplay, the characters, the settings, and even the visual style will all stem from this core idea. Taking the time to fully develop and refine your concept now will save you countless hours down the road, making the rest of the filmmaking process smoother and more focused.

As you continue to work on your film, always come back to the core of your concept. If you ever feel lost or unsure, revisit that initial spark of inspiration and the emotional and thematic elements that drew you to the idea in the first place. This will keep you grounded and ensure that your film remains true to the story you want to tell. In the end, finding your film's core is about passion, clarity, and focus. When you know what your film is truly about, the entire creative process becomes more cohesive and enjoyable. Your smartphone is the tool, but your concept is the heart of your film. With a strong core, you're ready to start building the rest of your project with confidence

Developing Your Idea: Expanding on the Spark

Once you've discovered the core of your film, the next step is to develop that idea into something rich, layered, and ready to become a full-fledged story. Expanding on the spark of inspiration involves fleshing out the details, deepening the characters, and building the world your film will inhabit. This is where your initial concept begins to grow and take shape, as you start to explore all the possibilities it holds.

The first task in developing your idea is to think about the central conflict and the characters involved. Conflict is the engine of any story—it's what drives the narrative forward and keeps the audience engaged. At the heart of this conflict is your protagonist, the main character who will carry the weight of the story. To develop your idea, start by asking yourself more about this character. Who are they? What do they want? And most importantly, what's standing in their way?

Let's take an example. Imagine your initial spark is the idea of a woman who discovers she has the ability to see glimpses of the future, but only a few seconds ahead. At first, this seems like an interesting concept, but to expand it, you need to dig deeper. Who is this woman? What is her life like before she discovers this power? How does the power change her? What kind of challenges does she face because of it? These questions are the beginning of character development, and as you answer them, you'll find that your story starts to come to life.

Developing your protagonist involves not just understanding their desires and motivations but also giving them depth. Characters aren't just defined by what they want; they're also shaped by their past experiences, fears, flaws, and relationships. To expand your idea, think about your protagonist's backstory. What events in their life have made them who they are today? Maybe the woman who can see the future was once a gambler, always trying to predict the next move. Or perhaps she's a scientist, obsessed with controlling the unknown. These details help to flesh out your character, making them more relatable and giving their actions more weight.

Of course, your protagonist isn't the only character in the story. Developing the antagonist, or the force opposing the protagonist, is just as crucial. Whether your antagonist is a person, an internal struggle, or a force of nature, this opposition provides the conflict that drives the plot forward. In our example, the antagonist could be a shadowy organization trying to exploit the woman's ability, or it could be the woman's own struggle with the ethical implications of her power. As you develop your antagonist, think about how their motivations clash with the protagonist's goals. A well-developed antagonist isn't just an obstacle—they should be a fully realized character or force that challenges the protagonist in meaningful ways.

Once you've started to develop your characters, the next step in expanding your idea is to think about the world they live in. The setting of your film isn't just a backdrop; it's an integral part of the story. A well-developed setting can add layers of meaning and atmosphere to your film, influencing the tone and mood. If your film is set in a dystopian future where everyone's every move is monitored, that changes how the characters behave and what's at stake. Alternatively, if your story takes place in a small, sleepy town, the challenges your protagonist faces will likely be more intimate and personal.

As you expand on your idea, think about how the setting affects your characters and their journey. What kind of world do they inhabit? Is it a realistic, present-day setting, or are there fantastical elements that shape the rules of this world? How does the setting influence the story's themes? In our example of the woman who can see the future, the setting could be a near-future society where technology allows for constant surveillance, making her ability both a blessing and a curse. The world you build around your characters will help to ground your story and give it a unique flavor. Another important aspect of developing your idea is to think about the themes you want to explore. Themes are the underlying messages or ideas that your story conveys. They give your film depth and make it resonate on a more profound level with the audience. As you expand your idea, consider what themes are emerging. In our example, a woman with the ability to see the future could lead to explorations of fate versus free will, the burden of knowledge, or the ethics of interfering with what's to come. Themes don't have to be heavy-handed, but having a sense of what your film is about on a thematic level can help guide your decisions as you continue to develop the story.

At this stage, you also want to think about the structure of your story. Expanding your idea means considering how the narrative will unfold. Will it follow a traditional three-act structure, with a clear beginning, middle, and end? Or will it be more experimental, perhaps told in a non-linear fashion? The structure of your film will determine how the audience experiences the story. In our example, you might choose to structure the film around the woman's gradual discovery of her power, with each act revealing more about the consequences of her ability. Alternatively, you could structure it as a series of vignettes, each showing how her power impacts different aspects of her life. The structure also ties into the pacing of your film. A well-paced story keeps the audience engaged, balancing moments of tension with quieter scenes of reflection. As you expand your idea, think about how the action will rise and fall. When will your protagonist face their biggest challenges? When will they experience their greatest moments of doubt or triumph? In our example, the pacing could build toward a climactic moment where the woman must decide whether to use her power to change a significant event, knowing it could have devastating consequences.

Another part of developing your idea is to think about how your film will look and feel. This is where you start to consider the visual style and tone of your film. What kind of atmosphere are you trying to create? Is your film dark and gritty, with a moody, noir-like aesthetic? Or is it bright and colorful, with a whimsical, surreal quality? The tone of your film will influence everything from the camera angles you use to the type of music you choose for the soundtrack. In our example, a story about a woman who can see the future might benefit from a slick, futuristic aesthetic, with sleek visuals and a tense, pulsating score that adds to the suspense. Finally, expanding your idea also means thinking about the audience. Who is your film for? What kind of emotional response do you want to evoke? Understanding your audience will help you make decisions about the tone, style, and pacing of your film. If your story is a dark psychological thriller, you'll want to build tension and suspense that keeps viewers on the edge of their seats. If it's a light-hearted comedy, your focus will be on creating moments of humor and levity. Tailoring your film to your intended audience will ensure that it resonates with the people who watch it.

Building the Story: Turning Concepts into Narrative

After developing your idea and expanding on the core concepts, the next critical step is building your story. Turning concepts into a coherent narrative is where you start shaping your raw ideas into a structured form that can guide the entire filmmaking process. This chapter focuses on how to take the ideas you've brainstormed and transform them into a solid, engaging narrative that will captivate your audience.

Building a story starts with understanding that storytelling is about more than just a series of events. It's about creating a journey—one that connects emotionally with the audience and keeps them invested from start to finish. To build this journey, you need to think about your story as a series of interconnected beats that push your characters and their world forward. But how do you do that?

The first thing to establish is the overall shape of your story. This is where the idea of structure comes into play. Most narratives follow a basic structure that helps guide the progression of events, giving the audience a clear sense of beginning, middle, and end. For many films, this structure is the classic three-act model. The first act introduces the world and the main characters, the second act explores the conflict and complications, and the third act resolves those conflicts and brings the story to a conclusion.

Let's take the example of the woman who can see glimpses of the future that we developed in the previous chapter. How can you turn that into a structured narrative? The first act might introduce her normal life, showing how she discovers her power and the initial shock and confusion it brings. The second act could explore the challenges she faces as she tries to navigate life with this new ability—perhaps she begins to misuse it, or others try to take advantage of her. The third act would bring everything to a head, forcing her to make a crucial decision about whether to keep using her power or abandon it entirely. This structure provides a clear framework for the story and ensures that the narrative has a logical flow.

Of course, not every story needs to follow the traditional three-act structure. Some narratives are better suited to more experimental or nonlinear approaches. But no matter the structure you choose, the key is to make sure that each part of the story connects logically and emotionally to the next. A well-structured story will keep the audience engaged because it gives them a sense of momentum—there's always something propelling the characters and the plot forward.

Now that you have a basic structure in mind, it's time to think about how to fill in the details. A story isn't just about the broad strokes; it's about the small moments that make it come alive. These are your story beats—the key events that define your narrative. Story beats can be thought of as the building blocks of your story. They're the turning points, revelations, and actions that move the plot forward and create emotional impact.

For example, let's return to our future-seeing protagonist. One important story beat could be the moment she first realizes she has this ability. Another might be the first time she uses it to change an outcome, setting off a chain of unforeseen consequences. Each of these beats should serve a purpose in the overall narrative, whether it's deepening our understanding of the character, raising the stakes, or moving the plot toward its eventual resolution.

As you build your story, it's crucial to think about pacing. Pacing refers to the rhythm of your narrative—the speed at which events unfold. Too slow, and you risk losing the audience's interest; too fast, and important emotional moments can get lost in the rush of action. A well-paced story balances moments of tension with moments of calm, allowing the audience to catch their breath and reflect on what they've seen.

In our example, the pacing might start slow as the protagonist's life is introduced and the strange new ability is revealed. As she begins to explore this power, the pacing would pick up, introducing more conflict and tension as the consequences of her actions become clear. Finally, the third act might slow down again, building suspense as she faces the final, difficult decision about whether to continue using her ability or give it up.

Another essential element of building a story is character development. Your characters are the heart of your narrative, and their growth and change over the course of the story are what make the audience care about what happens. As you build your story, think about how your characters evolve in response to the events of the plot. This is called the character arc—the journey a character takes from who they are at the beginning of the story to who they become by the end.

For example, in the case of the woman who can see the future, her arc might be one of self-discovery. At the beginning of the story, she's uncertain and overwhelmed by her new ability. She may use it carelessly, thinking it's a gift without consequences. But as the story progresses, she starts to understand the weight of her actions and the responsibility that comes with her power. By the end of the film, she's faced with a decision that forces her to take control of her life and accept the consequences of her choices.

This character arc isn't just about adding depth to the story—it's about creating emotional investment. The more the audience cares about the protagonist's journey, the more they'll be drawn into the narrative. A strong character arc helps to keep the audience engaged because they want to see how the character grows and changes. In many ways, the character's internal journey is just as important—if not more so—than the external events of the plot.

As you build your story, it's also important to think about conflict. Conflict is the driving force behind any narrative; it's what creates tension and makes the story interesting. Without conflict, your story will feel flat and aimless. Conflict can come in many forms—it might be a physical obstacle, an internal struggle, or a clash between characters. The key is to make sure that the conflict is meaningful and drives the plot forward.

In our example, the woman's conflict could be both internal and external. Externally, she might be pursued by people who want to exploit her ability for their own gain. Internally, she could wrestle with the morality of using her power—does she have the right to change the future, even if it benefits her? This combination of internal and external conflict adds complexity to the story and gives the protagonist multiple layers of challenges to overcome.

Themes also play an important role in building your story. Themes are the underlying messages or ideas that your film explores, and they give the narrative depth and meaning. As you develop your story, think about what themes are emerging. In our example, the story might explore themes of fate versus free will, the ethical implications of knowledge, or the cost of power. These themes don't need to be overt, but they can help to unify the story and give it a sense of purpose.

Finally, as you build your story, keep the audience in mind. The best stories resonate with viewers because they tap into universal emotions and experiences. Whether your film is a small, intimate drama or an epic sci-fi adventure, the core of your story should be something that viewers can connect with on an emotional level. This doesn't mean that every film needs to be about grand, philosophical ideas—sometimes, the most powerful stories are the ones that explore simple human truths. The key is to make sure that your story, no matter how big or small, has heart.

In conclusion, building a story is about turning your ideas into a structured, emotionally engaging narrative. By focusing on structure, pacing, character development, conflict, and theme, you can create a story that captures the audience's attention and keeps them invested from start to finish. The process of building a story is both creative and technical, but with a strong foundation, you'll be ready to bring your concept to life on the screen.

Crafting the Screenplay: Writing for the Smartphone Format

Once you've built your story and shaped the narrative, it's time to move on to crafting the screenplay. Writing a screenplay is a distinct process that requires careful attention to structure, dialogue, and visual storytelling. When writing for the smartphone format, you need to be especially mindful of the limitations and advantages of shooting with a mobile device. The goal is to create a script that works within the parameters of what a smartphone can achieve, while still delivering a compelling and cinematic story.

The first thing to understand about writing a screenplay for a smartphone film is that the principles of storytelling don't change. You still need a strong plot, engaging characters, and clear conflict. However, the way you write and structure scenes may need to be adjusted to fit the strengths of the smartphone format. Smartphones offer mobility, intimacy, and immediacy, but they also come with challenges like limited lens options, lighting control, and audio quality. Knowing these factors will help guide your writing process.

When writing a screenplay for a smartphone, it's essential to focus on the visuals. Since you're working with a smaller, more mobile camera, you'll need to think about how to make each shot dynamic and purposeful. In traditional filmmaking, you might rely on wide establishing shots or complex camera movements to convey the scope of a scene. With a smartphone, it's more effective to focus on close-ups, medium shots, and tight framing that draw the audience into the characters' emotional experiences. Write scenes that emphasize intimacy—scenes where the camera can get up close and personal with the actors, capturing subtle expressions and emotions.

For example, instead of setting a dialogue-heavy scene in a large, sprawling location, you might choose a smaller, more confined space where the camera can focus on the characters' faces. This not only plays to the strengths of the smartphone's camera but also adds a sense of immediacy to the film. The audience feels as though they're right there with the characters, experiencing the moment alongside them. This intimacy can make for a powerful viewing experience.

One of the most important aspects of crafting a screenplay for the smartphone format is writing with practicality in mind. Smartphones don't have the same capabilities as professional film cameras, so you need to be strategic about what you ask of the camera. Complex action sequences, elaborate set pieces, or scenes that require intricate special effects may not translate well on a smartphone. Instead, focus on writing scenes that play to the strengths of the format—scenes that emphasize character interactions, strong visuals, and simple, effective action.

For example, if your film involves a chase scene, you might write it in a way that focuses more on the tension and suspense of the moment rather than on large-scale stunts. A chase scene filmed on a smartphone might involve quick cuts between close-ups of the characters' faces, their feet pounding the pavement, and the environment rushing past them. By emphasizing the smaller, more intimate details of the chase, you can create a sense of urgency without needing to rely on sweeping camera movements or expensive special effects.

In addition to writing with practicality in mind, it's important to consider the locations you'll be using. Because smartphones are portable and discreet, they allow you to film in places that might be off-limits to traditional film crews. When writing your screenplay, think about how you can take advantage of this mobility. Write scenes that can be shot in real-world locations—streets, parks, coffee shops, apartments—without needing to build elaborate sets or secure filming permits. Guerrilla-style filmmaking is one of the strengths of smartphone filmmaking, and writing your screenplay with this in mind can help you create a film that feels spontaneous and authentic.

For instance, if your protagonist is a street performer trying to make it in a big city, you could write scenes that take place in real, bustling public spaces. Instead of relying on a controlled set, you can use the unpredictability of the environment to your advantage. The background noise, the passersby, and the natural light can all add to the realism of the scene. Writing your screenplay to fit locations that are easily accessible with a smartphone will save you time, money, and effort during production.

Another consideration when crafting the screenplay is sound. Sound is often the most challenging aspect of smartphone filmmaking because smartphones typically don't have the same high-quality microphones as professional cameras. As a result, you'll need to be mindful of how sound is handled in your screenplay. Avoid writing scenes that rely heavily on dialogue in noisy environments unless you plan to use external microphones or dub the audio later. You can also use sound strategically by incorporating moments of silence, ambient noise, or sound design elements that don't require pristine audio quality.

For example, instead of relying on long, exposition-heavy dialogue scenes, you could write visual storytelling moments where the characters' actions and the environment convey the necessary information. Show, don't tell. This not only helps overcome the limitations of smartphone sound recording but also makes your film more visually engaging. In scenes where dialogue is crucial, write them in quieter settings where you can better control the sound, or plan to record dialogue separately and add it during post-production.

Editing is another aspect you should consider while writing. Since smartphones allow for on-the-go shooting, it's helpful to write with the editing process in mind. Keep your scenes short and punchy, making it easier to piece them together during editing. The mobile filmmaking process lends itself well to fast cuts, snappy transitions, and dynamic pacing. When writing your screenplay, think about how each scene will flow into the next. Are there natural transitions between locations and actions? Does the dialogue flow smoothly, or will it require heavy editing to make it work?

Incorporating editing apps and tools available for smartphones, like LumaFusion or Adobe Premiere Rush, into your workflow can also influence how you write your screenplay. For instance, if you know you'll be using a particular app for color grading or special effects, you can write scenes that take advantage of those tools. Writing with the editing process in mind ensures that your film will have a cohesive, polished feel, even if it's made on a smartphone.

In terms of dialogue, writing for a smartphone film often means focusing on brevity. Because smartphone films tend to emphasize visual storytelling, the dialogue should be sharp and to the point. Avoid lengthy monologues or expository speeches unless they're absolutely necessary. Instead, aim for concise, impactful lines that get straight to the heart of the matter. The advantage of smartphone filmmaking is that the camera can get so close to the actors that even the smallest expressions and gestures can carry a lot of weight. Let the visuals do as much of the storytelling as possible, and use dialogue to enhance the emotional depth of the scenes rather than explain what's happening.

Lastly, when crafting your screenplay, think about the themes and tone of your film. Smartphone filmmaking naturally lends itself to certain styles and genres, particularly those that feel raw, personal, and immediate. Films shot on smartphones often have a more intimate, handheld feel, which can work well for character-driven stories, documentaries, or films with a "fly-on-the-wall" aesthetic. Write with this in mind, and tailor your tone to the strengths of the smartphone format. Whether your story is a gritty drama, a light-hearted comedy, or a tense thriller, let the immediacy of the smartphone's camera enhance the mood you're trying to create.

In conclusion, writing a screenplay for smartphone filmmaking requires a blend of traditional storytelling skills and an understanding of the medium's unique strengths and limitations. By focusing on practical, visual storytelling, using real-world locations, crafting concise dialogue, and keeping the editing process in mind, you can create a screenplay that works perfectly for the smartphone format. Embrace the limitations of the device and let them inspire creative solutions, making your film feel fresh, authentic, and deeply connected to the audience. With a well-crafted screenplay, you'll be ready to bring your smartphone film to life in a way that's both professional and personal.

Planning the Shoot: Organizing a Mobile Film Production

Once you've completed your screenplay, the next critical step is planning the shoot. Organizing a mobile film production requires careful attention to detail and an understanding of how to maximize the unique advantages of smartphone filmmaking. While the process may differ slightly from traditional film shoots, the principles remain the same: preparation is key to ensuring that the actual filming goes smoothly, efficiently, and creatively.

The first step in planning your shoot is breaking down your screenplay. This involves going through your script and identifying the various elements required for each scene. You'll need to look at everything, from the locations and props to the costumes, characters, and special effects. A thorough breakdown will help you identify what you need to have on hand for each day of shooting, allowing you to organize your production in the most efficient way possible. You can do this manually or use filmmaking software designed for script breakdowns, even on a smartphone.

Once you've broken down the screenplay, the next step is creating a shooting schedule. This schedule will serve as the roadmap for your entire production. When creating your schedule, it's important to think about several factors, such as the availability of actors and locations, the order in which scenes need to be shot, and how to make the most efficient use of your time. Since smartphones allow for more flexibility in terms of mobility and ease of use, you have the advantage of being able to shoot more spontaneously, but a well-organized schedule will still keep things running smoothly.

When creating your shooting schedule, it's important to consider the time of day for each scene. Since smartphones are more sensitive to lighting conditions than traditional film cameras, you'll want to schedule exterior scenes for times of day when you can take advantage of natural light. Early morning or late afternoon light is often ideal for outdoor scenes, as it provides soft, even lighting without the harsh shadows of midday. For interior scenes, think about how you can control the lighting to achieve the desired look. Portable lighting kits for smartphones are a great investment, but you can also get creative with lamps, natural light through windows, and even DIY lighting solutions like reflectors or white boards to bounce light where you need it.

Another key consideration in planning your shoot is the location. Since smartphones offer greater flexibility than traditional film cameras, you can shoot in locations that might be difficult or impractical for a full film crew. However, this doesn't mean you should just start filming anywhere without a plan. Scouting locations in advance is essential to ensure that the spaces fit the tone and look of your film. When choosing locations, think about the setting, the availability of power sources for charging your equipment, and the potential for ambient noise, which could interfere with sound recording.

One of the advantages of shooting with a smartphone is the ability to film in public places more easily and with less disruption. You can blend into the environment in ways that larger film crews cannot, which can be especially useful for guerrilla-style filmmaking. But even though smartphones are less conspicuous, you still need to respect location regulations, so check if you need permits for certain areas, especially if your production involves significant equipment or blocking traffic. Keep in mind that public spaces can be unpredictable, so have backup locations in mind in case your original plan falls through.

Organizing your crew is another important part of planning your mobile film production. While a smartphone film typically requires fewer people than a traditional film shoot, you'll still need a small, dedicated team to help with various tasks. For example, you'll likely need someone to handle sound, someone to manage lighting, and someone to assist with directing or acting as a second set of eyes for continuity and camera framing. Since smartphone filmmaking often relies on a smaller crew, you may find yourself wearing multiple hats—directing, shooting, and editing, for example—so plan your roles carefully to ensure you have the support you need to stay focused on the creative aspects of filmmaking.

If you're working with a cast, you'll need to organize rehearsals ahead of time. Even though smartphone filmmaking allows for more spontaneity, having your actors rehearse their scenes before shooting will save you time on set. It's particularly important to rehearse blocking—the actors' movement within the scene—since smartphone cameras often work best when they're in close quarters or when movement is minimal. This will help you determine how to frame the action and ensure that your shots are dynamic even within the constraints of the smaller screen size.

Another aspect of planning your shoot is preparing your equipment. Smartphones are versatile and capable, but they still benefit from some added tools to make the filmmaking process smoother and more professional. Invest in accessories like a gimbal or stabilizer for smooth tracking shots, external microphones for better sound quality, and portable lights for scenes shot in low-light conditions. If your film requires more elaborate shots, such as aerial views or crane movements, consider using a drone or creative DIY rigs that work with smartphones. Test all your equipment ahead of time to make sure it works properly and that you're familiar with how to use it on set.

Battery life and storage are two critical factors you'll need to manage during your shoot. Shooting video on a smartphone, especially in high-resolution formats like 4K, can quickly drain your phone's battery and eat up storage space. Be sure to have multiple backup batteries or portable chargers on hand, and consider using external storage options, such as cloud services or portable hard drives, to offload footage throughout the day. This will prevent any interruptions in filming due to low battery or insufficient storage. Also, be mindful of file organization as you transfer footage—label files clearly to avoid confusion during the editing process.

Once you have your equipment and crew ready, it's time to think about contingency plans. Every film shoot, no matter how well planned, is susceptible to unforeseen challenges. Whether it's bad weather, technical difficulties, or a last-minute location change, being prepared for unexpected events is crucial. Build flexibility into your shooting schedule, and have alternative shooting locations and backup equipment ready in case something goes wrong. By anticipating potential issues and having solutions in place, you can keep the production moving smoothly, even when things don't go as planned.

Finally, consider the post-production process as you plan your shoot. The way you capture footage on set will directly impact how easy or difficult the editing process is later. To make things easier in post-production, try to shoot with editing in mind. Pay attention to continuity between shots, ensure that your framing is consistent, and capture enough B-roll (supplemental footage) to give yourself options during editing. Organize your shots so that you can easily find and assemble them when you start working with your editing software. If you know you'll be using a particular editing app, familiarize yourself with its features ahead of time so you can shoot in a way that makes the editing process smoother.

In conclusion, planning a mobile film production involves many of the same elements as traditional filmmaking but with a focus on the unique advantages and limitations of the smartphone format. By carefully organizing your shoot, breaking down your screenplay, scheduling scenes efficiently, scouting locations, preparing your crew, managing equipment, and anticipating challenges, you can ensure that your production runs smoothly and stays on track. Smartphone filmmaking allows for incredible creative freedom and flexibility, but that freedom only works when you have a solid plan in place. With proper preparation, you'll be ready to bring your vision to life, all from the palm of your hand.

Choosing Your Genre: Finding the Right Tone for Your Film

Choosing the right genre is one of the most critical decisions you'll make when creating a film, especially when working within the constraints of smartphone filmmaking. The genre sets the tone for your entire project and influences everything from the writing and directing style to the visuals, sound, and pacing. It defines the kind of emotional experience you want to give your audience, whether it's suspenseful, humorous, heartwarming, or thrilling. In this chapter, we'll explore how to choose the right genre for your film and find the tone that best suits both your story and the medium of smartphone filmmaking.

The first step in choosing your genre is looking at the story you've developed and asking yourself what emotional reaction you want to evoke in the audience. Do you want them to laugh, cry, or sit on the edge of their seats? Is your story driven by action, emotions, or intellectual intrigue? Your answers to these questions will help point you toward the right genre. For example, if your story centers around a protagonist trying to solve a mystery or uncover hidden truths, you may be leaning toward the mystery or thriller genres. If your film explores relationships and emotional growth, you might consider a drama or romance.

When selecting a genre, it's essential to consider how it pairs with the unique strengths of smartphone filmmaking. Different genres lend themselves better to the intimacy, mobility, and raw authenticity that smartphones can capture. For example, smartphone filmmaking is particularly well-suited to genres like drama, documentary, and thriller, where close-ups, real-world locations, and a sense of immediacy enhance the storytelling. Let's explore how some genres might work within the smartphone format:

Drama

Drama is an ideal genre for smartphone filmmaking because it often focuses on character-driven stories, emotional arcs, and realistic settings. With a smartphone, you can easily capture intimate moments between characters, using close-up shots to highlight subtle facial expressions and emotional nuances. The portability of smartphones also allows for more natural and spontaneous performances, as actors can feel less restricted by the presence of large cameras and crews.

If your story is about personal struggles, family dynamics, or emotional growth, a drama might be the right genre for you. The smartphone's ability to film in everyday locations—homes, streets, parks—gives the film a more grounded and authentic feel, which is perfect for drama. Additionally, smartphones excel at capturing raw and unpolished moments, which can add a layer of realism that enhances the emotional weight of your film.

Thriller

Thrillers are another genre that pairs well with smartphone filmmaking, thanks to the camera's ability to get up close and create a sense of tension and immediacy. In a thriller, the audience is often on edge, waiting for the next unexpected twist or revelation. The smartphone's portability allows for dynamic shots—whether you're filming a chase sequence, a suspenseful conversation, or a sudden surprise. The fact that smartphones can shoot in real-world locations with minimal setup makes it easier to capture fast-paced or tense scenes without the need for elaborate camera rigs.

In a thriller, the tone is crucial. The atmosphere needs to be gripping, filled with suspense, and sometimes unsettling. Smartphones can help you achieve this tone through their natural handheld look, which creates a sense of instability and unpredictability. Shooting scenes with handheld motion or tight close-ups can increase the tension, making the audience feel as though they're right there with the characters, experiencing the fear or anxiety firsthand.

Horror

Horror films often rely on the audience's fear of the unknown, and smartphone filmmaking can amplify this effect. The handheld, often shaky quality of smartphone footage can make horror scenes feel more visceral and real, much like found-footage horror films such as *The Blair Witch Project* or *Paranormal Activity*. If your film involves a lurking danger, supernatural events, or psychological terror, the immediacy of smartphone footage can intensify the scares.

In horror, lighting and sound are key to building tension, and while smartphones may not have the best low-light capabilities compared to professional cameras, you can use creative lighting setups to enhance the atmosphere. For example, the dim glow of a flashlight or the flickering of a candle can create eerie shadows and contribute to the unsettling tone of a horror film. Sound design is equally important—creaking doors, distant whispers, or sudden loud noises can be added in post-production to heighten the fear factor.

Documentary

Smartphones are an excellent tool for documentary filmmaking. Their small size and unobtrusiveness make it easy to capture real-life moments without disrupting the natural flow of events. Whether you're filming interviews, following someone's daily life, or documenting an event, a smartphone allows you to get closer to your subjects and capture authentic, unguarded moments.

Documentaries often require a balance between planned shots and spontaneous filming, which is where smartphones excel. You can quickly switch from one location to another, capturing footage on the go, and record interviews in spaces where a full film crew might not fit. The tone of a documentary can range from educational and informative to emotional and intimate, depending on the subject matter. Smartphones allow for a more personal, handheld feel, which is perfect for documentaries that aim to tell human stories up close.

Comedy

Comedy is a genre that relies heavily on timing, both in dialogue and in visual gags. Smartphones can work well for comedy, especially if you're going for a light, quick, and modern feel. The casual, almost homemade look of smartphone footage can enhance comedic situations, making them feel more relatable to modern audiences who are accustomed to watching videos on their phones.

If your film involves quirky characters, witty dialogue, or humorous situations that arise in everyday life, comedy might be the right genre for your project. The key to shooting comedy with a smartphone is to make sure that the humor translates visually. Think about how you can use framing, editing, and even the portability of the smartphone to capture humorous reactions or visual punchlines. Smartphone filmmaking allows for quick, off-the-cuff shooting, which can be perfect for capturing spontaneous moments of humor.

Experimental

If your film idea doesn't fit neatly into any one genre or if you're drawn to more avant-garde, non-traditional storytelling methods, an experimental film might be the way to go. Smartphone filmmaking lends itself well to experimentation because it removes many of the barriers that typically restrict traditional filmmakers. With a smartphone, you can shoot in unusual places, use unconventional camera angles, or play with the visual style in ways that would be more difficult with larger cameras.

An experimental film gives you the freedom to break the rules of narrative structure, genre, or even visual storytelling. You might combine elements from multiple genres or create something entirely unique. For example, you could use a mix of handheld footage, animation, and voiceover to create a surreal and abstract narrative. The limitations of the smartphone's camera can also inspire creativity—perhaps you choose to film entirely in extreme close-ups or use apps to create visual distortions. In this genre, tone and mood are often created through unconventional means, allowing for artistic expression beyond the confines of traditional genres.

Action

Action films are often associated with big-budget productions, elaborate stunts, and complex choreography, but that doesn't mean you can't create an exciting action film on a smartphone. While you may not be able to pull off large-scale explosions or car chases, you can focus on smaller, more contained action sequences that still pack a punch. Smartphone filmmaking allows you to capture quick, dynamic shots, which can be used to create fast-paced action scenes. Fight sequences, for example, can be shot in tight spaces with rapid cuts to give the impression of intensity and speed. Handheld shots can also add to the chaotic feel of an action scene, making the audience feel like they're in the middle of the fight. The key is to work within the limitations of the smartphone while still delivering high-energy moments that thrill the audience.

Romance

If your story is focused on relationships, emotional connections, and love, romance is the genre to explore. Romance films often rely on intimate moments between characters, and smartphones are great for capturing these close, personal scenes. With the ability to film in everyday locations and focus on small, meaningful gestures, smartphones allow you to create a romance film that feels grounded and genuine.

The tone of a romance film can vary from lighthearted and fun to serious and emotional. With a smartphone, you can capture the subtle moments that define romantic relationships—the glances, the touch of a hand, the quiet conversations. The handheld feel of a smartphone film can make the romance feel more personal, drawing the audience into the emotional world of the characters.

In conclusion, choosing your genre is a crucial step in shaping your film, as it sets the tone and influences every aspect of the filmmaking process. Whether you're drawn to the intimacy of drama, the suspense of a thriller, the scares of horror, or the lightness of comedy, the genre you choose should align with both your story and the strengths of smartphone filmmaking. By understanding how your chosen genre interacts with the unique possibilities of shooting on a smartphone, you can create a film that not only fits the format but also maximizes its potential to tell a powerful, engaging story.

The Protagonist: Creating a Compelling Hero

Creating a compelling protagonist is one of the most important steps in storytelling. The protagonist is the character who drives the story forward and engages the audience, serving as their emotional anchor throughout the film. A well-developed protagonist is someone the audience can relate to, root for, and invest in emotionally, even if they don't always agree with their choices. In this chapter, we'll explore how to craft a protagonist that is dynamic, layered, and suited for the medium of smartphone filmmaking.

The first step in creating a compelling protagonist is understanding their central role in the story. The protagonist is more than just the main character; they are the driving force behind the narrative. Their goals, desires, and challenges shape the plot and give the story meaning. As you begin developing your protagonist, start by asking a fundamental question: What does this character want? The protagonist's desire—whether it's to find love, seek revenge, achieve a dream, or solve a mystery—gives them purpose and motivates their actions throughout the film.

For example, if your film is about a woman who discovers she can see the future, your protagonist's central desire might be to figure out how to control this ability and use it to her advantage. Or, on a deeper level, her real goal might be to reclaim control over her life, which has been thrown into chaos by this new power. Identifying your protagonist's goal will help clarify their motivation and make their journey compelling to the audience.

While the protagonist's goal is essential, it's their obstacles and struggles that make them truly engaging. No compelling hero has an easy path, and it's the conflicts they face—both internal and external—that create drama and tension. These conflicts should be personal to the protagonist, challenging their beliefs, values, and abilities. As you develop your protagonist, think about the obstacles that stand in their way. What forces oppose their goal? What internal struggles make their journey even more difficult?

In our example of the future-seeing protagonist, external obstacles could come from people who want to exploit her power for their own gain. Internally, she might struggle with ethical dilemmas—should she use her ability to alter the future for her own benefit, or should she let events play out as they're meant to? These internal conflicts add complexity to the protagonist's journey, making their decisions weightier and more dramatic.

A well-rounded protagonist also has flaws. Perfect characters are boring because they lack growth and relatability. Flaws make your protagonist human—they give them room to evolve throughout the story and allow the audience to connect with their struggles. Your protagonist's flaw might be a character trait that holds them back, such as arrogance, fear, insecurity, or impulsiveness. It could also be a limiting belief they need to overcome. For example, the woman who sees the future might initially be overconfident in her ability, thinking she can control fate. Over time, she might realize that trying to manipulate the future has consequences she didn't anticipate.

These flaws give your protagonist a starting point for their character arc—the journey of growth or change they undergo throughout the film. A strong character arc is one of the most satisfying elements of storytelling, as it shows the protagonist evolving in response to the challenges they face. In the case of our future-seeing woman, her arc might involve learning to accept the limits of her power and making peace with the uncertainty of life. By the end of the film, she could realize that not knowing the future is part of what makes life meaningful.

Another important aspect of crafting a compelling protagonist is giving them a backstory. While not every detail of a character's past needs to be revealed to the audience, knowing where your protagonist comes from will inform their motivations, fears, and relationships. A well-developed backstory helps you understand why your character behaves the way they do and what drives their decisions. For instance, if your protagonist grew up in a strict, controlling environment, their desire for freedom and autonomy might be a central theme in the story.

Backstory also helps you create internal conflict. What unresolved issues from the protagonist's past are they still grappling with? How do these past experiences shape their worldview and affect their relationships with other characters? For example, if your protagonist has a history of making bad decisions that hurt the people they care about, they might be reluctant to take risks or make bold choices, even when it's necessary. This internal conflict adds depth to the character and makes their journey more compelling.

When writing for smartphone filmmaking, it's important to keep in mind that much of your protagonist's character development will be conveyed visually. Smartphones allow for intimate, close-up shots that capture subtle expressions and emotions, so use this to your advantage. Rather than relying heavily on dialogue to convey your protagonist's thoughts and feelings, think about how you can show their internal struggles through their actions, facial expressions, and body language. For example, a lingering close-up of your protagonist's face as they hesitate before making a difficult decision can be more powerful than a lengthy monologue explaining their dilemma.

Smartphone filmmaking also lends itself to a more spontaneous and raw style of acting, which can enhance the authenticity of your protagonist. Since smartphones are less intrusive than traditional cameras, actors often feel more comfortable delivering natural, understated performances. This allows you to focus on the small, human moments that make your protagonist relatable. Whether it's a nervous glance, a hesitant smile, or a moment of vulnerability, these subtle details can bring your protagonist to life in a way that feels grounded and real.

Another way to create a compelling protagonist is to give them relationships that matter. The people your protagonist interacts with—whether they're friends, family, mentors, or enemies—help define who they are and what they care about. Relationships add emotional stakes to the story, as the protagonist's decisions often affect not only themselves but also the people they care about. In our example, the woman who can see the future might have a close friend or sibling who challenges her decisions and pushes her to think about the consequences of her actions. These relationships provide opportunities for conflict, growth, and emotional resonance.

It's also important to think about the theme of your film when crafting your protagonist. The protagonist's journey should align with the broader themes you want to explore. If your film is about fate versus free will, for example, your protagonist's arc should reflect their evolving beliefs about control and destiny. If your film is about overcoming fear, your protagonist's actions and decisions should be shaped by their struggle to confront and conquer that fear. The protagonist is the vessel through which the audience experiences the film's themes, so their journey needs to resonate on both a personal and thematic level.

Finally, remember that a compelling protagonist doesn't have to be a traditional hero. Some of the most interesting protagonists are flawed, morally ambiguous, or even anti-heroes. What matters most is that the audience can connect with them on an emotional level, whether through empathy, curiosity, or fascination. Even if your protagonist makes questionable decisions or has a darker side, as long as their motivations are clear and their journey is engaging, the audience will be invested in their story.

In conclusion, creating a compelling protagonist is about more than just giving your character a goal and placing them in a plot. It's about crafting a fully realized person with desires, flaws, internal conflicts, and relationships that feel authentic and engaging. Your protagonist should grow and change over the course of the story, allowing the audience to experience that evolution alongside them. By focusing on the emotional, visual, and narrative elements of your protagonist, you can create a character that not only drives the story forward but also resonates with the audience long after the film is over.

Developing Antagonists: Giving Your Story Depth

A compelling story isn't just about a well-crafted protagonist—it's equally important to develop a strong antagonist. The antagonist is the force that opposes the protagonist and creates the conflict that drives the narrative forward. While the antagonist is often thought of as a villain, they don't necessarily have to be evil or even a person. The key is that the antagonist stands in the way of the protagonist's goals, making their journey more difficult and giving the story depth and tension. In this chapter, we'll explore how to develop an antagonist that adds complexity to your film and makes your protagonist's journey more engaging.

The first step in creating a compelling antagonist is to understand their role in the story. At their core, the antagonist serves as the primary obstacle for the protagonist. They are the person, force, or circumstance that stands between the protagonist and what they want to achieve. A well-developed antagonist not only challenges the protagonist on a physical or external level but also forces them to confront their internal flaws, beliefs, and weaknesses.

When developing your antagonist, start by asking yourself: What does the antagonist want? Just like the protagonist, the antagonist should have clear goals and motivations. In fact, the best antagonists often believe they are the hero of their own story. They may see their actions as justified, necessary, or even noble, even if those actions conflict with the protagonist's goals. This complexity makes the antagonist more interesting and relatable, allowing the audience to understand their point of view, even if they don't agree with it.

For example, let's say your story is about a woman who discovers she can see glimpses of the future. The antagonist in this case could be a government agency or corporation that wants to exploit her ability for their own gain. While this antagonist might initially seem purely villainous, you could deepen their character by giving them a legitimate reason for wanting to control the protagonist's power. Perhaps they believe that using her ability is the only way to prevent a global catastrophe, even if it means taking away her freedom. This moral ambiguity makes the antagonist more compelling because their goals, while opposed to the protagonist's, are rooted in a belief that they are doing the right thing.

Another way to create a compelling antagonist is to ensure that they have a strong connection to the protagonist. The best conflicts arise when the protagonist and antagonist are deeply intertwined—whether through shared history, opposing values, or personal stakes. This connection adds emotional weight to their conflict and makes the stakes feel more personal. For example, if the antagonist is someone from the protagonist's past—a former friend, mentor, or family member—their opposition feels more charged, as both characters have a shared history that influences their actions.

In some cases, the antagonist may be more of a symbolic force rather than a traditional villain. For instance, in a survival film, the antagonist might be nature itself, with the protagonist battling against harsh weather conditions, wild animals, or the struggle for food and water. While this type of antagonist isn't a person, it still provides a powerful external conflict that challenges the protagonist physically and mentally. In these cases, the protagonist's internal journey often becomes the central focus, as they confront their fears, limitations, and resilience in the face of overwhelming odds.

When creating an antagonist, it's essential to think about how they complement the protagonist's character arc. A strong antagonist should not only create obstacles for the protagonist but also push them to grow and change. The antagonist should challenge the protagonist's beliefs, forcing them to confront their flaws and evolve over the course of the story. For example, if the protagonist begins the story with a belief in their ability to control their own destiny, the antagonist might represent a force that challenges this belief—whether it's an individual trying to manipulate the future or a larger force that reveals the unpredictability of life.

It's also important to consider the antagonist's flaws and weaknesses. Just as a protagonist with flaws is more relatable, an antagonist who isn't entirely invincible is more engaging. Giving your antagonist vulnerabilities—whether they're physical, emotional, or psychological—makes them feel more human and adds depth to the conflict. These weaknesses can also create opportunities for dramatic tension, as the protagonist may exploit them to gain an advantage in their struggle.

For example, an antagonist who is a powerful figure in a corporate or governmental organization may have an underlying fear of losing control or being exposed for unethical behavior. This fear could drive them to take increasingly desperate actions, creating additional layers of conflict as they try to maintain their position of power. Alternatively, an antagonist who is driven by personal grief or trauma may struggle with their own emotional demons, making their actions more complex and nuanced.

Another important element in developing an antagonist is their backstory. Just as with the protagonist, understanding the antagonist's past can help inform their motivations and actions in the story. Why do they oppose the protagonist? What events or experiences shaped their worldview and led them to their current position? A well-developed backstory adds depth to the antagonist, helping the audience understand their perspective and making them more than just a one-dimensional villain.

For instance, if your antagonist is a scientist who is trying to exploit the protagonist's ability to see the future, their backstory might reveal that they once lost a loved one in a preventable accident. This personal tragedy could drive their obsession with controlling future events, making them willing to do whatever it takes to prevent similar losses, even if it means disregarding the protagonist's autonomy. While their actions may be morally questionable, their motivation is rooted in something deeply personal and understandable.

When writing for smartphone filmmaking, developing a visually compelling antagonist is also key. Smartphones are great for capturing intimate, close-up shots, so use this to your advantage when portraying the antagonist's emotions and psychological state. Rather than relying solely on grand, over-the-top villainy, focus on the subtle moments that reveal the antagonist's inner conflict or motivations. A fleeting look of doubt, a clenched fist, or a moment of vulnerability can speak volumes about the antagonist's character and make them more compelling.

Smartphones also allow for dynamic, on-the-go shooting, which can be particularly effective in scenes involving the antagonist. Think about how you can use the smartphone's mobility to capture tense confrontations between the protagonist and antagonist, or how you can play with framing to visually emphasize the power dynamics between the two characters. For example, shooting the antagonist from a low angle can make them appear more imposing and powerful, while shooting them in tight close-ups can reveal moments of vulnerability or doubt.

Another consideration when developing your antagonist is how they fit into the overall theme of your film. The antagonist should embody the opposing side of the theme you are exploring. If your film is about free will versus fate, for example, the antagonist might represent the forces of control and determinism, pushing the protagonist to question their ability to change their destiny. If your film explores the cost of power, the antagonist might be someone who is willing to sacrifice everything for control, serving as a cautionary figure for the protagonist.

Finally, it's worth remembering that an antagonist doesn't always have to be a traditional villain. In some stories, the antagonist can be more of a rival or a competitor—someone who isn't necessarily evil but whose goals conflict with the protagonist's. This type of antagonist can add complexity to the story, as the conflict is less about good versus evil and more about two opposing forces or ideologies. In these cases, the antagonist may even be sympathetic in their own right, which adds depth and nuance to the story.

In conclusion, developing a compelling antagonist is essential for giving your story depth and creating meaningful conflict. By giving your antagonist clear motivations, complex backstory, and personal flaws, you can create a character who challenges the protagonist in ways that go beyond mere opposition. Whether your antagonist is a traditional villain, a symbolic force, or a morally ambiguous figure, their presence should force the protagonist to grow, evolve, and confront their deepest fears. With a well-developed antagonist, your film will have the tension, drama, and emotional stakes necessary to keep the audience fully engaged in the protagonist's journey.

Supporting Characters: Bringing Your Cast to Life

While the protagonist and antagonist are often the central figures in your film, the supporting characters are just as crucial for adding depth, richness, and complexity to your story. They help flesh out the world your protagonist inhabits, provide emotional resonance, and often serve as catalysts for key moments in the plot. Well-crafted supporting characters can elevate a film by offering different perspectives, creating subplots, and deepening the protagonist's journey. In this chapter, we'll explore how to develop supporting characters that bring your story to life. The first step in developing supporting characters is understanding their role in the story. Supporting characters don't just exist to fill space; they each have a purpose that serves the overall narrative. Some will help the protagonist on their journey, others will act as obstacles, and some may simply provide a window into different aspects of the story's world or themes. When crafting your supporting cast, it's essential to ask: What function does each character serve? How do they relate to the protagonist, and how do they help drive the plot forward?

For example, if your protagonist is a woman who can see the future, one supporting character might be her best friend, someone who grounds her and provides emotional support. Another might be a mentor figure who helps her understand and control her power. Perhaps there's also a rival, someone who envies her ability and creates tension in her personal life. Each of these characters serves a specific purpose, whether it's to support, challenge, or complicate the protagonist's journey.

One way to think about supporting characters is to categorize them by the roles they play in the protagonist's life. Some common types of supporting characters include:

The Mentor

A mentor character is someone who provides guidance, wisdom, or expertise to the protagonist. They help the protagonist grow, offering advice or teaching valuable skills that the protagonist will need to succeed in their journey. In many stories, the mentor is a figure who has already faced similar challenges and can offer insight into the protagonist's struggles. However, mentors are not always perfect; they may have their own flaws or limitations, which can add depth to their character.

For example, in a film where the protagonist can see the future, the mentor could be a mysterious figure who has had a similar ability in the past. They might teach the protagonist how to harness her power but also warn her of the dangers of meddling with fate. The mentor's guidance is crucial to the protagonist's growth, but the mentor may also have their own past failures, which add a layer of complexity to their relationship.

The Ally

An ally is a character who supports the protagonist, often helping them through difficult times or assisting them in achieving their goals. Allies provide emotional support, friendship, or practical help. They often act as sounding boards for the protagonist, offering advice or alternative perspectives. A well-developed ally has their own motivations and personality, making them more than just a sidekick.

In the example of a protagonist who can see the future, an ally might be a close friend who helps her navigate the ethical dilemmas of her power. This friend might not have any special abilities but serves as a moral compass, pushing the protagonist to consider the broader implications of her actions. The ally could also provide moments of levity, humor, or emotional relief, balancing the tension of the main plot.

The Foil

A foil is a character who contrasts with the protagonist, highlighting their strengths and weaknesses by comparison. While not necessarily an antagonist, the foil often challenges the protagonist, offering a different perspective or worldview. A well-written foil can reveal aspects of the protagonist's personality that wouldn't otherwise come to light and can serve as a catalyst for the protagonist's growth.

For instance, in the story of a woman who can see the future, the foil could be another character who believes in living fully in the present, rejecting the idea of trying to control or predict what's to come. This character's philosophy might directly oppose the protagonist's need for control, creating tension between them. The foil challenges the protagonist's worldview, forcing her to question whether she's using her ability wisely.

The Love Interest

A love interest is a common supporting character in many stories, adding a layer of emotional complexity and personal stakes for the protagonist. The love interest often helps the protagonist explore their vulnerabilities and grow on a personal level. However, to avoid clichés, it's important to give the love interest their own goals, desires, and challenges, rather than making them exist solely for the protagonist's development.

In our example, the love interest might be someone who doesn't know about the protagonist's ability at first. As their relationship develops, the protagonist's struggle to hide or reveal her power creates conflict and tension. The love interest could represent a normal life that the protagonist craves but fears she can never have, adding an emotional dimension to the main plot.

The Comic Relief

A comic relief character is someone who lightens the tone of the story with humor, offering moments of levity amidst the tension. While comic relief can add entertainment value, it's essential that these characters also have depth and purpose beyond providing laughs. Well-developed comic relief characters can still have meaningful relationships with the protagonist and contribute to the overall narrative.

In a story about seeing the future, the comic relief might be a quirky sidekick who is fascinated by the protagonist's ability and constantly speculates about future events in humorous ways. While they provide much-needed humor, their loyalty and friendship also offer emotional support to the protagonist when things get tough.

The Rival

A rival character is someone who competes with the protagonist, creating tension and conflict. Unlike an antagonist, the rival might not be trying to harm the protagonist directly but may represent a competing force that drives the protagonist to work harder, question their abilities, or reassess their goals. Rivals can push the protagonist out of their comfort zone, forcing them to confront their weaknesses.

In our example, the rival might be someone else who has discovered a way to predict future events, but they use this knowledge in a self-serving, manipulative way. Their presence serves as a dark mirror to the protagonist, showing what could happen if she abuses her power. This rivalry creates both external conflict and internal tension as the protagonist grapples with her own choices.

The Antagonist's Ally

Just as the protagonist has allies, the antagonist often has their own supporters. These characters can serve to amplify the antagonist's power and create additional obstacles for the protagonist. They might be loyal followers, hired help, or people who share the antagonist's worldview. Antagonist's allies can also be complex characters with their own motivations, which may not always align perfectly with the antagonist's goals.

For example, in a story where a government agency is trying to control the protagonist's future-seeing abilities, the antagonist's ally might be a scientist who works for the agency. While the scientist believes in the project's goals, they might also have ethical concerns about how the protagonist is being treated, creating internal conflict within the antagonist's camp. This complexity adds depth to the narrative and can lead to interesting character dynamics.

Writing Well-Rounded Supporting Characters

Once you've identified the role each supporting character plays in the story, it's important to flesh them out into well-rounded individuals with their own motivations, personalities, and backstories. Supporting characters should feel like real people with lives that exist beyond their interactions with the protagonist. Even if they don't have as much screen time or focus as the protagonist, they should still have their own desires, fears, and growth throughout the film.

For example, the best friend of the protagonist who helps her navigate her future-seeing ability might have their own personal struggles. Maybe they're dealing with a difficult relationship, career challenges, or a personal loss. By giving them their own mini-arc, you add layers to their character and make their relationship with the protagonist feel more authentic.

Supporting characters also play a vital role in shaping the tone of the film. For example, a sarcastic or light-hearted ally can bring humor to an otherwise tense story, while a mentor who is world-weary and wise can add a somber, reflective tone. The way supporting characters interact with the protagonist can highlight different facets of the protagonist's personality—whether it's their sense of humor, their vulnerabilities, or their determination.

Visual Storytelling with Supporting Characters

When writing for smartphone filmmaking, much of the development of supporting characters can be achieved through visual storytelling. Smartphones allow for intimate, close-up shots, which can be used to reveal subtle aspects of a character's personality—whether it's a nervous tic, a fleeting expression, or the way they interact with their environment. Use these visual cues to show how supporting characters feel about the protagonist and their situation, rather than relying solely on dialogue.

Additionally, smartphones are great for capturing real-world locations and natural environments, which can add to the authenticity of your supporting characters. Showing a character in their personal space—whether it's their home, office, or favorite coffee shop—can reveal a lot about who they are without needing extensive exposition. These small, human moments make your supporting characters feel more alive and relatable.

Supporting characters are the backbone of any story, providing depth, emotional resonance, and new dimensions to the protagonist's journey. By carefully crafting a cast of well-rounded, purposeful characters, you can enrich your film's narrative and create a world that feels vibrant and real. Whether they're allies, mentors, rivals, or comic relief, supporting characters play a crucial role in shaping the protagonist's growth and adding complexity to the story. When developed thoughtfully, these characters will not only bring your cast to life but also leave a lasting impression on your audience.

Themes and Messages: What Is Your Film Saying?

Every film, whether consciously or unconsciously, carries themes and messages that reflect the filmmaker's intentions and worldview. These underlying ideas give your story depth and meaning, elevating it beyond the surface-level plot and engaging the audience on an emotional and intellectual level. Themes help unify your film and provide a lens through which the audience can interpret the events and characters. In this chapter, we'll explore how to identify the themes and messages of your film, and how to weave them into the narrative in a way that feels natural and impactful.

What Are Themes?

Themes are the universal ideas or concepts that your film explores. They represent the bigger picture, the underlying message that transcends the specific events of the plot. Common themes in storytelling include love, power, freedom, justice, identity, and the nature of good and evil. A theme might explore human relationships, societal issues, or personal growth, often speaking to the audience's emotions and experiences in ways that make the story more relatable.

For example, if your film is about a protagonist who can see the future, the theme might revolve around fate versus free will. Does the protagonist have the power to change the future, or are they bound by what they see? This theme could explore the tension between accepting one's destiny and striving to forge a different path. Another theme could be the ethical implications of possessing knowledge that others don't have—should the protagonist intervene in other people's lives, or is it morally wrong to manipulate the future for personal gain?

How to Identify Your Film's Themes

To identify the theme of your film, start by looking at the central conflict and the protagonist's journey. What challenges are they facing, and what lessons are they learning along the way? The theme often arises naturally from the protagonist's internal struggle. If your protagonist is grappling with questions about their identity, for example, then a theme of self-discovery or the search for belonging might emerge. If they are navigating complex relationships, a theme of love, trust, or betrayal could take center stage.

Another way to discover your theme is to ask yourself, "What is this story really about?" Beyond the plot's surface, what deeper message do you want to communicate to the audience? It's important to distinguish between the plot—the series of events that happen—and the theme, which is the underlying idea behind those events. For instance, in a heist film, the plot might focus on a group of criminals pulling off a robbery, but the theme could explore issues of loyalty, greed, or justice.

Weaving Themes into Your Narrative

Once you've identified your theme, the next step is to weave it naturally into your narrative. A theme shouldn't feel forced or overly explicit, like a lesson being taught to the audience. Instead, it should emerge through the characters' actions, decisions, and the consequences of those actions. When done well, the theme will be present throughout the film without needing to be spelled out.

One of the most effective ways to integrate a theme into your film is through the protagonist's character arc. The protagonist's internal growth and the decisions they make should reflect the theme. For example, if your film's theme is about the struggle between fate and free will, your protagonist's arc might involve learning to accept that they can't control everything, or it could involve them fighting against destiny to carve out their own path. Their journey should mirror the thematic question at the heart of the film, with each major decision they make contributing to their overall growth.

The antagonist can also play a crucial role in reinforcing the theme. Often, the antagonist represents the opposing side of the thematic argument, embodying the idea or value that contrasts with the protagonist's beliefs. For example, if your theme is about the balance between freedom and control, your antagonist might be someone who believes in strict order and control over people's lives, while the protagonist values freedom and autonomy. This ideological conflict between the protagonist and antagonist deepens the central theme and adds layers to their struggle.

Supporting characters, too, can reflect different facets of the theme. Each character in your film doesn't need to align perfectly with the protagonist's journey; in fact, it's often more interesting if they challenge or provide alternative perspectives on the theme. For example, in a film about fate versus free will, one supporting character might be a fatalist, resigned to the idea that everything is preordained, while another character might fiercely advocate for the idea that people create their own destinies. These contrasting views enrich the film and provide the protagonist with different viewpoints to consider.

Using Visual and Symbolic Storytelling

Themes don't have to be conveyed solely through dialogue or character arcs. Visual and symbolic storytelling can be powerful tools for expressing your film's themes. In fact, films often communicate their most profound messages through imagery, metaphors, and motifs rather than through words.

For example, if your film's theme involves the tension between freedom and control, you might use recurring imagery of open skies or wide landscapes to represent freedom, contrasted with tight, confined spaces to symbolize control or restriction. A protagonist trapped in a small room could visually reflect their internal struggle with feeling trapped by fate. Visual motifs, such as recurring symbols or objects, can also be used to reinforce the theme throughout the film. For instance, if your theme involves the passage of time, you might include clocks, hourglasses, or other time-related imagery to subtly remind the audience of the protagonist's battle against the clock.

Another example of symbolic storytelling could be in a story where the theme revolves around knowledge and its consequences. Light could be used as a metaphor for enlightenment or understanding, with scenes of increasing brightness as the protagonist uncovers more truths. Conversely, darkness might symbolize ignorance or danger, with pivotal moments shrouded in shadows to heighten the tension. These visual choices add layers of meaning to the story without needing to be explicitly addressed in the dialogue.

Sound and music can also be powerful tools for expressing your film's themes. A recurring musical motif or specific sound design can reinforce the emotional tone and thematic content of the film. For example, in a film about control versus chaos, you might use structured, rhythmic music when the antagonist is present, contrasting with more erratic, dissonant sounds during scenes where the protagonist is struggling against losing control. These subtle auditory cues help create an immersive thematic experience.

Avoiding Heavy-Handedness

One of the challenges of working with themes is striking the right balance between making your theme clear and avoiding heavy-handedness. It's tempting to make the theme explicit by having characters state the message outright, but this can feel forced and reduce the emotional impact. Instead, allow the theme to emerge naturally through the characters' actions, choices, and the consequences they face.

For example, instead of having a character deliver a monologue about the dangers of trying to control the future, you could show the protagonist experiencing the fallout from attempting to manipulate events. Let the audience see the consequences unfold, and they'll grasp the theme on a deeper, more emotional level. Show, don't tell, is an important rule when it comes to integrating themes effectively.

One way to avoid heavy-handedness is to allow room for ambiguity. While your film should have a clear thematic direction, it doesn't need to provide a definitive answer to the thematic question. In fact, leaving some aspects open to interpretation can make your film more thought-provoking. If your film explores the theme of fate versus free will, for example, you don't need to definitively answer which one is "right." Allowing the audience to wrestle with the question themselves makes the theme more engaging and memorable.

Thematic Consistency

Another important aspect of working with themes is ensuring consistency throughout the film. The theme should resonate in every major decision, conflict, and resolution within the story. If your theme is about the struggle for control, then every key moment in the film should reflect that struggle in some way, whether it's through the protagonist's internal conflict, the antagonist's actions, or the world the characters inhabit.

However, thematic consistency doesn't mean that every scene needs to directly address the theme. Instead, the theme should act as an undercurrent, subtly influencing the tone, atmosphere, and emotional weight of the film. Even scenes that seem unrelated to the central plot can contribute to the overall thematic texture. For instance, a quiet moment between two characters in a film about control might reveal how one of them has let go of control in their personal life, adding another layer to the theme without explicitly stating it.

Themes and messages are the heart of any great film, giving it depth and resonance beyond the immediate plot. By identifying your film's themes early in the creative process and weaving them into the story through character development, visual storytelling, and symbolic imagery, you can create a film that not only entertains but also provokes thought and emotion. Whether your theme explores personal growth, societal issues, or philosophical questions, it should feel like a natural extension of the story rather than a forced message. When done well, the theme will leave a lasting impression, making your film memorable and meaningful for your audience.

Setting the Scene: Choosing Locations for Mobile Shoots

Choosing the right locations is a key part of setting the scene for your mobile film. Since you're working with the flexibility of a smartphone, you have a unique opportunity to explore diverse, real-world environments without the logistical challenges of traditional film equipment. Mobile filmmaking allows you to be more agile and spontaneous in your choice of locations, but it also requires careful planning to ensure that each setting supports the story and maximizes the strengths of your smartphone's capabilities. In this chapter, we'll explore how to choose the right locations for your mobile shoots, focusing on practical considerations and creative opportunities that will bring your story to life.

Understanding the Importance of Location

Locations play a crucial role in storytelling. They provide the backdrop against which the narrative unfolds, establish the mood, and contribute to the visual tone of the film. A well-chosen location can enhance the emotional impact of a scene, reflect the internal state of the characters, and even serve as a metaphor for the themes of the story. When selecting locations for your mobile shoot, it's important to think about how each setting complements the narrative and what it adds to the audience's experience.

For example, if your film is a thriller about a protagonist being chased through a city, the choice of narrow, winding alleyways could heighten the sense of danger and claustrophobia. On the other hand, if your story revolves around a character seeking freedom, wide-open landscapes or expansive city views might visually symbolize that quest. The location doesn't just provide a physical space for the action—it becomes a character in its own right, shaping the mood and meaning of the scene.

The Benefits of Mobile Filmmaking for Location Scouting

One of the biggest advantages of mobile filmmaking is the freedom to shoot in a wide variety of locations without the constraints of heavy equipment or large crews. Smartphones are lightweight, easy to carry, and unobtrusive, allowing you to film in places that might be difficult or impossible for a traditional film crew to access. This flexibility opens up a world of creative possibilities, from shooting in bustling public spaces to capturing intimate moments in confined or unconventional settings.

For example, if you're filming a dialogue scene in a crowded café, a smartphone allows you to blend in with the environment, avoiding the disruption that a large camera setup might cause. This can result in more natural, authentic performances from your actors, as well as a more organic feel to the scene. Additionally, smartphones allow you to capture spur-of-the-moment opportunities, whether it's a stunning sunset, an unexpected crowd reaction, or a unique architectural detail you hadn't planned for.

However, with this flexibility comes the need for careful planning. While it's easier to shoot in a variety of locations with a smartphone, you still need to ensure that the setting enhances the story and meets the practical requirements of the shoot. Let's look at some of the key factors to consider when scouting locations for your mobile film.

Considerations When Choosing Locations

Story Relevance

The first and most important consideration is whether the location serves the story. Every setting should contribute to the narrative, either by reflecting the emotional tone of the scene or by offering practical benefits for the action taking place. Ask yourself: What does this location say about the characters? How does it support the themes of the film? Does it visually enhance the mood of the scene?

For example, if your film is about isolation and loneliness, a desolate, abandoned building or an empty park at dusk might convey that emotional state better than a busy, populated area. On the other hand, if your film is a romantic drama, locations like cozy cafés, vibrant streets, or scenic outdoor spots might help create the right atmosphere for the story's tone.

Practicality

While creativity is important, practicality is key when working with mobile shoots. Consider the logistics of filming in each location. Is it easily accessible for your cast and crew? Does it provide enough space for movement and different camera angles? Are there noise issues that could interfere with recording sound, such as traffic, wind, or crowds?

Smartphones are great for shooting in small or tight spaces, but you'll still need to plan for practical needs like power sources for recharging your phone, nearby restrooms, or shelter from the weather. If you're shooting outdoors, make sure to consider lighting conditions throughout the day, as smartphones are more sensitive to lighting than professional cameras.

If your scene involves dialogue, you'll need to ensure that the location is quiet enough for clear sound recording or plan to use external microphones. For instance, a city street might look visually dynamic, but if it's too noisy, you may struggle to capture clean audio, which can distract from the overall quality of the film.

Lighting Conditions

Lighting is one of the most critical factors in mobile filmmaking, as smartphones have limited capabilities in low-light environments. When choosing locations, consider the available natural light, particularly if you're shooting outdoors. Early morning or late afternoon, often referred to as the "golden hour," provides soft, even lighting that works well for many scenes. Midday sun, on the other hand, can cast harsh shadows and overexpose the image, making it more difficult to capture visually pleasing shots.

If you're shooting indoors, think about how you can control the lighting to create the right mood. Large windows that let in natural light can be a valuable asset, especially when shooting on a smartphone. You can also use practical lighting from lamps, candles, or even string lights to add ambiance to a scene. Since you're working with a mobile device, experimenting with available light sources can create a more intimate and organic feel to the visuals.

For example, if your film involves a dramatic scene set in a dimly lit bar, you might use the warm, ambient lighting of the bar itself, supplemented by small LED lights to enhance the actors' faces without overpowering the scene. The goal is to work with the lighting conditions of the location to achieve the desired visual effect.

Permits and Permissions

While smartphones allow for a certain level of stealth when filming in public, it's still essential to check whether you need permits to shoot in certain locations, especially if you're using public spaces, private property, or busy urban environments. Even though you might be able to blend into the crowd, getting permission to film ensures that you don't run into legal issues or get interrupted mid-shoot.

Some locations may have restrictions on filming, especially if they are tourist attractions, government buildings, or commercial areas. Do your research ahead of time to understand the local laws and regulations regarding filming. In some cases, you may be able to get away with guerilla-style filmmaking using your smartphone, but always weigh the risks and plan for potential challenges.

Weather and Environmental Conditions

Outdoor shoots are particularly vulnerable to changes in weather, which can affect lighting, sound, and overall filming conditions. When scouting locations, keep an eye on the weather forecast and plan for contingencies in case conditions change unexpectedly. Rain, wind, or extreme temperatures can pose challenges, especially when filming on a smartphone that might not handle adverse weather conditions as well as traditional film equipment.

For example, if you're filming a scene in an outdoor park, make sure to have backup plans for shelter if it starts raining or extra lighting options in case the weather turns cloudy and reduces natural light. Additionally, be prepared with portable chargers or battery packs, as cold weather can drain smartphone batteries more quickly.

Creating Visual Contrast

Choosing locations that provide visual contrast can add depth and variety to your film. Think about how you can juxtapose different types of settings to reflect changes in mood, character development, or shifts in the story's tone. For instance, starting a scene in a chaotic, crowded city street and then transitioning to a quiet, empty room can create a powerful contrast, reflecting the protagonist's emotional journey.

For example, if your film explores themes of isolation, you might shoot some scenes in wide-open, barren landscapes, while other scenes take place in confined, cluttered indoor spaces. This contrast can visually reinforce the protagonist's internal state or highlight the tension between freedom and confinement.

Working with Real Locations

One of the most exciting aspects of mobile filmmaking is the ability to shoot in real locations, often without the need for elaborate set designs. This can bring an authentic, grounded quality to your film, as real locations often have textures, details, and atmosphere that are difficult to replicate on a set. Think about how you can use these real-world environments to your advantage, incorporating the unique features of each location into the storytelling.

For example, if your protagonist lives in a gritty urban environment, shooting in real city streets, with all the natural noise, movement, and life of the city, can add realism to the film. Alternatively, if your film is set in a rural area, capturing the wide, sweeping landscapes and natural beauty of the environment can enhance the film's visual impact and emotional tone.

Maximizing Smartphone Capabilities in Locations

When shooting in your chosen locations, remember to take full advantage of the capabilities and strengths of your smartphone. Smartphones are great for capturing dynamic movement and tight spaces, so don't be afraid to experiment with handheld shots, unusual angles, or even point-of-view perspectives. The compact size of a smartphone allows you to get shots that would be challenging with larger cameras, such as filming from within a car, inside a closet, or through small openings.

You can also make use of smartphone stabilizers or gimbals to create smooth tracking shots or pans, adding a professional touch to your mobile filmmaking. Additionally, smartphones are ideal for quick transitions between locations, allowing you to shoot multiple scenes in different settings within a short time frame, which can be a significant advantage for time-sensitive or low-budget productions.

Choosing the right locations for your mobile film is a balance between creativity, practicality, and storytelling. Each location should serve a purpose within the narrative, enhancing the emotional and visual impact of the scenes. With the flexibility of smartphone filmmaking, you have the opportunity to explore a wide range of real-world environments, allowing for a more spontaneous and authentic approach to location shooting. By carefully considering the story's needs, lighting conditions, sound, and logistical factors, you can maximize the potential of your smartphone to create visually stunning, immersive settings that bring your film to life.

Casting for a Smartphone Film: How to Find the Right Talent

Casting is one of the most critical aspects of filmmaking, and this is just as true for a smartphone film as it is for a big-budget production. The right cast brings your characters to life, deepens the emotional impact of your story, and helps the audience connect with the narrative on a personal level. In a smartphone film, where intimacy and natural performances are often emphasized, casting becomes even more important. Finding the right talent can make the difference between a film that feels authentic and engaging and one that falls flat. In this chapter, we'll explore how to cast effectively for your smartphone film, considering practical tips, creative strategies, and how to work within the unique constraints and opportunities of mobile filmmaking.

Understanding the Importance of Casting in Smartphone Filmmaking

In any film, the actors are the audience's primary connection to the story. They bring the script to life through their performances, embodying the emotions, motivations, and conflicts that drive the plot. In smartphone filmmaking, this connection can be even more intimate due to the close-up nature of mobile shooting. Smartphones allow for tight, personal shots that capture subtle expressions and movements, making it essential to cast actors who can convey depth and nuance, even with minimal dialogue.

The performances in a smartphone film are often rawer and more natural because of the smaller, less intrusive equipment. Actors may feel more comfortable and relaxed without the imposing presence of a large camera and crew, leading to performances that feel more genuine. Because of this, casting the right actors—those who can embrace the smartphone's immediacy and adapt to the more intimate shooting style—becomes key to the success of your film.

Defining Your Characters

Before you begin the casting process, it's essential to have a clear understanding of your characters. Who are they, and what drives them? What do they want, and what are their flaws or internal struggles? Defining your characters will help you identify the traits and qualities you're looking for in your actors. Consider the following:

Personality: Is your protagonist introverted and quiet, or outgoing and bold? Is the antagonist charming but ruthless, or more reserved and calculated? Understanding each character's personality will guide you in finding an actor whose natural demeanor aligns with the role.

Age and Appearance: While appearance is not the most critical factor in casting, it's still important to consider whether the actor's look fits the character's description. Age, physicality, and other visual traits should support the narrative, but don't be afraid to think outside the box if an actor brings something unique to the role.

Emotional Range: Smartphone filmmaking often involves close-up shots that capture even the smallest facial expressions and gestures, so you'll need actors who can convey a wide range of emotions without relying on exaggerated movements or heavy dialogue. Think about how much emotional depth the character requires and whether the actor can express that in a subtle, realistic way.

Once you have a solid understanding of your characters, you can begin the casting process with a clear idea of what you're looking for in each role.

Where to Find Actors for Your Smartphone Film

Finding the right talent doesn't have to be a daunting task, even if you're working on a small budget or with limited resources. Here are several ways to find actors for your smartphone film:

Local Talent

One of the easiest and most cost-effective ways to find actors is to look locally. Check out community theater groups, acting classes, or university drama programs in your area. Many actors who are just starting out are eager to build their portfolios and gain experience, making them more likely to participate in indie or low-budget projects. Attending local theater performances or film screenings can also help you discover talent and network with actors who may be interested in your film.

Online Casting Platforms

Several online platforms allow filmmakers to post casting calls and search for actors based on specific criteria. Websites like Backstage, Casting Networks, and Mandy are popular options for finding actors of all experience levels. These platforms allow you to post detailed descriptions of your project, including the characters you're casting, the type of film you're making, and any other relevant information.

Online casting platforms are particularly useful for mobile filmmakers because they give you access to a wider pool of talent beyond your local area. You can find actors who are specifically looking for indie, low-budget, or experimental projects, which can make the casting process more efficient.

Social Media

Social media can be a powerful tool for finding actors, especially if you're working within a specific community or niche. Platforms like Instagram, Facebook, and Twitter allow you to connect with actors, filmmakers, and creative professionals. Posting casting calls in relevant Facebook groups, Reddit forums, or Instagram pages dedicated to filmmaking can help you reach actors who may be interested in your project.

If you already have a small following on social media, you can use your own platform to promote your casting call. Encouraging your followers to share the post can help spread the word and attract actors who align with your film's vision.

Word of Mouth and Networking

Sometimes the best way to find talent is through personal connections. If you've worked with actors before, reach out to them to see if they're available for your project or if they know someone who might be a good fit. Word of mouth is a powerful tool in the filmmaking community, and recommendations from trusted sources can lead you to actors who may not be actively seeking roles but are open to new opportunities.

Networking events, film festivals, or local filmmaker meetups are also great places to connect with actors and other professionals who may be interested in collaborating on your smartphone film.

Non-Actors

Depending on the style and tone of your film, you may also consider casting non-actors. Since smartphone films often emphasize realism and intimacy, casting someone with little or no acting experience can sometimes bring an authenticity to the performance that professional actors might not capture. Non-actors, especially if they share characteristics with the character they're playing, can offer a fresh, unpolished energy that feels genuine and spontaneous.

For example, if your film is a documentary-style drama or a film with a very naturalistic tone, casting someone with lived experience that mirrors your character's life may add authenticity to the film. However, non-actors may need more guidance and direction, so be prepared to spend extra time on rehearsals and establishing trust.

Holding Auditions

Once you've found potential actors, the next step is holding auditions. Even if you're working on a small, low-budget film, auditions are crucial for determining whether the actor is the right fit for the role. Smartphone films often rely on subtle, nuanced performances, so it's important to see how the actor delivers their lines, expresses emotion, and interacts with others.

In-Person Auditions

In-person auditions give you the opportunity to work directly with the actors and observe how they respond to your direction. You can run through key scenes from your script, focusing on moments that reveal the character's personality or emotional arc. Pay attention to how the actor handles the material, their chemistry with other potential cast members, and their ability to adapt to feedback.

Since smartphones allow for close-up, intimate shots, use your phone to film the audition. This will give you a sense of how the actor looks on camera, their facial expressions, and whether their performance resonates in the close-up style of mobile filmmaking.

Self-Tape Auditions

Self-tape auditions are another great option, especially if you're casting actors from outside your local area or if scheduling in-person auditions is difficult. Ask actors to film themselves performing a scene or monologue from your script and send you the video. Watching self-tapes allows you to compare multiple actors' performances and assess their suitability for the role from the comfort of your own home.

For smartphone filmmaking, self-tapes are particularly useful because they give you an idea of how the actor handles recording themselves with mobile devices. If they have the technical skill to shoot a decent self-tape, they may also be more comfortable adjusting to the style and limitations of smartphone filmmaking.

Callbacks and Chemistry Reads

After initial auditions, you may want to hold callbacks to see how the final contenders for a role interact with each other. Chemistry between actors, especially if they're playing close relationships like friends, lovers, or rivals, is crucial. A chemistry read involves pairing actors together and observing how they play off one another in key scenes.

For example, if you're casting for a love interest, it's important to see whether the two actors have a natural connection that feels believable on screen. A chemistry read allows you to see if the actors' energies align and whether they can create a convincing dynamic that serves the story.

Directing Actors in Smartphone Films

Directing actors in a smartphone film requires a slightly different approach than directing for a traditional film, especially because the equipment you're working with is less intimidating and offers more flexibility. The goal is to create an environment where the actors feel comfortable, natural, and ready to give authentic performances. Here are some key tips for directing actors in a smartphone film:

Embrace Intimacy

One of the greatest strengths of smartphone filmmaking is its ability to capture intimate, close-up moments. Since you'll likely be working with tighter shots and more personal framing, encourage your actors to focus on subtle facial expressions and body language. Small gestures, a fleeting look, or a quiet moment of hesitation can have a powerful impact when filmed up close on a smartphone.

Remind your actors that they don't need to overact. In fact, less is often more when working with a smartphone's camera, which excels at picking up subtle emotional shifts. Because the audience will be physically closer to the characters (due to the nature of the filming style), the performances should feel grounded and natural.

Foster a Relaxed Atmosphere

One of the benefits of smartphone filmmaking is that it often feels less formal than a traditional film set. Without the presence of large cameras, bulky equipment, and a massive crew, the set can feel more relaxed and less intimidating. This environment can help your actors feel more at ease, which often leads to more natural, uninhibited performances.

As a director, work to maintain this relaxed atmosphere by keeping the crew small and the energy positive. The less pressure your actors feel, the more likely they are to experiment with their performances and deliver something raw and real. Since smartphone filmmaking often involves improvisation and flexibility, create space for your actors to explore their characters and try different approaches to the scenes.

Prioritize Rehearsals

While smartphone films offer spontaneity, rehearsals are still essential for getting the best performances. Take the time to rehearse key scenes before filming, especially those that involve complex emotions, dialogue, or physical interaction. Rehearsing allows your actors to get comfortable with the material and each other, leading to smoother, more organic performances on set.

Use rehearsals to explore the characters' motivations and relationships in depth. Encourage your actors to ask questions about their characters and experiment with different line readings or movements. Since smartphone filmmaking often involves quick, on-the-go shooting, rehearsals help eliminate any awkwardness or uncertainty, ensuring that the actors are ready to perform once the camera starts rolling.

Give Specific Direction

When working with actors, always give clear, specific direction. Vague instructions like "be more emotional" or "act natural" aren't helpful. Instead, provide concrete guidance based on the character's motivation or the scene's context. For example, if a character is supposed to be frustrated but trying to hide it, you might say, "Try clenching your fists subtly or tapping your fingers while speaking, as if the frustration is bubbling under the surface."

Specific direction helps actors better understand the emotional beats of the scene and gives them actionable steps to take in their performance. Because smartphone films tend to focus on smaller, more intimate moments, paying attention to these details can make a big difference in the overall tone and effectiveness of a scene.

Be Open to Improvisation

One of the joys of smartphone filmmaking is its flexibility. Without the constraints of traditional film sets, actors can often be more spontaneous and take creative risks. Don't be afraid to encourage improvisation, especially during emotionally charged scenes or moments of dialogue. Sometimes the best performances come from an actor's instinctive response to the material, rather than a strictly rehearsed line delivery.

If an actor feels particularly connected to a moment or a piece of dialogue, allow them to explore that instinct. You may discover unexpected gems during these improvisational moments. This spontaneity can make your film feel more authentic and alive, adding to the natural, unpolished aesthetic that smartphone films often excel at.

Work with Non-Actors Thoughtfully

If you've chosen to cast non-actors, take extra care to guide them through the process, as they may not have the same experience with character development, memorization, or understanding direction as trained actors. Non-actors often excel when playing roles that closely mirror their real-life experiences or personalities, so leverage this authenticity by encouraging them to act as naturally as possible.

Provide non-actors with clear, simple instructions. Instead of focusing on the technical aspects of performance, engage them by asking them to imagine how they would naturally react in the situation their character faces. Be patient, and if possible, try to create a comfortable, informal setting to ease any nerves they might have about being on camera.

Capture Multiple Takes and Angles

Smartphone filmmaking makes it easy to capture multiple takes quickly without needing extensive setup changes. Take advantage of this by shooting scenes from different angles and capturing a variety of takes. This flexibility in editing can give you more options when piecing the film together and allows the actors to try different approaches to the scene.

Since smartphones are lightweight and easy to move, experiment with unique angles and perspectives to see how the actors' performances change depending on the framing. For example, filming a conversation from a low angle might emphasize a power dynamic between characters, while filming at eye level creates a more equal, intimate feel.

Use the Smartphone's Mobility to Enhance Performance

The mobility of a smartphone allows you to shoot scenes in a way that follows the actors' natural movements. You can easily follow them through tight spaces, capture spontaneous interactions, and film from unconventional angles without the need for complex rigs. This can enhance the performances, making them feel more natural and less rehearsed.

For example, if a character is walking through a busy street, you can follow them with the phone in hand, capturing their facial expressions and body language in real-time, while seamlessly transitioning between action and emotion. This immersive approach helps the audience feel as if they're right there with the character, experiencing the moment alongside them.

Casting the right talent for your smartphone film is a vital step in creating a compelling, emotionally resonant story. By carefully defining your characters, searching for actors in local communities or online platforms, and holding thoughtful auditions, you can find the perfect performers to bring your story to life. Once cast, fostering a relaxed, collaborative environment and embracing the unique opportunities of smartphone filmmaking—such as mobility, intimacy, and improvisation—will allow your actors to deliver their best work. Whether you're working with seasoned professionals or non-actors, the right casting choices and direction can make all the difference, turning your smartphone film into a powerful, engaging cinematic experience.

Directing with a Smartphone: Maximizing Performance

Directing a film with a smartphone presents unique opportunities and challenges, especially when it comes to maximizing performance. While traditional filmmaking requires extensive equipment, a large crew, and rigid setups, smartphone filmmaking allows for a more flexible, intimate, and spontaneous approach. This means that as a director, you can be more agile and responsive to your actors' performances, giving them the space to experiment, improvise, and deliver authentic, emotionally resonant portrayals. In this chapter, we'll explore the strategies for directing with a smartphone and maximizing the performances of your cast to bring out the best in your film.

Embrace the Flexibility of Smartphone Filmmaking

One of the key advantages of using a smartphone is its portability and ease of use. Unlike a traditional film set, where large cameras, lighting rigs, and crews can sometimes limit the actors' freedom, smartphones allow for more movement and fluidity. As a director, you can take advantage of this flexibility to create a more relaxed and organic atmosphere for your actors. You're no longer confined to pre-determined setups or restricted by the need for heavy equipment; instead, you can move quickly, change angles, and capture spontaneous moments on the fly.

This freedom also allows your actors to perform in a more natural, unguarded way. Because the smartphone is less imposing than a traditional camera, your actors may feel more comfortable and open to experimentation. They can interact with their environment and each other more freely, leading to performances that feel authentic and grounded. Encourage your actors to use this flexibility, whether it's moving naturally within a space, reacting to unexpected stimuli, or engaging with real-life locations.

Create an Intimate Atmosphere

Smartphone filmmaking naturally lends itself to more intimate, close-up shots, which means the emotional core of your film will often be conveyed through small gestures, subtle facial expressions, and nuanced body language. As a director, it's essential to create an environment that fosters this intimacy, allowing your actors to feel safe and comfortable enough to explore the emotional depths of their characters.

Here are a few ways to create an intimate atmosphere:

Keep the crew small: The more people on set, the more pressure the actors might feel. With a smartphone, you don't need a large crew, which allows for a more personal, less formal shooting environment. A smaller crew also enables you to shoot in tight spaces or real-world locations without drawing attention, which can help actors stay focused on their performances.

Use natural settings: Since smartphones are highly portable, you can take advantage of real-world locations that fit your story. These settings often feel more authentic and less controlled than a studio environment, allowing the actors to engage more naturally with the space around them.

Encourage close collaboration with the actors: Because you won't be bogged down by technical setups, you can spend more time communicating directly with your actors, working with them to shape their performances. This personal attention helps them understand your vision while giving them the confidence to take creative risks.

Focus on Subtlety and Nuance

Smartphones are great for capturing small, intimate details, which is why subtlety and nuance should be a priority in your direction. Unlike larger productions, where actors may have to "play to the camera" due to distance or wide shots, smartphone filmmaking allows you to capture the tiniest movements, changes in facial expression, and shifts in emotion. These subtle moments can add depth and realism to a performance, drawing the audience into the emotional world of the characters.

Encourage your actors to avoid overacting and instead focus on conveying their character's inner emotions through small, authentic gestures. A slight shift in body language, a flicker of hesitation, or a glance can often communicate more than lengthy dialogue. Help your actors understand the importance of these micro-expressions and give them the space to explore how their character might respond naturally to each situation.

Experiment with Movement and Framing

One of the advantages of smartphone filmmaking is the ability to experiment with movement and framing without the need for complicated equipment. Handheld shots, tracking movements, and close-ups can all be achieved effortlessly with a smartphone. As a director, you can use this mobility to enhance the performances and create a more immersive experience.

Handheld shots for dynamic scenes: For scenes that require tension or high energy, a handheld shot can amplify the intensity and urgency of the moment. Following your actor's movements closely with the smartphone can create a sense of immediacy, making the audience feel like they are part of the action. This can be particularly effective in chase sequences, arguments, or emotionally charged confrontations.

Tracking shots for immersion: If your scene involves characters walking or moving through a space, use your smartphone to track their movements in a smooth, flowing shot. This technique creates a sense of fluidity and immersion, bringing the audience along with the characters. It also helps actors stay in the moment, allowing them to move naturally without worrying about hitting specific marks for traditional camera setups.

Close-ups for emotional resonance: Close-up shots are a powerful tool in smartphone filmmaking. They allow you to capture your actor's facial expressions in detail, highlighting the emotions that might otherwise be lost in a wider shot. Use close-ups strategically to convey the most important emotional beats of the scene, whether it's a moment of quiet reflection, a decision being made, or a reaction to a dramatic event.

Creative framing: Smartphones can fit into spaces that larger cameras can't, giving you the freedom to experiment with framing. Consider unusual angles, such as filming through windows, mirrors, or doorways, to add depth and interest to the shot. These creative framing techniques can also reflect the character's emotional state or the themes of the story, adding a layer of visual storytelling to the performance.

Direct with Clarity and Purpose

Even though smartphone filmmaking allows for more improvisation and flexibility, it's important to maintain clarity in your direction. Actors rely on the director to guide them through the emotional beats of the story, so be clear about the tone, pacing, and motivations for each scene. While you may encourage experimentation, make sure your actors understand the character's objectives and what's at stake in each moment.

Here are a few tips for clear and purposeful direction:

Give specific feedback: Avoid vague directions like "act more sad" or "be angrier." Instead, offer concrete guidance that helps the actor connect with the character's emotions. For example, you might say, "In this moment, you're trying to hide your frustration, but it's seeping through. Try tightening your jaw or looking away when you speak."

Use verbs, not emotions: Directing with verbs—such as "convince," "comfort," or "challenge"—can help actors focus on what their character is trying to accomplish in the scene, rather than how they're supposed to feel. This approach encourages more dynamic and action-oriented performances.

Focus on objectives: Every character in a scene should have a clear objective. What does your protagonist want, and what's stopping them from getting it? By reminding actors of their character's objectives, you help them play the scene with purpose and direction, creating more engaging and believable performances.

Encourage Improvisation and Play

Because smartphone filmmaking allows for more spontaneous shooting, it's a great opportunity to encourage improvisation and creative play. While you'll want to stick to your script's key plot points, giving your actors the freedom to improvise within a scene can lead to unexpected moments of brilliance. Improvised dialogue, reactions, or even physical movements can bring authenticity and energy to the film, especially in emotionally charged scenes.

For example, during a scene of tension between two characters, let the actors play off each other's reactions and emotions, allowing them to improvise their lines or responses. You may find that these unscripted moments feel more genuine and engaging than what was initially planned.

Improvisation is also useful when working in real-world locations, where unpredictable elements—such as passersby, background noise, or changes in the environment—can be incorporated into the scene. Allow your actors to react naturally to these elements, using them to enhance the realism of the performance.

Keep the Set Relaxed and Focused

A relaxed set is often the key to getting the best performances from your actors. Smartphone filmmaking allows you to create a more laid-back atmosphere, free from the pressures of a traditional film set. However, it's still important to maintain focus and ensure that your actors understand the tone and pace of the production.

Minimize distractions: Keep the set as quiet and distraction-free as possible to help your actors stay in the moment. Since smartphones are less intrusive, you don't need to worry about large equipment getting in the way, but make sure that everyone on set is focused on the scene being shot.

Give your actors time: Even in a more flexible, fast-paced environment, actors still need time to prepare mentally and emotionally for each scene. Allow them moments of quiet reflection or discussion before the camera rolls, especially if the scene is emotionally demanding.

Use the Smartphone's Strengths to Enhance Performance

Ultimately, directing with a smartphone allows you to harness the unique strengths of mobile filmmaking to enhance your actors' performances. The immediacy, flexibility, and portability of the device give you the ability to capture moments that feel raw, intimate, and authentic. By embracing these strengths—whether through tight close-ups, spontaneous movement, or on-the-go shooting—you can create a film that feels personal, dynamic, and deeply connected to the emotional core of your characters.

Directing with a smartphone is about maximizing the opportunities for natural, authentic performances while maintaining clarity and purpose in your storytelling. By embracing the flexibility of mobile filmmaking, creating an intimate environment, and focusing on subtlety, you can guide your actors toward delivering powerful, emotionally resonant performances. Whether you're encouraging improvisation, experimenting with movement and framing, or capturing nuanced expressions, your smartphone is the perfect tool to bring out the best in your cast and make your film truly come

Filming in Limited Spaces: Creative Use of Locations

Filming in limited spaces is a common challenge for many filmmakers, especially those working with smaller budgets or shooting with a smartphone. But rather than seeing limited space as a restriction, it can be an opportunity to get creative with how you use your environment. With the flexibility of smartphone filmmaking, tight or unconventional spaces can be transformed into dynamic, visually interesting settings that enhance the story and offer a unique cinematic experience. In this chapter, we'll explore strategies for making the most of limited spaces and using them to your creative advantage in your smartphone film.

Embrace the Strengths of Smartphone Filmmaking

One of the key advantages of using a smartphone is its ability to fit into spaces that traditional cameras cannot. Whether you're shooting in a cramped apartment, a narrow alley, or even inside a car, smartphones allow you to capture unique angles and perspectives that larger, bulkier equipment would struggle with. The portability and compact size of smartphones make them perfect for navigating tight spaces, allowing you to capture shots from unconventional positions that add visual interest to your film.

Instead of thinking of limited space as a constraint, view it as a way to push the boundaries of traditional filmmaking. Use the smartphone's mobility to your advantage by filming from low angles, high angles, or even handheld as you follow your actors through the scene. These creative choices can add dynamic energy to your shots, making the most of the space you have.

Maximize Depth with Framing and Composition

When filming in a small space, it's important to think about how you frame your shots to create a sense of depth and movement. Smart framing can help you avoid making the space feel too claustrophobic or flat. Here are a few ways to maximize depth in tight locations:

Foreground and background elements: Including both foreground and background elements in your shots can create a sense of depth, even in a small room. For example, you can position objects like furniture, windows, or doorways in the foreground while your actors move in the background. This layering technique draws the audience's eye through the shot, making the space feel larger and more dynamic.

Mirrors and reflective surfaces: Using mirrors or other reflective surfaces in your framing can add visual complexity to tight spaces. Mirrors can reflect parts of the room or the characters, creating the illusion of more space while adding depth and texture to the scene. Reflections can also be used creatively to capture unique angles or to show multiple perspectives of the same action.

Strategic use of doors and windows: Doors and windows are natural framing devices that can help break up a scene and add layers of depth. Filming a character through a doorway or a window can create a sense of distance, provide a voyeuristic or isolating effect, or allow you to divide the frame into distinct sections, adding visual interest.

Frame within a frame: A great technique for adding depth to small spaces is to use a "frame within a frame," where you position your subject within a natural frame created by the environment, such as a window, doorway, or even the shape of furniture. This technique focuses the audience's attention on the subject while giving the impression of a larger, more structured space.

Play with Angles and Camera Movement

In a small space, static shots can sometimes make the scene feel confined. To counter this, experiment with different angles and camera movements to create a sense of fluidity and make the most of the environment. Since smartphones are lightweight and easy to maneuver, you can be more flexible with your shot choices. Consider the following approaches:

Low and high angles: Filming from low or high angles can create a dramatic effect and add visual interest to an otherwise confined space. For example, a low-angle shot can make a character appear more powerful or imposing, while a high-angle shot can make the audience feel like they are looking down on the character, adding to a sense of vulnerability or isolation.

Tracking shots: Use the portability of the smartphone to create tracking shots that follow the actors through the space. This technique adds movement and energy to the scene and helps the audience feel more connected to the characters' actions. For example, you can follow a character as they move from room to room, or track their movements as they interact with objects in a tight space.

Handheld movement: Handheld shots can create a sense of intimacy or tension, especially in confined environments. By moving the camera naturally with the actors, you can heighten the realism and make the audience feel like they are inside the space with the characters. This technique works well in emotional or intense scenes, where the closeness and movement of the camera can amplify the drama.

Overhead shots: If the space allows, consider using overhead shots to create an unusual perspective. Shooting from directly above can make a small space look larger and give the audience a new way to view the action. Overhead shots work particularly well for scenes involving physical movement, like a character lying down, a fight sequence, or a group of people moving within a confined area.

Use Lighting to Create Atmosphere

Lighting is one of the most effective tools for transforming small spaces into visually interesting environments. Since smartphone cameras are more sensitive to lighting conditions than traditional cameras, carefully controlling the light in a limited space can enhance the mood and tone of the scene.

Here are some tips for using lighting in small spaces:

Natural light: Take advantage of natural light whenever possible, especially if you're shooting in a small room with windows. Position your actors near windows to let soft, natural light illuminate their faces, or use the sunlight to cast interesting shadows across the room. Natural light can help brighten up a small space and create a more open, airy feeling.

Practical lighting: Incorporate practical light sources—such as lamps, candles, or even string lights—into the scene to add atmosphere and texture. Since smartphone films often have a more intimate and DIY aesthetic, using practical lights can make the space feel more realistic and lived-in. Experiment with different types of light to create contrast and highlight key elements of the room.

Low light and shadows: Don't be afraid to play with shadows and darkness, especially if the mood of the scene calls for it. In a small space, strategic use of shadows can create depth and mystery, hiding parts of the room while drawing attention to the characters. Low lighting can also enhance the atmosphere, adding tension or a sense of isolation.

LED or portable lights: If you need more control over the lighting, portable LED lights are a great option for small spaces. They are compact, easy to adjust, and can provide soft, even lighting that complements the smartphone's camera. You can use LED lights to fill in dark corners, highlight specific areas, or create dramatic lighting effects.

Use the Space to Reflect the Characters

The location in a film isn't just a backdrop—it can also serve as a reflection of the characters' internal state or the film's themes. In a confined space, you have the opportunity to use the environment to emphasize the characters' emotions, relationships, and struggles.

For example, a cluttered, disorganized room might represent a character's chaotic mental state, while a small, stark, empty space could symbolize isolation or emotional withdrawal. Pay attention to the details of the space and think about how they reflect the character's journey. Is the room filled with personal items that reveal something about the character's personality? Is the setting oppressive, with no escape, mirroring the character's situation? Use the space as an extension of the character's story.

Make Use of Off-Screen Space

Even if you're filming in a small room, you can create the illusion of a larger world by making use of off-screen space. This technique involves suggesting action, sounds, or events happening outside the frame, giving the audience the sense that the story extends beyond the immediate environment.

For example, you can film a conversation where one character is off-screen, letting the audience imagine their presence while focusing on the reaction of the character in frame. Similarly, sounds like footsteps, distant voices, or ambient noise from outside the room can suggest a world beyond the walls of the small space, expanding the film's scope without physically changing the location.

Transform the Space with Set Design

Even if you're working with a limited location, you can transform the space with creative set design. Small adjustments like rearranging furniture, adding props, or changing the color scheme can dramatically alter the mood and appearance of the room. Set design allows you to tailor the environment to the needs of the story while adding layers of visual storytelling.

For example, a cramped living room can be turned into a cozy, intimate space by adding warm lighting, soft fabrics, and personal touches like books or artwork. On the other hand, the same room can feel cold and distant with harsher lighting, minimalist décor, and fewer personal items. Think about how the design of the space aligns with the characters and the themes of your story, and make changes accordingly.

Filming in limited spaces doesn't have to be a limitation—it can be an opportunity to get creative and make bold choices that enhance your film. With a smartphone, you have the flexibility to explore unique angles, dynamic camera movements, and unconventional framing that maximize the potential of tight environments. By paying attention to lighting, composition, and set design, you can transform a small space into a visually compelling setting that supports the story and brings your characters' emotions to life. Ultimately, your creativity in using the space will add depth and richness to your film, turning limitations into strengths.

Lighting for Mobile Filmmaking: Techniques on a Budget

Lighting is one of the most critical elements of filmmaking, directly influencing the mood, tone, and visual quality of your film. While smartphones have advanced significantly in terms of camera capabilities, they are still more sensitive to lighting conditions than professional cameras, meaning good lighting is essential to getting the best results. Fortunately, creating effective lighting setups for your smartphone film doesn't require a big budget or expensive equipment. In this chapter, we'll explore budget-friendly lighting techniques that can elevate the look of your mobile film and help you craft compelling visuals.

The Importance of Lighting in Mobile Filmmaking

Smartphone cameras are often less forgiving in low-light conditions, producing grainy or noisy images if not properly lit. Lighting not only helps improve the overall clarity and quality of your footage but also sets the emotional tone of a scene. Whether you're aiming for a soft, natural feel or a dramatic, high-contrast look, lighting helps convey the mood and atmosphere of your story.

Good lighting can also be used to guide the viewer's attention, highlight key elements in the frame, and reveal or conceal aspects of the scene. By understanding the basics of lighting, you can use it to enhance your storytelling without the need for expensive gear.

Understanding the Basics of Lighting

Before diving into specific techniques, it's important to understand some basic lighting principles:

Key Light: The primary source of light in your scene. It illuminates the subject and sets the overall tone. The key light is usually placed to the side of the camera, creating depth and shadows.

Fill Light: Used to soften or fill in the shadows created by the key light. The fill light is often placed opposite the key light and is usually softer or less intense to maintain some contrast.

Backlight: Positioned behind the subject, the backlight helps separate the subject from the background and adds depth to the image. It can create a halo effect around the subject, especially when used subtly.

Natural Light: Light from the sun, which can be a powerful and free resource for outdoor and indoor shoots. However, natural light can be unpredictable, so learning to harness and control it is key.

Practical Lights: Light sources that exist within the scene itself, such as lamps, candles, or streetlights. Practical lights can add atmosphere, and since they are part of the set, they feel organic and realistic.

Maximizing Natural Light

When working on a budget, natural light is your best friend. The sun provides a free and powerful source of light, but it requires some planning and creativity to make the most of it. Here are some tips for using natural light effectively:

Golden Hour

The "golden hour"—the period shortly after sunrise and before sunset—provides some of the most flattering, soft, and even natural light for filming. During this time, the sun is low in the sky, casting a warm glow and creating gentle shadows. Shooting during golden hour can give your film a cinematic quality without needing any additional lighting equipment.

Positioning Your Subject

When filming outdoors, always be mindful of the position of the sun. Placing the sun directly behind the subject can create a beautiful backlit effect, highlighting the subject's outline while softening their features. You can also place the sun at an angle to create a more dramatic lighting setup, with one side of the subject in light and the other in shadow. If the sunlight is too harsh (especially around midday), you can use reflectors or whiteboards to bounce light back onto the subject's face. This will help reduce the harsh shadows and even out the lighting.

Using Windows

When filming indoors, windows are a great source of natural light. Position your subject near a window to let soft, diffused light illuminate their face. North-facing windows generally provide the most consistent and even light throughout the day, as they don't receive direct sunlight.

If the light from the window is too strong, you can soften it by hanging a white curtain, sheet, or even a shower curtain over the window to diffuse the sunlight. This creates a natural softbox effect that smooths out shadows and reduces harshness.

Budget-Friendly Lighting Solutions

While natural light is ideal, it isn't always available or reliable, especially for indoor shoots or nighttime scenes. Fortunately, there are several low-cost lighting options that can significantly improve your smartphone footage.

Household Lamps

Household lamps are an easy and budget-friendly way to add light to your scenes. Desk lamps, floor lamps, or even bedside lamps can be repositioned to act as key or fill lights. You can experiment with different bulb types and wattages to achieve the desired brightness and color temperature.

Soft light: If you need softer, more diffused lighting, place a lampshade over the bulb or drape a piece of white fabric or parchment paper in front of the lamp (but keep it at a safe distance from the heat of the bulb). This will reduce harsh shadows and create a more flattering light for close-up shots.

Directional light: For a more dramatic look, remove the lampshade and use the bare bulb to create strong, directional light. Position the lamp to the side or behind the subject to cast bold shadows and enhance contrast.

LED Lights

Portable LED lights are affordable, energy-efficient, and easy to set up. You can find small LED panels or handheld LED lights at low prices, many of which are designed specifically for mobile filmmaking. LEDs are versatile and can be used as key, fill, or backlights.

Some LED lights come with adjustable brightness and color temperature settings, allowing you to control the intensity and warmth of the light. This flexibility is useful when you're working in different lighting conditions or trying to match the color of existing light sources.

DIY Reflectors

Reflectors are an inexpensive way to manipulate light, especially when working with natural light or household lamps. You can create DIY reflectors using everyday materials, such as white poster boards, aluminum foil, or even a car sunshade.

White reflectors: These bounce soft, even light back onto the subject and are great for filling in shadows. You can use white foam boards or poster boards to reflect light onto your subject's face.

Silver reflectors: Aluminum foil or metallic surfaces reflect more intense, focused light. This can create a sharper fill or add dramatic highlights to the scene.

Position the reflector opposite the key light to bounce light back onto the shadowed side of the subject. Reflectors are particularly useful for outdoor shoots when you need to even out lighting without introducing additional light sources.

String Lights and Fairy Lights

String lights or fairy lights can add ambiance and visual interest to your scenes without costing much. These lights work well as practical lighting in the background, adding a warm, magical glow to night scenes or creating a cozy atmosphere in indoor settings.

You can also use string lights as a soft, diffused source of light for close-ups. By positioning them around your subject or draping them over a surface, you can create a dreamy, intimate vibe that enhances the scene's mood.

Smartphone LED Flashlight

In a pinch, the LED flashlight on your smartphone can be used as a quick source of light. While not ideal for every situation, the flashlight can work for close-up shots or when you need a small amount of fill light in darker environments.

To avoid harsh shadows or overexposure, try diffusing the flashlight by covering it with a piece of wax paper or a thin white cloth. This will soften the light and create a more flattering effect on the subject.

Lighting Techniques to Create Mood

Lighting isn't just about illuminating your scene—it's a powerful tool for establishing the mood and tone of your film. Here are some lighting techniques you can use to create specific atmospheres:

High-Key Lighting

High-key lighting is bright, even, and minimizes shadows. It's commonly used in comedies, feel-good films, or scenes where you want to create a light, optimistic, or happy atmosphere. You can achieve high-key lighting by using multiple light sources (such as two or three lamps) to eliminate deep shadows and create an evenly lit scene.

Low-Key Lighting

Low-key lighting, on the other hand, is characterized by strong contrasts between light and dark areas. It creates a more dramatic, moody, or mysterious atmosphere and is often used in genres like horror, noir, and thrillers. To create low-key lighting, use a single, strong light source (such as a bare bulb or LED panel) placed at an angle to cast deep shadows across the subject's face. You can also turn off or dim the fill light to maintain those shadows and increase contrast.

Silhouette Lighting

Silhouette lighting creates a striking visual effect by placing the subject in front of a bright light source (such as a window, lamp, or even the setting sun) while keeping the foreground unlit. This creates a dark outline or silhouette of the subject, obscuring their facial features and focusing the viewer's attention on their shape or movements.

Practical Lighting for Atmosphere

Using practical lights—like desk lamps, neon signs, or even candles—can add atmosphere and realism to a scene while also serving as the primary light source. Practical lights are great for scenes that require a more intimate, natural feel. Since practical lights are already part of the set, they feel more integrated and organic to the environment, helping to enhance the authenticity of the film.

Controlling Color Temperature

Color temperature refers to the warmth or coolness of the light in your scene, measured in Kelvin (K). Warmer light (lower Kelvin, around 2000-4000K) gives off a yellowish glow, while cooler light (higher Kelvin, around 5000-6500K) produces a bluish tint. Controlling color temperature allows you to set the tone of the scene and ensure consistency across shots.

Warm light: Use warmer tones to create a cozy, inviting, or nostalgic atmosphere. Warm light works well in interior scenes or moments of emotional intimacy.

Cool light: Cool light can create a more clinical, detached, or eerie feel. It's often used in sci-fi, crime dramas, or to create tension in darker scenes.

If you're working with multiple light sources, make sure they have similar color temperatures to avoid inconsistencies in your footage. You can adjust the color temperature by changing the type of bulbs you use or by adding colored gels to your lights.

Lighting for mobile filmmaking doesn't have to be expensive or complicated. With a few budget-friendly tools and a solid understanding of lighting principles, you can create visually striking and emotionally powerful scenes that elevate the quality of your film. Whether you're using natural light, household lamps, DIY reflectors, or creative lighting techniques, the key is to experiment and find what works best for the mood, tone, and visual style of your story. By mastering the art of lighting on a budget, you can bring a professional look to your smartphone film and create compelling visuals that captivate your audience.

Sound on Set: Recording Audio with Your Phone

Good audio is just as important—if not more important—than good visuals when it comes to filmmaking. While audiences may tolerate slightly grainy or low-resolution footage, poor sound quality can quickly take them out of the experience. This is especially true for smartphone filmmaking, where you're often working with smaller, less advanced equipment. Fortunately, recording high-quality audio with your phone is entirely possible with the right techniques and a few affordable tools. In this chapter, we'll explore how to record great sound on set using your smartphone, covering essential equipment, tips for minimizing background noise, and methods for syncing audio in post-production.

Why Audio is Crucial in Mobile Filmmaking

In film, sound helps immerse the audience in the world of the story, conveying emotions, setting the atmosphere, and delivering essential dialogue. Even with strong visuals, poor sound can make a film feel amateurish or disengaging. Clear dialogue, ambient sounds, and appropriate sound effects bring depth and authenticity to your film.

Smartphones can produce decent sound with their built-in microphones, but they're far from ideal for professional-quality audio. They tend to pick up a lot of ambient noise, have limited range, and lack the ability to focus on specific sounds. Therefore, investing in external audio equipment and employing smart recording techniques can dramatically improve the sound quality of your film.

Basic Smartphone Audio Equipment

While you can certainly record audio directly with your smartphone's built-in microphone, external microphones offer better sound clarity and noise isolation. Here's a look at some of the key audio equipment to consider for your mobile filmmaking setup:

Lavalier (Lapel) Microphones

Lavalier microphones, or lapel mics, are small, clip-on microphones that attach directly to your actor's clothing. They are ideal for capturing clear dialogue, especially in scenes with lots of movement or background noise. Lavalier mics are discreet, allowing you to get the microphone close to the speaker's mouth without being visible on camera.

Many lavalier mics are designed to work with smartphones and plug directly into your phone's headphone jack or Lightning/USB-C port. These mics are affordable and offer a significant improvement over your phone's internal microphone, making them a great option for dialogue-heavy scenes.

Shotgun Microphones

Shotgun microphones are directional mics designed to capture sound from a specific direction, reducing background noise from other angles. These mics are ideal for recording clean audio on set, as they can be pointed directly at the speaker while filtering out unwanted ambient sounds.

A shotgun mic can be mounted on your smartphone using a cold shoe mount or held off-camera using a boom pole. Some small, affordable shotgun mics are designed specifically for smartphones and come with adapters to plug directly into your device. Using a shotgun mic with a boom operator allows you to position the mic close to the actors without it appearing in the frame, capturing high-quality sound from a distance.

External Recorders

If you want to take your audio quality to the next level, consider using an external audio recorder. While this requires syncing audio in post-production, external recorders often provide superior sound quality compared to a smartphone's internal microphone. Popular options like the Zoom H1n or Tascam DR-05 are portable, easy to use, and can be connected to external mics for professional-grade sound recording.

External recorders give you more control over audio levels and recording settings, allowing you to capture crisp, clean sound that you can easily adjust in post. They also come in handy when you need to record ambient sounds or foley (sound effects created after the shoot) to enhance your film.

Audio Adapters

If you're using an external microphone with your smartphone, you may need an adapter to connect the mic to your phone's input. Modern smartphones often have either Lightning ports (for iPhones) or USB-C ports (for Android devices), so ensure that your microphone is compatible or use an adapter that works with your phone's input.

For example, the Rode SC6 is an adapter that allows you to connect two microphones and headphones to a smartphone for monitoring audio during recording. Investing in a high-quality audio adapter ensures that you're capturing the best possible sound from your external microphone.

Windscreens and Shock Mounts

Windscreens and shock mounts are essential accessories for improving the quality of your recordings, particularly when shooting outdoors or in noisy environments.

Windscreens: Windscreens (also known as "deadcats") are furry covers that go over your microphone to block out wind noise during outdoor shoots. Even a slight breeze can cause unpleasant distortion in your recordings, so using a windscreen is a simple yet effective way to protect your audio.

Shock mounts: Shock mounts prevent handling noise and vibrations from being picked up by the microphone. These mounts isolate the microphone from physical movement, ensuring cleaner sound when the mic is moved or adjusted during a shoot.

Tips for Recording Clear Audio on Set

Once you have the right equipment, it's important to employ good recording practices to ensure the best possible sound quality. Here are some tips to help you record clear, professional audio with your smartphone:

Record in Quiet Environments

Choosing a quiet location for recording is the most important factor in getting clear audio. Avoid filming in areas with excessive background noise, such as busy streets, crowded public spaces, or areas near loud machinery. If you must shoot in a noisy environment, consider recording the dialogue separately in a quieter location (called ADR or Automated Dialogue Replacement) and syncing it with the visuals later.

If you're indoors, turn off any fans, air conditioners, or other electronic devices that could create unwanted background noise. Also, listen for small noises like ticking clocks, footsteps, or creaky floors that might interfere with the clarity of your audio.

Get the Microphone Close to the Subject

One of the most important rules of sound recording is to get the microphone as close to the subject as possible. The closer the mic is to the actor's mouth, the better the clarity of the sound and the less background noise it will pick up. Using a lavalier mic attached to the actor's clothing or a shotgun mic held just outside of the frame on a boom pole are effective ways to get close to the subject without compromising the shot. If you're recording with a built-in microphone, try to position the smartphone close to the actor while ensuring that the framing still works for the scene.

Monitor the Audio in Real-Time

Whenever possible, use headphones to monitor the audio while recording. This allows you to catch any issues, such as unwanted noise, distortion, or uneven levels, before it's too late. If your phone supports it, connect a pair of headphones directly to the device or use an external recorder that allows for real-time audio monitoring.

Monitoring your audio ensures that you're aware of any potential problems, such as wind interference or handling noise, and allows you to adjust the microphone or settings accordingly.

Control Audio Levels

Most smartphones and external recorders allow you to manually adjust the audio levels, which is crucial for avoiding distortion or clipping (when the sound is too loud and gets cut off). Aim for audio levels that peak around -6 dB, leaving enough headroom to prevent distortion during loud moments while ensuring the sound is still clear.

If you're using an external microphone or recorder, adjust the gain levels based on the volume of the speaker's voice or the ambient noise in the environment. Always test your audio levels before you start filming to ensure they're set appropriately.

Record Room Tone and Ambient Sound

It's a good practice to record room tone (the natural sound of the environment when no one is speaking) and ambient sound (background noise that adds atmosphere) at every location you shoot. Room tone is essential for smoothing out audio transitions in post-production and can help make cuts between dialogue feel seamless.

For example, after shooting a dialogue scene in a quiet room, record 30 seconds of the room's natural ambient noise. This audio can then be used to fill any gaps or smooth out the transition between different takes. Ambient sound can also be useful for enhancing the setting, such as birds chirping in a park or distant city traffic in an urban environment.

Syncing Audio in Post-Production

If you're using an external audio recorder, you'll need to sync the recorded sound with the video footage during editing. Syncing audio manually can be time-consuming, but it's much easier if you follow these steps:

Use a Clapboard or Hand Clap

A traditional clapboard (or slate) or a simple hand clap before each take provides a visual and audio reference point for syncing the audio in post-production. When editing, you can align the visual of the clap with the corresponding spike in the audio waveform to ensure perfect synchronization.

Label and Organize Your Audio Files

Keeping your audio files organized is key to a smooth post-production process. Label each audio file with the scene number and take number so that you can easily match it with the corresponding video footage during editing. Organizing your audio and video files properly will save you time and frustration in the editing room.

Use Audio Syncing Software

Many editing programs, such as Adobe Premiere Pro, Final Cut Pro, and DaVinci Resolve, offer automatic audio syncing features that match external audio with your video clips based on the sound waveform. These tools can greatly speed up the process and ensure accurate syncing, allowing you to focus more on the creative aspects of editing.

Recording high-quality audio is crucial to creating a professional, polished film, even when shooting on a smartphone. With the right equipment and techniques, you can capture clear dialogue, ambient sound, and atmospheric audio that enhances your film's storytelling.

Shooting Techniques: Framing and Angles for Mobile Films

When it comes to mobile filmmaking, one of the most powerful tools at your disposal is how you frame and shoot your scenes. Thoughtful framing and the right angles can elevate your film from simple to cinematic, creating depth, mood, and meaning without the need for expensive equipment. Smartphones allow for flexibility and experimentation, giving you the ability to capture unique perspectives and dynamic shots that enhance the storytelling process. In this chapter, we'll explore various shooting techniques for framing and angles to help you maximize the visual impact of your mobile film.

Understanding Framing in Mobile Filmmaking

Framing refers to how you position your subject within the boundaries of the shot. The way you frame a shot can change how the audience perceives the action, emotion, or setting. Strong framing can guide the viewer's eye, emphasize important elements, and create a sense of balance and composition. Since smartphone screens are smaller than traditional camera monitors, careful framing becomes even more crucial to ensure clarity and impact.

Here are some key concepts to consider when thinking about framing in mobile filmmaking:

The Rule of Thirds

The rule of thirds is a fundamental composition technique that involves dividing the frame into a 3x3 grid. The idea is to place key elements of the scene along the grid lines or at the intersections of these lines, rather than simply centering the subject in the frame. This creates a more visually balanced and dynamic shot.

When using the rule of thirds, think about what you want the audience to focus on. Placing your subject off-center can create a sense of movement or tension, while using the intersecting points to position important visual elements can draw the viewer's attention naturally.

For example, if you're shooting a conversation, you might position the actor's eyes along the upper third line, with their body placed on one of the vertical grid lines. This technique not only frames the subject well but also leaves space for the background, adding context and depth to the shot.

Leading Lines

Leading lines are visual elements in the scene that naturally guide the viewer's eye toward the subject. These can be actual lines, such as roads, walls, or railings, or implied lines, such as the way light falls on a surface. Leading lines create a sense of direction and depth, drawing the audience into the shot and helping them focus on the most important elements.

When composing your shot, look for natural or architectural lines in the environment. Position your subject where these lines converge or direct attention, adding a dynamic flow to the scene. For example, filming an actor walking down a long hallway with the walls and floor forming leading lines toward them can create a powerful sense of focus and movement.

Symmetry and Balance

Symmetrical framing involves placing the subject directly in the center of the frame, creating a sense of balance and harmony. This type of framing works well when you want to emphasize stability, order, or importance. Symmetrical shots can be visually striking, particularly in scenes that involve formal environments or where you want to draw attention to the symmetry of the setting.

For example, shooting a character sitting alone in a perfectly symmetrical room can create a feeling of isolation or power. While symmetry is visually pleasing, it's best used sparingly to avoid making the composition feel too static.

Negative Space

Negative space refers to the empty or unused areas of a frame that surround the subject. It can be a powerful tool for creating mood and emphasizing isolation, vulnerability, or freedom. By allowing more negative space around your subject, you create room for the audience to contemplate the scene and the character's emotional state.

For example, framing a character off to the side of the frame with a vast amount of empty space around them can evoke feelings of loneliness or tension. Negative space can also create a sense of minimalism, directing focus solely on the character or action while stripping away unnecessary details.

Exploring Angles in Mobile Filmmaking

The angle from which you shoot your subject can significantly alter the emotional impact of the scene. Different angles can change the way the audience perceives the character, the action, and the environment. Here are some of the most commonly used angles in filmmaking and how you can use them to enhance your mobile film:

Eye-Level Shots

The eye-level shot is one of the most common and natural angles, placing the camera at the same height as the subject's eyes. This creates a sense of equality and neutrality, making the shot feel grounded and relatable. Eye-level shots are ideal for dialogue scenes, as they mimic how we typically engage with people in real life.

Since smartphone cameras are small and portable, achieving eye-level shots is easy, whether your subject is sitting, standing, or moving. This angle is perfect for scenes where you want to create an intimate connection between the audience and the character, offering a direct, unfiltered perspective.

Low-Angle Shots

A low-angle shot is filmed from below the subject, looking up. This angle can make the subject appear more powerful, dominant, or intimidating. Low-angle shots are often used in films to emphasize a character's authority or strength, as they make the subject look larger and more imposing.

In a smartphone film, you can easily achieve low-angle shots by positioning the phone on the ground or holding it just below the subject. This angle is great for action scenes, moments of confrontation, or when you want to visually convey that a character is in control of the situation.

High-Angle Shots

A high-angle shot looks down on the subject from above. This angle tends to make the subject appear smaller, weaker, or more vulnerable, creating a sense of inferiority or submission. High-angle shots are effective for portraying characters who are in difficult or compromising situations.

To shoot a high-angle shot with a smartphone, simply raise the phone above the subject's head, either by hand or using a stabilizer. High-angle shots work well in emotional scenes where a character is experiencing fear, defeat, or loneliness. They can also be used in establishing shots to give a broad overview of the setting.

Bird's-Eye View

A bird's-eye view shot is taken from directly overhead, looking straight down on the scene. This angle provides a unique, often abstract perspective and is great for showing spatial relationships between characters or creating a sense of distance or isolation. Bird's-eye view shots can also be used to reveal patterns or movements that are not visible from other angles.

In smartphone filmmaking, you can achieve a bird's-eye view by holding the phone directly above the subject or using a drone for outdoor shots. This angle works well for scenes that involve large groups of people, intricate choreography, or when you want to create a stylized, detached look.

Dutch Angle (Tilted Angle)

A Dutch angle involves tilting the camera so that the horizon line is slanted, creating a sense of unease, tension, or disorientation. This angle is often used in thriller or horror films to visually convey instability or conflict. The Dutch angle is great for moments of emotional or psychological distress, heightening the sense of chaos or danger in the scene.

To create a Dutch angle, simply tilt your smartphone slightly when framing the shot. Use this technique sparingly, as it can become visually overwhelming if overused. It's most effective in scenes where the character's world is figuratively or literally off-balance.

Over-the-Shoulder Shots

Over-the-shoulder (OTS) shots are commonly used in dialogue scenes to show one character's perspective while framing the other character in the shot. The camera is positioned just behind the shoulder of one character, focusing on the person they are interacting with. This angle creates a sense of involvement in the conversation, allowing the audience to feel like they are part of the interaction.

Smartphones are perfect for capturing OTS shots because of their lightweight design, allowing you to get close to the actors without being intrusive. OTS shots are useful for building tension or intimacy between characters, as they place the viewer within the personal space of the actors.

Point-of-View Shots

Point-of-view (POV) shots show the audience what the character is seeing, creating a direct connection between the viewer and the character's experience. This technique is highly immersive, making the audience feel like they are living through the character's perspective.

In mobile filmmaking, POV shots are easy to achieve by holding the smartphone at the character's eye level and capturing what they see. POV shots are effective for action scenes, horror moments, or any situation where you want the audience to feel directly involved in the character's journey.

Camera Movement in Mobile Filmmaking

Camera movement adds energy, emotion, and dynamism to a scene. With a smartphone, you can experiment with various types of movement to enhance your shots without the need for expensive equipment:

Tracking Shots: A tracking shot follows the movement of a character or object, often using a handheld or stabilizer-mounted camera. This type of shot is ideal for scenes where characters are walking, running, or moving through a space, as it creates a sense of forward momentum.

Panning and Tilting: Panning involves moving the camera horizontally from left to right (or vice versa), while tilting involves moving the camera vertically up or down. Both techniques are great for revealing new elements of a scene or transitioning between different subjects.

Handheld Shots: Handheld shots offer a raw, intimate, and sometimes chaotic feel, as the camera moves naturally with the operator. Smartphone cameras are well-suited for handheld shooting because they are light and easy to carry. This technique works well for action scenes, chase sequences, or any moment where you want to create a sense of immediacy or realism.

Dolly Shots: A dolly shot involves moving the camera toward or away from the subject, creating a sense of depth and scale. While you may not have access to a traditional dolly, you can mimic this effect by walking smoothly toward or away from the subject with your smartphone or using a wheeled platform like a skateboard.

Framing and angles are key elements of storytelling in filmmaking, and smartphones offer the flexibility to experiment with a wide range of techniques. By using thoughtful framing, such as the rule of thirds, leading lines, and symmetry, you can create visually compelling shots that enhance the narrative. Exploring different angles, from eye-level and low-angle shots to bird's-eye views and Dutch angles, allows you to shape how the audience perceives the characters and the action. With the mobility of a smartphone, you can also incorporate dynamic camera movement, such as tracking, panning, or handheld shots, to bring energy and emotion to your film.

Visual Effects: Adding Magic with Your Phone

Visual effects (VFX) can add a layer of magic and creativity to your mobile film, transforming ordinary scenes into extraordinary moments. With advancements in smartphone technology, it's easier than ever to incorporate professional-quality visual effects into your films without needing a Hollywood budget or extensive technical expertise. Whether you want to enhance an action sequence, create a fantasy world, or add subtle touches that improve the realism of your scenes, your smartphone and a few key apps can help bring your vision to life. In this chapter, we'll explore how to add visual effects to your film using your phone, covering basic techniques, apps, and tips for seamless integration.

Why Visual Effects Matter in Mobile Filmmaking

Visual effects can serve multiple purposes in your film. They can create illusions or manipulations that would be difficult or impossible to achieve during filming, such as explosions, supernatural elements, or futuristic settings. VFX can also be used more subtly, enhancing everyday scenes with environmental effects like weather, lighting changes, or digital enhancements to make them more immersive and visually engaging.

The key to using visual effects effectively in your film is to ensure that they serve the story. Whether you're creating fantastical creatures, altering the setting, or adding cinematic touches, the VFX should enhance the narrative and not feel like a distraction. The right visual effects can elevate the production value of your smartphone film, making it more captivating and dynamic.

Tools and Apps for Adding Visual Effects

There are several powerful and user-friendly apps available for creating and editing visual effects on your smartphone. These apps allow you to add everything from simple animations to complex VFX elements directly onto your footage, transforming your scenes without requiring a deep understanding of visual effects software.

Here are some popular VFX apps you can use for mobile filmmaking:

Adobe after Effects (via Adobe Rush)

Adobe After Effects is one of the most widely used tools in the film industry for creating visual effects. While it's a desktop application, you can integrate After Effects into your mobile workflow by using Adobe Rush, a mobile editing app that connects with Adobe Creative Cloud. Rush allows you to edit your footage and import it into After Effects for advanced VFX work.

For filmmakers who are familiar with desktop VFX tools or want to take their visual effects to a professional level, this is a powerful option. After Effects offers endless possibilities, from adding explosions and particle effects to creating complex animations and green screen compositions.

Action Movie FX

Action Movie FX is an app that allows you to easily add Hollywood-style visual effects to your scenes. The app offers a wide range of effects, including explosions, missile attacks, alien invasions, car crashes, and more. It's particularly useful for action-packed scenes where you want to add drama and intensity.

This app is designed to be user-friendly, making it perfect for beginners. You simply shoot the footage with your smartphone, select an effect, and the app automatically integrates it into your scene. While the effects are pre-designed, you can still adjust their positioning and timing to fit your footage, making it an accessible and quick way to enhance your action sequences.

Videoleap by Lightricks

Videoleap is a powerful mobile editing app that includes features for adding visual effects, overlays, and animations to your footage. It offers tools like green screen keying, blending modes, and layering, allowing you to combine multiple visual elements into a single shot. Videoleap is great for adding creative effects, such as glitch transitions, light leaks, and color enhancements.

What sets Videoleap apart is its intuitive interface and ability to layer effects on top of your video. For instance, you can easily add particle effects like dust, sparks, or rain to create atmospheric scenes, or use its masking tools to blend different elements seamlessly. The app also supports 4K resolution, making it ideal for high-quality smartphone filmmaking.

Alight Motion

Alight Motion is another mobile app that offers advanced motion graphics, visual effects, and compositing features. It's one of the most versatile apps available for smartphone filmmakers, allowing you to create everything from simple effects to complex VFX sequences. You can animate elements, use keyframe animation, add visual distortions, and apply blending modes to create professional-looking effects.

Alight Motion also includes vector and bitmap support, so you can create custom graphics and integrate them with your live-action footage. This app is perfect for filmmakers who want to push the boundaries of what's possible with VFX on a smartphone, creating everything from animated title sequences to complex visual compositions.

Filmr

Filmr is a mobile video editor that offers basic visual effects tools like transitions, overlays, and text animations. It's user-friendly and suitable for filmmakers who want to add simple effects to enhance their storytelling. You can add cinematic transitions, light effects, and visual filters that improve the look and feel of your film.

While Filmr doesn't offer the extensive VFX capabilities of apps like Videoleap or After Effects, it's a great option for filmmakers who want to keep things simple and add subtle visual enhancements without spending too much time on post-production.

Key Visual Effects Techniques for Smartphone Films

Now that you have an understanding of the tools available, let's explore some essential VFX techniques you can use to enhance your mobile film. These effects range from simple, subtle touches to more complex creations that can dramatically transform your scenes.

Green Screen (Chroma Keying)

Green screen or chroma keying is one of the most versatile VFX techniques available, allowing you to replace the background of a shot with virtually anything you can imagine. By filming your subject in front of a green (or blue) screen, you can later remove the green background and replace it with a new environment, such as an alien planet, a bustling cityscape, or a fantasy realm.

Many mobile editing apps, including Videoleap and Alight Motion, offer built-in chroma keying tools, making it easy to implement green screen effects in your smartphone film. To achieve the best results, ensure that the green screen is evenly lit, and avoid shadows or wrinkles that could interfere with the keying process.

Particle Effects (Rain, Snow, Fire, Dust)

Particle effects, such as rain, snow, fire, or dust, can add realism and atmosphere to your scenes. These effects are particularly useful when you want to create environmental conditions that would be difficult or impractical to film on location. For example, you can add rain to an outdoor scene or simulate falling snow for a winter setting.

Apps like Videoleap and Action Movie FX offer built-in particle effects that can be easily layered onto your footage. You can adjust the size, density, and direction of the particles to fit the scene, creating a more immersive atmosphere.

For instance, adding light dust particles can give an outdoor scene a sense of age or mystery, while fire or sparks can intensify an action sequence.

Slow Motion and Time Manipulation

Manipulating time—either by speeding it up or slowing it down—can create dramatic visual effects that captivate the audience. Slow motion is particularly effective for action sequences, highlighting key moments like a punch, a car crash, or an explosion. Speeding up time can create a sense of urgency or excitement, such as during a chase scene.

Most smartphones come with built-in slow-motion and time-lapse capabilities, allowing you to capture footage directly in these modes. You can also manipulate time in post-production using apps like Alight Motion or Videoleap. These apps allow you to control the speed of specific sections of your footage, creating dynamic shifts in the pacing of your scenes.

Tracking and Motion Graphics

Motion tracking allows you to attach visual effects or animations to specific points in your footage, ensuring they move naturally with the action. For example, you could track a character's hand as they cast a spell, adding glowing energy effects that follow their movement. Motion graphics, such as animated text or objects, can also be used to enhance your scenes with digital elements.

Alight Motion and Adobe After Effects offer motion tracking tools that make it easy to attach effects or animations to specific points in your footage. You can use this technique to create dynamic visual elements that interact with the live-action shots, adding depth and engagement to the film.

Lighting Effects (Lens Flares, Light Rays)

Lighting effects can add a cinematic touch to your scenes, giving them a polished, professional feel. Lens flares, light rays, and glows can create a dramatic atmosphere or emphasize important moments in your film. These effects are often used in sci-fi, action, or fantasy genres to heighten the intensity of a scene.

Videoleap, Alight Motion, and other VFX apps allow you to add lighting effects to your footage. You can use lens flares to mimic the look of sunlight or artificial lights, or add glows and light rays to enhance magical or supernatural elements. Be careful not to overuse these effects, as too many can make the scene feel artificial or overwhelming.

Color Grading and Filters

While not a traditional visual effect, color grading can dramatically alter the mood and tone of your film. By adjusting the color balance, contrast, and saturation of your footage, you can create a cohesive visual style that supports your story. For instance, cooler tones might convey a sense of isolation or sadness, while warmer tones evoke comfort or nostalgia.

Many mobile apps, including Videoleap and Filmr, offer color grading tools and filters that allow you to enhance your footage with different looks. Color grading can help unify your film's visual style, ensuring that each scene feels like part of the same world.

Tips for Seamless Visual Effects Integration

To ensure that your visual effects feel natural and cohesive within your film, follow these tips:

Plan Ahead: Think about how you'll integrate visual effects into your scenes before you start filming. Knowing where and when you'll need VFX can help you plan shots, lighting, and camera movement to accommodate the effects more smoothly.

Blend Effects with Reality: Make sure your visual effects blend naturally with the live-action footage. This involves matching the lighting, perspective, and movement of the VFX elements to the environment and characters. For example, if you're adding a digital explosion, ensure that the lighting and shadows cast by the explosion align with the rest of the scene.

Use Effects to Serve the Story: Avoid overloading your film with unnecessary effects. The best visual effects are those that enhance the narrative, not distract from it. Always ask yourself how the VFX contribute to the storytelling, whether by creating atmosphere, adding drama, or visualizing something that can't be done practically.

Test and Adjust: Experiment with different effects, settings, and placements to see what works best for your scene. Don't hesitate to adjust and fine-tune the effects until they feel seamless and integrated into the action.

With the right tools and techniques, you can add high-quality visual effects to your smartphone film, transforming it into a cinematic experience that rivals larger productions. Whether you're using green screen, particle effects, motion graphics, or lighting enhancements, these VFX can help you create stunning visuals that captivate your audience. By carefully integrating effects that serve the story and using mobile apps to streamline the process, you can add magic and realism to your film, elevating it from simple smartphone footage to a creative, professional-level production.

Practical Effects: Using DIY Techniques for Stunning Results

Practical effects are an essential tool in filmmaking, allowing you to create tangible, physical effects that can be captured directly on camera. These effects can range from simple visual tricks to elaborate setups that mimic explosions, weather, or other dramatic elements. While visual effects (VFX) can be added in post-production, practical effects add a sense of realism and authenticity that is often hard to replicate digitally. The best part is that you can create stunning practical effects on a budget using DIY techniques and everyday materials. In this chapter, we'll explore how to use practical effects in your mobile film, offering creative ideas and techniques to achieve professional-quality results.

The Power of Practical Effects in Mobile Filmmaking

Practical effects bring a tactile, realistic quality to your film, allowing actors and environments to interact with real-world elements. This can lead to more authentic reactions and performances, as your actors have something tangible to respond to. Additionally, practical effects reduce the need for extensive post-production work, making the filmmaking process more efficient and grounded.

From smoke and fog to rain, fire, and even miniature models, practical effects offer countless ways to elevate your film's visual impact. With a bit of creativity and planning, you can achieve stunning effects with DIY methods that don't require expensive equipment or materials.

Essential DIY Practical Effects Techniques

Here are several effective and budget-friendly practical effects that you can incorporate into your smartphone film to achieve cinematic results.

DIY Rain Effects

Rain is a powerful visual tool that can add drama, tension, or melancholy to a scene. While you could wait for a real rainstorm, it's often easier to create your own rain effect on set. Here's how you can simulate rain using simple DIY techniques:

Garden Hose or Sprinkler: One of the easiest ways to create rain is by using a garden hose with a spray nozzle or a lawn sprinkler. Position the hose or sprinkler just out of the frame and let the water fall naturally over the actors or setting. Make sure to adjust the water pressure for the desired intensity, whether it's a light drizzle or a downpour.

Watering Can: For more localized rain, you can use a large watering can to pour water over specific areas. This is ideal for close-up shots where you don't need to drench the entire set.

Overhead Protection: If you're worried about your smartphone or lighting equipment getting wet, create a canopy or cover for your gear. A simple plastic sheet or umbrella can protect your camera while still allowing the rain effect to fall in front of the lens.

Backlight for Visibility: Rain is often hard to see on camera, so consider backlighting the rain with a soft light source to make the droplets sparkle and catch the light. This technique will make the rain more visible and enhance the overall cinematic effect.

Smoke and Fog Effects

Smoke and fog can add atmosphere and mystery to your film, creating a sense of danger, otherworldliness, or intensity. Here are a few easy ways to produce smoke and fog on a budget:

Smoke Machine: Affordable smoke machines are available for as little as $30 and can be used to create thick clouds of smoke for dramatic scenes. You can control the density of the smoke, making it perfect for everything from eerie horror settings to intense action sequences.

Dry Ice: Dry ice, when placed in water, produces a thick, low-lying fog that can drift across the floor, creating a spooky or magical effect. Be cautious when handling dry ice, as it can cause burns, but with proper safety precautions, it's a highly effective and visually stunning tool for atmospheric effects.

Incense or Cigarettes: For smaller smoke effects, such as smoke rising from a character's cigarette or a smouldering object, you can use incense sticks. The thin stream of smoke can be easily controlled and directed, making it great for subtle effects in close-up shots.

Fog with Glycerin and Water: You can create a homemade fog effect by mixing glycerin with water in a spray bottle. Lightly misting the set with this solution creates a fine, foggy appearance that works well for small indoor scenes.

Fire and Explosions

Fire and explosions can be dangerous to handle on set, but there are safe, DIY alternatives that mimic the appearance of fire or blast effects without the risk. Here are a few creative ways to simulate fire and explosions:

Flashing Lights for Fire: To simulate the glow of a fire without using real flames, use a flickering LED light or string of Christmas lights with orange and red gels over them. These lights can be placed just out of frame, casting a warm, flickering glow onto the actors and surroundings, giving the illusion of fire.

Dust and Debris for Explosions: Instead of using real explosives, you can simulate the aftermath of an explosion by throwing dust, dirt, or small debris into the air as the actors react. Combine this with sound effects in post-production for a convincing explosion scene. Use a fan or leaf blower to scatter debris across the scene for added realism.

Compressed Air for Small Blasts: If you need a small blast effect, you can use a compressed air canister (often used for cleaning electronics) to shoot air and dust into the scene. This works well for quick, close-up shots where an object is being knocked over or impacted.

Miniature Models

Miniature models are a classic technique for creating large-scale effects, such as cityscapes, buildings, or vehicles, in a controlled environment. Here's how you can use miniature models effectively:

Model Buildings and Vehicles: Use model kits or create your own miniature buildings and vehicles to simulate large structures or settings. By filming these miniatures at a low angle, you can make them appear much larger on screen. Add details like tiny lights, miniature cars, or debris to make the scene more convincing.

Forced Perspective: Forced perspective is a technique where you position a small model or object close to the camera while keeping the actors farther away, creating the illusion that the object is much larger. This works well for scenes where you want to make a small object, like a toy car or action figure, appear life-sized on camera.

Blood Effects

Blood effects are often essential for action, horror, or thriller films, but creating realistic-looking blood on a budget is easier than you might think:

DIY Fake Blood: You can create realistic fake blood using a mixture of corn syrup, red food coloring, and a few drops of blue or green food coloring to darken the shade. For a thicker consistency, add cornstarch. This mixture is non-toxic and looks great on camera.

Blood Splatter: For splattering effects, dip a sponge in the fake blood mixture and gently squeeze it in the direction of the camera or surface. You can also use a spray bottle filled with diluted fake blood to create fine mist effects, simulating blood spray from an impact.

Blood Tubes: If you want blood to spurt or drip from a wound, you can use small rubber tubing hidden under the actor's clothing. By squeezing the tube, the fake blood will flow out, simulating a bleeding injury.

DIY Camera Rigs for Effects

Sometimes the way you move or position your camera is just as important as the practical effect itself. Here are a few DIY camera rig ideas to enhance your practical effects:

Dolly or Slider: You can create a DIY camera dolly or slider using items like a skateboard, a rolling office chair, or even PVC pipes. This allows you to add smooth, controlled movement to your shots, especially when capturing practical effects like explosions or dynamic action.

Handheld Shake for Impact: For scenes that involve an explosion or intense action, you can simulate the shockwave by shaking the camera slightly during the moment of impact. A gentle, controlled shake will give the illusion of the ground shaking, intensifying the effect of the scene.

Makeup and Prosthetics

Makeup and prosthetic effects are invaluable for creating realistic wounds, scars, and other physical transformations. With a little creativity, you can make convincing special effects makeup using everyday household items:

Liquid Latex and Tissue: For creating wounds, burns, or scars, apply liquid latex to the skin and layer tissue paper over it. Once dry, you can tear or cut the tissue to create the appearance of torn flesh, which can be painted with fake blood and makeup for a realistic look.

Gelatin for Burns: You can create the appearance of burned or blistered skin by using gelatin. Apply warm gelatin to the skin, let it cool, and then paint over it with dark makeup and fake blood. The texture of the gelatin mimics the rough, uneven look of burns.

Face Paint for Monsters or Creatures: Use face paint or costume makeup to transform actors into otherworldly creatures or monsters. With a few simple tools like sponges, brushes, and stencils, you can create intricate designs that are perfect for fantasy or horror films.

Combining Practical Effects with VFX

While practical effects can often stand alone, combining them with visual effects (VFX) can produce truly stunning results. For example:

Fire and Explosion Effects: You can combine practical debris and smoke with digital fire or explosions using VFX apps like Videoleap or Action Movie FX. This creates a layered effect that feels more immersive.

Blood Effects: Start with practical blood splatters and enhance them with digital blood spray or dripping effects in post-production. This combination allows you to control the scale and intensity of the effect.

Weather Effects: Use a fog machine for practical smoke, then enhance the atmosphere by adding digital rain, snow, or wind effects during post-production.

Practical effects are a powerful and cost-effective way to create cinematic moments in your smartphone film. From DIY rain and smoke to miniature models and fake blood, these hands-on techniques can add realism, intensity, and visual interest to your scenes. By experimenting with household materials and simple tools, you can achieve stunning practical effects that elevate the overall production value of your film. Whether you're working with a small budget or simply love the tactile nature of practical effects, these techniques will help you bring your creative vision to life in a tangible, immersive way.

Editing on Your Phone: Choosing the Right Apps

Editing is where your film truly comes to life, transforming raw footage into a cohesive, polished final product. With today's powerful smartphones, you can easily edit an entire film on your device, making the process more accessible than ever. The key to successful mobile editing is choosing the right apps that suit your needs and budget. Whether you're looking for a simple editing tool for basic cuts or a more advanced app with professional-grade features, there are a variety of options available. In this chapter, we'll explore some of the best mobile editing apps, their features, and how to choose the right one for your mobile film project.

Why Editing on Your Phone Is a Game-Changer

Editing on your phone offers unparalleled convenience and flexibility. You can edit on the go, making adjustments wherever you are, without needing to transfer footage to a desktop computer. This can speed up your workflow, especially for smaller projects, and allows you to maintain creative momentum throughout the post-production process. Additionally, mobile editing apps have become increasingly sophisticated, with many offering features that rival desktop editing software.

Editing on your phone also reduces the amount of gear you need, making it easier for independent filmmakers and those working on tight budgets to produce professional-quality films. Let's dive into some of the best apps for mobile editing and what they offer.

Top Mobile Editing Apps

Here's a breakdown of the best mobile editing apps, from beginner-friendly options to more advanced tools for experienced filmmakers.

Adobe Premiere Rush

Best for: Filmmakers looking for a powerful, professional tool with seamless cross-device integration.

Adobe Premiere Rush is one of the most versatile and comprehensive mobile editing apps available. Designed with mobile filmmaking in mind, Rush allows you to shoot, edit, and share high-quality videos from your phone, tablet, or desktop. It offers a range of professional features like multi-track editing, advanced color correction, audio mixing, and motion graphics, all in a user-friendly interface.

One of the biggest advantages of Premiere Rush is its integration with Adobe Creative Cloud, allowing you to sync your project across devices and continue working from where you left off on another device, including Adobe Premiere Pro on your desktop.

Key Features:

Multi-track timeline

Advanced color grading

Motion graphics templates

Seamless cross-device workflow with Creative Cloud

Integrated soundtracks and sound editing tools

Pros:

Powerful editing features

Cross-device integration

Professional-level color grading and audio tools

Cons:

Some advanced features require a Creative Cloud subscription

LumaFusion

Best for: Experienced filmmakers who need robust features for professional-quality films.

LumaFusion is widely regarded as the gold standard for mobile video editing and is particularly popular among filmmakers looking to produce high-quality films entirely on their smartphones or tablets. It offers a comprehensive set of tools, including multi-track editing (up to 12 video and audio tracks), keyframing for animations, professional color correction, and support for 4K video. LumaFusion's interface is intuitive yet powerful, with drag-and-drop functionality, precision editing, and customizable effects.

One of the standout features of LumaFusion is its advanced audio editing capabilities, which include multi-channel audio support, audio filters, and real-time audio mixing. This makes it an excellent choice for filmmakers who want precise control over both their visuals and sound design.

Key Features:

12-track editing for video and audio

Advanced keyframing for animation and effects

Professional color correction tools

4K resolution support

Real-time audio mixing and multi-channel support

Pros:

Desktop-level editing power on a mobile device

Advanced audio and color correction features

Intuitive user interface with professional-grade tools

Cons:

Steeper learning curve for beginners

Only available for iOS devices

KineMaster

Best for: Filmmakers looking for a feature-rich editor with a user-friendly interface.

KineMaster is one of the most popular mobile editing apps for both beginners and more experienced filmmakers, thanks to its balance of powerful features and an easy-to-navigate interface. It supports multi-layer editing, chroma key (green screen), blending modes, and advanced audio controls, all of which can be accessed through an intuitive, touch-friendly timeline.

KineMaster offers a wide range of visual effects, transitions, and filters, making it perfect for filmmakers who want to add creative flair to their projects. Additionally, it includes built-in asset libraries with music, sound effects, stickers, and fonts that can be easily incorporated into your film.

Key Features:

Multi-layer editing for video, images, and text

Chroma key (green screen) support

Blending modes for creative effects

Built-in asset library (music, sound effects, stickers, etc.)

Frame-by-frame trimming for precision editing

Pros:

Easy to use for beginners while offering advanced features

Powerful green screen and blending options

Available for both iOS and Android

Cons:

Free version includes watermarks; full features require a subscription

InShot

Best for: Filmmakers looking for a simple, user-friendly app for quick edits.

InShot is a highly popular mobile editing app known for its simplicity and ease of use. While it's geared more toward short-form content like social media videos, it's also a great tool for filmmakers who need to quickly cut and edit their footage. InShot offers basic editing tools like trimming, splitting, and merging clips, as well as features for adding filters, music, voiceovers, and text.

The app also includes a selection of transition effects, background blurring, and video speed adjustments, making it a solid choice for anyone looking to create polished edits without diving into more complex software.

Key Features:

Easy-to-use interface for quick editing

Basic trimming, splitting, and merging tools

Filters, transitions, and music overlays

Supports aspect ratio adjustments for different platforms

Pros:

Perfect for quick, simple edits

Great for beginners

Wide selection of filters and transitions

Cons:

Limited advanced editing features

Free version includes watermarks

FilmoraGo

Best for: Filmmakers who want a balance between ease of use and advanced tools.

FilmoraGo is a versatile mobile editing app that offers a blend of simplicity and powerful features, making it suitable for both beginners and intermediate filmmakers. The app includes a drag-and-drop timeline for easy editing, as well as tools for trimming, adding music, and applying effects. FilmoraGo also offers more advanced features like multi-layer editing, chroma key, and slow-motion effects.

For filmmakers who want to add professional touches to their film, FilmoraGo provides built-in templates for titles, transitions, and effects. The app also includes a royalty-free music library, allowing you to easily add background music or sound effects to your scenes.

Key Features:

Easy drag-and-drop editing timeline

Multi-layer editing for video, audio, and text

Built-in templates for transitions, titles, and effects

Royalty-free music library

Pros:

Combines ease of use with more advanced tools

Wide variety of creative effects and transitions

Available on both iOS and Android

Cons:

Some features require in-app purchases

Watermark included in free version

Factors to Consider When Choosing an Editing App

To choose the right mobile editing app for your film, it's important to consider a few key factors based on your project's needs and your level of experience:

Complexity of the Project

If your film involves advanced editing techniques, multiple layers of footage, or complex audio mixing, an app like LumaFusion or Adobe Premiere Rush will be ideal. For simpler projects, or if you're new to editing, apps like InShot or FilmoraGo can get the job done quickly and efficiently.

User Interface

Ease of use is an important consideration, especially if you're new to editing or prefer a straightforward workflow. KineMaster and InShot offer highly intuitive interfaces, making them perfect for beginners. On the other hand, more feature-rich apps like LumaFusion may take some time to learn but offer greater flexibility and control.

Editing Features

Consider the types of effects, transitions, and editing tools you'll need for your project. If you require advanced features like chroma key, multi-track editing, or motion graphics, apps like Premiere Rush or KineMaster will serve you well. For basic cuts, filters, and transitions, simpler apps like InShot or FilmoraGo may suffice.

Budget

Many mobile editing apps offer free versions, but they often include watermarks or limited features. If you're serious about filmmaking and need access to premium tools, consider investing in a paid app or subscription plan. Apps like LumaFusion and Adobe Premiere Rush offer great value for their professional-grade features.

Platform Compatibility

Make sure the app you choose is compatible with your device. While most apps are available for both iOS and Android, some—like LumaFusion—are iOS-exclusive. Additionally, if you plan to edit across multiple devices, consider apps like Adobe Premiere Rush that offer cross-device syncing.

Editing is a crucial part of the filmmaking process, and with the right mobile app, you can bring your film to life with professional-level quality. Whether you're looking for a simple, user-friendly app or an advanced tool with powerful editing capabilities, there's an option for every filmmaker. By choosing the right app based on your needs, experience level, and budget, you'll be able to create polished, cinematic films directly from your smartphone.

Music and Sound Design: Enhancing Your Story with Audio

Sound is an essential component of filmmaking, and it goes beyond just recording clean dialogue. Music and sound design are powerful tools that can shape the emotional tone of your film, elevate storytelling, and immerse the audience in your world. When used effectively, music and sound design not only enhance the visual elements but also add depth to characters, environments, and actions, creating a richer, more engaging experience for viewers. In this chapter, we'll explore how to use music and sound design to enhance your mobile film, covering key techniques, tools, and tips for incorporating sound in a way that complements and elevates your story.

The Role of Music in Filmmaking

Music has the ability to evoke emotions, create tension, build atmosphere, and guide the audience's experience of the story. Whether you're using a full orchestral score, an ambient soundscape, or carefully selected songs, the right music can make your film more memorable and impactful.

Music serves many roles in film:

Setting the tone: The style, tempo, and mood of the music can quickly establish the emotional tone of a scene. Whether it's a suspenseful thriller or a heartwarming drama, the music helps set expectations for the audience.

Building tension and release: Music can create tension by introducing unsettling or dissonant elements and then provide emotional release when the tension resolves, guiding the audience through the film's emotional beats.

Supporting character development: The music associated with specific characters can help the audience connect emotionally to their journey. A recurring theme or motif can signify character growth, changes in mood, or emotional turning points.

Enhancing pacing: Music can drive the pace of a scene, making it feel faster or slower depending on the tempo. Fast-paced music can energize an action sequence, while slow, contemplative music can make a dramatic scene more introspective.

The Power of Sound Design

While music often takes the spotlight, sound design is equally crucial in shaping the auditory experience of a film. Sound design involves creating and manipulating audio elements like ambient sounds, sound effects, and foley (recreated sounds) to enhance realism, build atmosphere, and support the narrative. Good sound design blends seamlessly with the visual elements, immersing the audience in the world of the film.

Sound design can:

Create immersion: By using realistic soundscapes (such as background noises of a city, forest, or office), you can make the setting feel more authentic and help the audience feel grounded in the scene.

Build tension: Subtle sounds like the hum of machinery, distant footsteps, or the rustling of leaves can create a sense of unease or suspense. As the sound design intensifies, it can heighten the tension before a major event unfolds.

Accentuate action: Sound effects, like a punch landing or a car screeching to a halt, add weight to action scenes. Well-timed effects can make every movement feel more impactful and engaging.

Support world-building: In genres like sci-fi or fantasy, sound design can help create a sense of place by introducing unique sounds that distinguish the world from reality. Alien landscapes, futuristic technology, or magical elements can all be brought to life through sound.

Tools for Adding Music and Sound Design to Your Film

There are a variety of apps and tools available for adding music and sound design to your mobile film. Whether you're using pre-recorded music, creating your own sounds, or designing a custom soundscape, here are some helpful tools to consider:

GarageBand

Best for: Composing original music and creating custom sound effects.

GarageBand is a powerful music creation app available for iOS users, allowing you to compose original music, create soundscapes, and record sound effects. With a wide range of virtual instruments, loops, and sound samples, GarageBand is perfect for filmmakers who want to create their own score or custom sound effects. You can record live instruments, use pre-made loops, or even compose orchestral music with the app's built-in tools.

Key Features:

Virtual instruments for creating custom scores

Multi-track recording for complex compositions

Built-in loops and samples for various genres

Ability to record live instruments and vocals

Pros:

Ideal for filmmakers who want to create original music

Wide range of instruments and loops

Easy to use for both beginners and experienced musicians

Cons:

Available only on iOS

Soundtrap

Best for: Cloud-based music and sound creation with collaboration features.

Soundtrap is a cloud-based digital audio workstation (DAW) that lets you create music and sound design for your film from any device. One of its standout features is real-time collaboration, meaning multiple users can work on the same audio project simultaneously from different locations. Soundtrap offers a variety of instruments, loops, and sound effects, making it a great option for filmmakers who want to design custom soundscapes or scores.

Key Features:

Cloud-based multi-track recording

Built-in loops, instruments, and sound effects
Real-time collaboration for remote teams
Supports live audio recording
Pros:
Accessible on any device (iOS, Android, desktop)
Collaboration tools for team-based projects
Large library of pre-recorded sounds and music
Cons:
Some advanced features require a subscription

Filmstro
Best for: Dynamic music scoring that adapts to the film's mood and pacing.
Filmstro is a unique app that allows you to dynamically score your film by adjusting the momentum, depth, and power of the music in real-time. This flexibility allows you to tailor the music to perfectly match the tone and pacing of your scenes. Filmstro's intuitive interface makes it easy to use, and the app provides access to a library of customizable soundtracks across various genres.
Key Features:
Dynamic music adjustment (momentum, depth, power)
Extensive library of customizable tracks
Intuitive interface for scoring in real-time
Pros:
Allows real-time adjustments to fit the scene
High-quality music tracks across genres
Easy-to-use controls for filmmakers without musical experience
Cons:
Limited to pre-made music tracks (no original composition)
Freesound.org
Best for: Finding royalty-free sound effects and ambient sounds.
Freesound.org is an online library of royalty-free sound effects, ambient noises, and audio samples contributed by a global community of sound designers. It's an excellent resource for filmmakers who need specific sound effects, such as footsteps, rain, machinery, or crowd noise, without creating them from scratch. You can search by category, tags, or keywords to find the exact sound you need for your scene.
Key Features:
Large database of royalty-free sound effects
Easy search and filtering options
Free to use with proper attribution
Pros:
Free access to a wide variety of sound effects
Community-driven platform with frequent updates
Simple to download and integrate into your film
Cons:
Requires attribution for each sound used
Audacity
Best for: Editing and mixing sound effects and music.

Audacity is a free, open-source audio editing tool available on both desktop and mobile. It's ideal for filmmakers who want to fine-tune audio elements, mix soundtracks, and edit sound effects for their film. Audacity allows for multi-track editing, noise reduction, and precise control over audio levels, making it perfect for sound design and mastering your film's audio.

Key Features:

Multi-track audio editing and mixing

Advanced tools for noise reduction and equalization

Supports a wide range of audio file formats

Pros:

Free and open-source

Powerful audio editing and mixing tools

Compatible with most operating systems

Cons:

Steeper learning curve for beginners

Tips for Integrating Music and Sound Design in Your Film

To effectively use music and sound design in your film, it's important to ensure that the audio complements the visual storytelling rather than overshadowing it. Here are some tips for achieving the best results:

Match the Mood to the Scene

Always consider the emotional tone of the scene when choosing music or sound design elements. For example, a fast-paced action scene might benefit from intense, rhythmic music, while a quiet, contemplative moment may require a more subdued, atmospheric soundscape. Avoid using music that feels out of place or distracts from the action on screen.

Use Music Sparingly

While music is a powerful tool, it's important not to overuse it. Strategic use of silence or minimal sound can create tension, enhance emotional moments, or make dialogue more impactful. Music should elevate key scenes, but allowing quiet moments can make the music stand out when it returns.

Layer Sound Effects for Realism

When creating sound design, consider layering multiple sound effects to build a realistic environment. For instance, if you're designing the soundscape for a city street, layer the sounds of cars, distant voices, footsteps, and ambient traffic noise to create a fully immersive experience. The more detailed the sound design, the more believable the scene will feel.

Balance Dialogue with Music and Effects

It's essential to ensure that the dialogue remains clear and audible, even when music and sound effects are present. Use audio mixing tools to balance the levels of dialogue, music, and effects. You can adjust the volume of background sounds to avoid overpowering the characters' voices or use EQ to reduce competing frequencies.

Sync Sound to Action

Timing is everything in sound design. Make sure that sound effects sync perfectly with on-screen actions, such as doors closing, punches landing, or objects falling. This helps maintain the illusion of realism and ensures that the audience remains engaged with the action.

Use Sound to Foreshadow Events

Sound design can also be used to foreshadow events or hint at something that is about to happen. For example, introducing an eerie, distant sound before a character enters a dangerous area can heighten suspense and set the stage for an upcoming conflict. Music cues can similarly prepare the audience for a shift in tone or narrative development.

Royalty-Free Music and Sound Resources

Using copyrighted music without permission can lead to legal issues, so it's important to source royalty-free music and sound effects for your film. Here are some popular resources for finding royalty-free audio:

Freesound.org: As mentioned earlier, this is a free library of sound effects and ambient sounds contributed by the community.

Artlist: Offers a subscription-based service with a vast collection of royalty-free music that can be used in films.

Epidemic Sound: Another subscription service providing high-quality royalty-free music and sound effects.

YouTube Audio Library: Free music and sound effects that can be used in videos and films with proper attribution. Music and sound design are vital components of any film, transforming simple footage into an emotionally rich and immersive experience. By carefully selecting and integrating music, sound effects, and ambient sounds, you can create a dynamic auditory landscape that enhances your storytelling and deepens audience engagement. With a wide array of tools and resources available for mobile filmmakers, creating high-quality soundscapes and custom scores has never been easier. By applying these techniques and using the right apps, you can elevate your film's audio to match its visual brilliance.

Color Grading for Smartphone Films: Making Your Film Pop

Color grading is one of the final steps in the filmmaking process, but it plays a crucial role in determining the overall look and feel of your film. By adjusting the colors, contrast, and brightness, color grading can help unify the visual tone of your film, enhance the mood of specific scenes, and make your footage feel more cinematic. Even if you've shot your film on a smartphone, color grading can elevate your work, making it look polished and professional. In this chapter, we'll explore the essentials of color grading for smartphone films, including techniques, tools, and tips for making your film stand out visually.

Why Color Grading Matters in Filmmaking

Color grading is more than just enhancing the look of your film—it's a storytelling tool. It helps communicate the emotional tone of a scene, guide the audience's focus, and create a consistent visual style throughout the film. Whether you're aiming for a warm, nostalgic feel, a cold and clinical look, or something more vibrant and bold, color grading allows you to reinforce your film's themes and characters.

Here are some ways color grading enhances your film:

Mood and Atmosphere: The color palette you choose can dramatically impact the mood of a scene. Warmer tones often evoke feelings of comfort, nostalgia, or romance, while cooler tones can create tension, unease, or sadness.

Visual Continuity: Color grading ensures that your film has a consistent look, even if the footage was shot under varying lighting conditions or at different locations. A unified color grade makes your film feel cohesive and professional.

Character and Theme Development: Color can be used to visually represent the journey of a character or the overarching themes of your film. For example, you might use a muted color palette to reflect a character's emotional struggle or transition to brighter, more saturated colors as they find hope or resolution.

Cinematic Style: Color grading adds a layer of polish that can make even smartphone footage feel cinematic. Subtle adjustments in contrast, saturation, and hue can make your film visually striking and elevate its overall production value.

Key Concepts in Color Grading

Before diving into specific apps and techniques, it's important to understand the basic concepts of color grading. These will help guide your creative decisions and ensure that you achieve the desired look for your film.

Color Correction vs. Color Grading

It's important to distinguish between color correction and color grading, as they serve different purposes:

Color Correction: This is the first step in the process and involves fixing any color imbalances in your footage. The goal is to make sure that skin tones look natural, exposure is correct, and white balance is accurate. Essentially, color correction ensures that your footage looks clean and neutral before you start adding stylistic elements.

Color Grading: Once the footage has been corrected, color grading is where you can get creative. This step involves adjusting the overall color palette, contrast, saturation, and brightness to achieve a specific look or mood. It's during this stage that you can stylize your film and create a unique visual aesthetic.

Hue, Saturation, and Luminance (HSL)

These three elements form the foundation of color grading. Understanding how they work will give you greater control over the look of your film:

Hue: Refers to the actual color itself (red, blue, green, etc.). Adjusting the hue allows you to shift the color palette of your scene. For example, you can shift blues toward teal for a more cinematic look or change greens to a warmer yellow to evoke a sunny, nostalgic vibe.

Saturation: Saturation refers to the intensity of the color. Highly saturated colors are vivid and bold, while desaturated colors appear more muted. Depending on the mood of your film, you can either dial up the saturation to make the colors pop or reduce it for a more subdued, moody aesthetic.

Luminance: Luminance controls the brightness of a color. Increasing luminance makes the color lighter and more vibrant, while reducing luminance makes it darker and more subdued. This can be useful for highlighting certain colors while pushing others into shadow.

Contrast

Contrast refers to the difference between the light and dark areas of your image. High contrast creates a more dramatic, punchy look, while low contrast gives a softer, more muted feel. By adjusting contrast, you can control the depth and dimension of your shots, making them feel either flat or dynamic.

Shadows, Midtones, and Highlights

Color grading tools often allow you to make adjustments to specific parts of your image:

Shadows: The darkest areas of your image.

Midtones: The middle range of your image's brightness, where most of the detail is found.

Highlights: The brightest areas of your image.

By adjusting the shadows, midtones, and highlights separately, you can fine-tune the color and contrast, ensuring that each part of the image looks exactly how you want it.

Top Apps for Color Grading on Smartphones

Many smartphone editing apps now offer robust color grading tools that allow you to adjust the look of your footage directly on your device. Here are some of the best apps for color grading smartphone films:

LumaFusion

Best for: Professional-level color grading and editing on iOS devices.

LumaFusion is one of the most powerful mobile editing apps, offering a comprehensive suite of color grading tools. With LumaFusion, you can adjust exposure, saturation, contrast, and apply LUTs (Look-Up Tables) to quickly achieve cinematic color grades. It also allows for precise control over individual color channels, giving you the flexibility to manipulate specific hues in your footage.

Key Features:

Multi-layer video editing

Professional color grading tools (HSL adjustments, LUTs, etc.)

Real-time color correction and grading

Keyframe animations for dynamic color changes

Pros:

High-level color grading controls

Supports 4K video editing and export

LUT support for consistent color grading across multiple clips

Cons:

iOS only

More complex for beginners

Adobe Premiere Rush

Best for: Filmmakers seeking an all-in-one mobile editing solution with strong color grading options.

Adobe Premiere Rush is a user-friendly app that offers powerful color correction and grading tools. You can use preset filters to quickly apply a color grade or manually adjust exposure, contrast, shadows, and highlights. Premiere Rush also integrates seamlessly with Adobe Premiere Pro, allowing you to start editing on your phone and finish on a desktop if needed.

Key Features:

Built-in color presets for quick grading

Manual adjustments for exposure, contrast, highlights, and shadows

Cross-device syncing with Adobe Creative Cloud

LUTs support for professional color grading

Pros:

Easy-to-use color grading tools

Presets for quick adjustments

Seamless workflow with Adobe Premiere Pro

Cons:

Subscription required for full features

KineMaster

Best for: Filmmakers who need a versatile mobile editing app with strong color grading features.

KineMaster is a popular mobile editing app that includes a range of color grading tools. You can adjust brightness, contrast, saturation, and hue, and apply filters to achieve different looks. KineMaster also allows you to fine-tune individual clips or apply consistent color grading across multiple scenes.

Key Features:

Multi-layer video editing

Color correction and grading tools (brightness, contrast, hue, saturation)

Wide range of filters and effects

Available for both iOS and Android

Pros:

Intuitive interface with easy color grading controls

Available for both major platforms

Suitable for both beginners and advanced users

Cons:

Free version includes watermarks

Some advanced features require a subscription

Filmic Pro

Best for: Filmmakers who want full control over color settings while shooting.

Filmic Pro is one of the most advanced camera apps for mobile filmmakers, offering extensive control over exposure, focus, and color settings. While Filmic Pro is primarily a shooting app, its built-in color grading tools allow you to adjust white balance, tone mapping, and apply real-time LUTs while filming. This makes it an excellent choice for filmmakers who want to fine-tune their footage as they shoot, reducing the need for extensive post-production color grading.

Key Features:

Real-time color adjustment during filming

Custom white balance settings

LUT support for real-time color grading

Full manual control over exposure and focus

Pros:

Gives you control over color while shooting

Reduces the need for post-production grading

Professional-level camera features

Cons:

Primarily a shooting app, limited post-production tools

iOS and Android versions differ slightly in features

VSCO

Best for: Filmmakers looking for simple, stylized color grading tools.

VSCO is a popular app known for its stylish filters and color grading presets. While it's primarily used for photography, VSCO's video editing tools are ideal for filmmakers who want to quickly apply a consistent look to their footage. The app offers a wide range of filters that mimic the look of film stock, and you can adjust exposure, saturation, temperature, and other settings to fine-tune the grade.

Key Features:

Stylized color grading presets

Manual adjustment of exposure, contrast, temperature, and saturation

Simple interface for quick edits

Pros:

Easy to use for beginners

Wide selection of filters for different moods

Quick and consistent color grading across multiple clips

Cons:

Limited advanced editing features

Subscription required for full access to filters

Tips for Effective Color Grading

To make the most of your color grading process, follow these tips to ensure your film has a cohesive, polished look:

Start with Color Correction

Before diving into the creative side of color grading, make sure your footage is properly color corrected. Adjust the white balance, exposure, and contrast so that your colors look natural and balanced. This gives you a clean slate to work with when applying more stylized color grades.

Keep the Story in Mind

Always remember that color grading should serve the story. Think about the emotions you want to evoke in each scene, and choose colors that support those feelings. For example, desaturated colors may work well in scenes of conflict or emotional tension, while warm, saturated tones can add to moments of joy or nostalgia.

Use LUTs for Consistency

LUTs (Look-Up Tables) are pre-designed color profiles that can be applied to your footage to achieve a specific look. Using a consistent LUT throughout your film can help maintain visual continuity and give your project a unified aesthetic. Many editing apps, like LumaFusion and Adobe Premiere Rush, support LUTs, and there are countless LUTs available online to match different styles.

Don't Overdo It

Subtlety is key when it comes to color grading. Overly saturated or extreme color adjustments can distract from the story and make your film look unnatural. Focus on enhancing the colors that are already present in the scene, rather than completely altering the look of the footage.

Match Shots for Continuity

When color grading, make sure to match shots across scenes for visual continuity. If two shots are part of the same scene but have different lighting conditions (such as an indoor and outdoor shot), use color grading to balance them so they appear cohesive. This ensures that the audience remains immersed in the story without being distracted by jarring visual differences.

Color grading is an essential part of filmmaking, allowing you to refine and enhance the visual style of your film. Whether you're using powerful tools like LumaFusion or more straightforward apps like VSCO, the ability to control color, contrast, and saturation will help you create a visually compelling story. By starting with color correction, using LUTs for consistency, and being mindful of the mood and tone you want to convey, you can make your smartphone film look polished and professional. With the right approach to color grading, your film will pop on screen, drawing viewers into its world and enhancing the overall storytelling experience.

Creating a Consistent Visual Style: A Cinematic Look with a Phone

Creating a consistent visual style is key to giving your film a professional, cinematic look. While smartphone filmmaking offers flexibility, it also presents challenges in maintaining visual continuity due to varying lighting conditions, camera capabilities, and the limitations of mobile lenses. However, with the right techniques and tools, you can achieve a cohesive, cinematic aesthetic that enhances your storytelling and elevates the quality of your film. In this chapter, we'll explore how to create a consistent visual style using your smartphone, covering everything from framing and lighting to color grading and shot composition.

Why Consistency Matters in Filmmaking

A consistent visual style helps unify your film, making it feel like a cohesive piece of art rather than a collection of disjointed scenes. By maintaining consistency in lighting, color, framing, and camera movement, you can create a specific mood or tone that supports the narrative and keeps your audience engaged.

Consistency in visual style also reinforces the emotional journey of your characters and the atmosphere of your settings. Whether you're aiming for a gritty, raw aesthetic or a polished, vibrant look, consistency ensures that your audience remains immersed in the story, rather than being distracted by visual inconsistencies.

Key Elements of a Cinematic Look

To achieve a cinematic look with your smartphone, focus on the following elements. These techniques will help you create a film that not only looks professional but also has a strong and cohesive visual identity.

Aspect Ratio

The aspect ratio refers to the width and height of your film's frame. Most traditional cinematic films are shot in a widescreen aspect ratio (2.35:1 or 16:9), which gives a more expansive, cinematic feel. Shooting in widescreen can add visual depth to your film and make it feel more like a feature film than a typical video.

Many smartphone cameras default to 16:9, which is ideal for cinematic framing. If you're aiming for a wider aspect ratio, you can use apps like Filmic Pro or editing software that allows you to crop your footage to 2.35:1, giving your film a widescreen effect.

Tip: When shooting in widescreen, pay special attention to framing and composition, as the extra width can create opportunities for dynamic visual storytelling.

Lighting

Lighting is one of the most important factors in achieving a cinematic look. Good lighting helps create mood, enhances the subject, and adds depth to your scene. Even if you're shooting on a smartphone, careful attention to lighting can dramatically improve the quality of your footage.

Use Natural Light: Smartphones handle natural light well, and shooting outdoors during golden hour (just after sunrise or before sunset) can provide soft, cinematic lighting. Indoors, position your subjects near windows for diffused natural light.

Control Shadows: Cinematic lighting often plays with light and shadow to create contrast. Use key lights, fill lights, and backlights to sculpt your subject and create depth. A single light source, positioned at an angle, can create dramatic shadows and emphasize your subject's features.

Practical Lights: In addition to external lighting equipment, use practical lights (such as lamps, candles, or streetlights) in your scene. These natural sources of light add realism and texture to the environment while also contributing to the mood.

Tip: Avoid overexposing your footage, as blown-out highlights can make your film look amateurish. Instead, aim for a balanced exposure with well-defined highlights and shadows.

Camera Movement

Cinematic films often use smooth, controlled camera movements to enhance storytelling and create a sense of flow. While smartphones are small and lightweight, it's important to avoid shaky handheld footage unless you're going for a specific effect, such as in a found-footage or documentary-style film.

Here are a few ways to achieve cinematic camera movement:

Use a Gimbal or Stabilizer: A gimbal or smartphone stabilizer allows you to capture smooth, fluid shots, even when moving. This can make tracking shots, pans, and tilts look professional and polished.

Dolly Shots: You can create DIY dolly shots by moving your camera on a stable surface like a skateboard or sliding it along a smooth surface. Dolly shots add dynamic movement to a scene and are often used in cinematic films to follow characters or reveal new elements in the frame.

Slow Camera Movement: Subtle, slow camera movement is a hallmark of cinematic filmmaking. Whether it's a slow pan or a gentle push-in toward a subject, this kind of movement adds tension and draws the viewer's attention without being too distracting.

Tip: If you don't have access to stabilizing equipment, try holding your phone with both hands and bracing your arms against your body to reduce shake.

Framing and Composition

Strong composition is essential for creating visually compelling shots that feel cinematic. By paying attention to the arrangement of elements within the frame, you can guide the viewer's eye and add depth to your shots.

Rule of Thirds: One of the most basic principles of composition is the rule of thirds. Imagine your frame divided into a 3x3 grid. Placing your subject along the lines or at the intersection points creates a balanced and dynamic composition, rather than simply centering the subject in every shot.

Leading Lines: Leading lines are visual elements in the scene that guide the viewer's eye toward a specific point, usually the subject. These could be natural lines like roads, hallways, or rivers, or more abstract lines created by lighting or objects within the frame.

Symmetry and Asymmetry: Symmetrical shots can create a sense of stability and order, while asymmetry can evoke tension or unpredictability. Use symmetry when you want a formal or controlled look, and asymmetry to create visual interest or imply imbalance in the story.

Depth: Cinematic films often use multiple layers of depth within a shot, placing objects in the foreground, midground, and background. This creates a three-dimensional feel and adds visual richness to your film.

Tip: Avoid overusing close-ups. Cinematic films balance wide shots, medium shots, and close-ups to give the audience a sense of the environment and context for each scene.

Color Grading

Color grading, as discussed in the previous chapter, is a powerful tool for creating a consistent visual style. By adjusting the color palette of your film, you can unify the look across different scenes and establish a specific mood or tone.

Choose a Color Palette: Before you start color grading, consider what kind of color palette suits your film. Are you going for warm, golden tones to evoke nostalgia, or cooler, desaturated colors to create a sense of detachment? Sticking to a consistent palette helps reinforce the emotional tone of the film.

Use LUTs for Consistency: LUTs (Look-Up Tables) are pre-designed color profiles that can be applied to your footage to achieve a consistent color grade. Many mobile editing apps like LumaFusion and Adobe Premiere Rush allow you to apply LUTs, which can be particularly useful for maintaining a cohesive look across multiple scenes.

Tip: Don't overdo color grading—subtle adjustments are often more effective than extreme changes. The goal is to enhance the footage, not distract from it.

Shallow Depth of Field

One of the hallmarks of cinematic filmmaking is the use of shallow depth of field, where the subject is in focus while the background is blurred. This effect draws attention to the subject and creates a professional, polished look.

While smartphones have limited ability to achieve natural shallow depth of field due to their small sensors, there are ways to mimic this effect:

Portrait Mode: Some smartphones have a portrait or cinematic mode that simulates shallow depth of field by digitally blurring the background. This feature can be useful for close-up shots where you want to emphasize the subject.

Distance from Background: Another way to achieve shallow depth of field is by placing your subject far from the background while keeping the camera relatively close to the subject. This increases the perceived depth and helps blur the background naturally.

Tip: Avoid using digital zoom, as it can degrade the quality of your footage. Instead, move the camera closer to the subject for a more natural, shallow depth of field.

Consistent Camera Settings

To ensure consistency across your shots, it's important to lock your camera settings when shooting. Changes in exposure, white balance, and focus can lead to noticeable variations between scenes, making the film feel disjointed.

Manual Exposure and Focus: Use apps like Filmic Pro or the native camera app on your smartphone to manually set and lock exposure and focus. This prevents automatic adjustments that can result in uneven lighting and inconsistent focus.

White Balance: Lock your white balance to avoid shifts in color temperature between shots. This is especially important when shooting in different lighting conditions, as the color temperature can vary dramatically between natural light, artificial light, and mixed light sources.

Tip: Shoot at the highest possible resolution and frame rate your phone allows (such as 4K at 24 or 30fps) to give yourself more flexibility in post-production.

Developing Your Film's Visual Identity

While it's important to follow the principles above, it's equally important to develop your own unique visual style that reflects the story you're telling. The visual identity of your film should serve the narrative, character arcs, and emotional beats. As you plan your shots, think about how the visual elements—lighting, composition, color, and camera movement—support the themes and atmosphere of your film.

Research and Inspiration: Look to films, TV shows, or photography that inspire you and reflect the tone of your project. Analyze how lighting, framing, and color are used to create mood and guide the story.

Previsualization: Create storyboards or shot lists to plan your visual style ahead of time. This will help you stay consistent and ensure that each shot contributes to the overall look and feel of your film.

Experimentation: Don't be afraid to experiment with different techniques during production. While consistency is important, allowing room for creative exploration can lead to unique visuals that enhance your film.

Achieving a consistent visual style is one of the key steps to making your smartphone film look cinematic and professional. By focusing on elements such as aspect ratio, lighting, camera movement, composition, and color grading, you can create a cohesive visual language that enhances your storytelling. While smartphone filmmaking may come with some limitations, these techniques will help you overcome them and deliver a visually stunning, polished final product. With thoughtful planning and execution, you can make your smartphone film stand out with a cinematic look that rivals larger-scale productions.

Developing Character Arcs: Growth through the Story

Character arcs are at the heart of storytelling, and they play a vital role in engaging the audience emotionally and driving the plot forward. A well-crafted character arc allows viewers to connect with the character's journey, watching them evolve, grow, and change as a result of the challenges they face. In this chapter, we'll explore the process of developing strong character arcs, focusing on how growth and transformation can be woven into your story to create compelling, relatable characters. Whether you're writing for a film, television series, or a short story, understanding character arcs is essential to building a narrative that resonates with your audience.

What Is a Character Arc?

A character arc is the transformation or inner journey a character undergoes over the course of a story. This change often occurs in response to the events of the plot, the character's personal challenges, and the relationships they form. While plot-driven stories focus on external events, character-driven stories are propelled by the internal evolution of the characters.

A successful character arc takes a character from one state of being to another. This might mean overcoming a personal flaw, learning a valuable lesson, discovering inner strength, or experiencing a shift in perspective. The journey should feel natural and necessary, as it is often tied to the central theme of the story.

Types of Character Arcs

There are three main types of character arcs, each representing a different form of transformation. Choosing the right type of arc for your character will depend on the themes and goals of your story.

Positive Arc (Growth Arc)

In a positive character arc, the protagonist starts with a flaw, limitation, or misconception and grows throughout the story, ultimately overcoming this weakness. By the end, the character has evolved into a better, stronger, or more self-aware version of themselves. This is the most common type of arc and is often found in stories of personal triumph or redemption.

For example, in *The Lord of the Rings*, Frodo Baggins begins as an ordinary hobbit, reluctant and naive. Through his journey, he gains strength, courage, and wisdom, ultimately accepting the burden of the ring and fulfilling his role in saving Middle-earth.

Key Elements of a Positive Arc:

The character starts with a flaw, misconception, or fear.

They face challenges that force them to confront this flaw.

Through their struggles, they grow and change.

By the end, they have transformed in a meaningful, positive way.

Negative Arc (Fall Arc)

In a negative character arc, the character starts from a position of relative strength or neutrality but experiences a decline throughout the story. Rather than overcoming a flaw, the character succumbs to their weaknesses, leading to their downfall. This arc is often used in tragedies or stories of corruption.

An example of a negative arc is Walter White in *Breaking Bad*. Initially, Walter is a mild-mannered high school teacher, but as he becomes more deeply involved in the drug trade, his moral compass deteriorates. By the end of the series, he has transformed into a ruthless, power-hungry criminal, far removed from the man he once was.

Key Elements of a Negative Arc:

The character starts from a place of strength or neutrality.

They encounter challenges that exacerbate their flaws or weaknesses.

Instead of growing, they regress, make poor decisions, or lose sight of their moral center.

The story concludes with the character's downfall, failure, or tragic end.

Flat Arc (Steadfast Arc)

In a flat arc, the character remains fundamentally the same throughout the story, but they affect the world around them. Rather than undergoing personal growth, they remain steadfast in their beliefs or values, and their actions lead to changes in the people or society around them. These characters often serve as the moral compass or anchor in the story.

For example, in *Mad Max: Fury Road*, Max himself doesn't experience much personal growth—he remains a hardened survivor throughout the film. However, his presence and actions help Furiosa and the other characters achieve freedom, changing their world for the better.

Key Elements of a Flat Arc:

The character starts with strong convictions or beliefs.

They face external challenges but remain true to themselves.

Their actions influence or inspire others to change.

The story ends with the character unchanged, but the world around them is transformed.

Building a Strong Character Arc

To create a compelling character arc, you need to ensure that the character's journey is well-structured and tied closely to the narrative. Here's a step-by-step guide to building a strong character arc in your story.

Define the Character's Starting Point

The first step is to establish where your character begins. What are their flaws, fears, goals, or misconceptions? This starting point is essential because it sets up the journey they will undergo. Ask yourself the following questions:

What internal struggles is the character facing?

What do they believe about themselves or the world?

What are their primary goals or desires at the start of the story?

The more clearly you define the character's starting point, the more satisfying their arc will be as they undergo changes throughout the story.

Identify the Character's End Point

Next, think about where the character will be at the end of the story. How will they have changed? What lesson will they have learned, or what flaw will they have overcome? The end point should reflect the transformation that has taken place over the course of the narrative.

For a positive arc, the character will likely have grown in strength, wisdom, or self-awareness. For a negative arc, they may have succumbed to their darker impulses, leading to their downfall. In a flat arc, the character remains the same but will have had a profound impact on the world around them.

Map Out the Key Turning Points

Character arcs are driven by key turning points—moments in the story where the character faces challenges, makes important decisions, or experiences emotional growth. These turning points force the character to confront their flaws or beliefs, pushing them toward change.

Here are some typical turning points in a character arc:

Inciting Incident: The event that sets the story in motion and presents the character with a challenge or conflict. This forces the character out of their comfort zone.

Midpoint: A significant event or revelation that forces the character to make a critical decision. At this point, the character may begin to realize their flaw or the truth they've been avoiding.

Climax: The character faces their greatest challenge, and the decisions they make here will determine how they change or grow. This is often where the character confronts their deepest fear or flaw.

Resolution: The final outcome of the character's arc. They have either grown (positive arc), fallen (negative arc), or remained steadfast while changing the world around them (flat arc).

Tie the Arc to the Story's Theme

A strong character arc is often closely tied to the theme of the story. The arc should reflect the central message or question the story is exploring. For example, if your theme is about the importance of family, the character's arc might revolve around learning to reconnect with loved ones after years of isolation.

Ask yourself how the character's journey supports or challenges the theme. Does the character's growth reflect the story's deeper meaning? The more integrated the arc is with the theme, the more emotionally resonant it will be for the audience.

Show, Don't Tell

One of the most important rules in writing character arcs is to show the character's growth through their actions and decisions, rather than through exposition or dialogue. The audience should be able to see the character changing through what they do, how they react to situations, and the choices they make.

For example, if a character is learning to overcome their fear of failure, don't have them say, "I'm no longer afraid of failing." Instead, show them taking a bold risk that they would have avoided at the start of the story. The audience should experience the character's growth organically through the narrative.

Maintain Consistency

While characters should grow and evolve, they should also maintain a sense of consistency. Sudden, unearned changes in behavior or beliefs can make the character arc feel forced or unrealistic. Ensure that the character's evolution is gradual and driven by the events of the story, rather than happening abruptly.

Each decision or turning point should feel like a natural progression from the character's previous state. This builds a believable arc that resonates with the audience.

Examples of Character Arcs in Popular Films

Luke Skywalker (Star Wars): Luke starts as a naive farm boy, dreaming of adventure but unsure of his place in the world. Throughout the trilogy, he learns to trust the Force, confronts his lineage, and ultimately becomes a Jedi, embracing his destiny.

Tony Stark (Iron Man/Avengers): Tony Stark begins as an arrogant, self-serving billionaire, but over the course of multiple films, he evolves into a selfless hero willing to sacrifice himself for the greater good. His arc is one of redemption and personal growth.

Michael Corleone (The Godfather): Michael's arc is a classic example of a negative arc. He begins as an outsider to his family's criminal empire but gradually becomes more ruthless and corrupt, ultimately taking control of the mafia at the cost of his morality and personal relationships.

A well-developed character arc is essential to creating a compelling, emotionally resonant story. Whether your character is undergoing personal growth, experiencing a tragic downfall, or remaining steadfast while changing the world around them, their journey should feel organic and meaningful. By carefully mapping out your character's arc, integrating it with the theme of the story, and showing the progression through action and decision-making, you can craft characters that engage and captivate your audience, making your story unforgettable.

Conflict and Resolution: Structuring Drama for Film

Conflict and resolution are the driving forces behind any compelling story. They give the narrative its structure, fuel character development, and engage the audience by creating tension and anticipation. In film, conflict is what keeps viewers invested in the plot, while resolution provides a satisfying conclusion that ties the story's threads together. Understanding how to structure conflict and resolution effectively can make the difference between a flat narrative and one that captivates your audience from start to finish. In this chapter, we'll explore how to build conflict, the different types of conflict, and how to craft a powerful resolution that leaves a lasting impact.

The Importance of Conflict in Storytelling

At its core, conflict is the struggle between opposing forces—whether internal, external, or both—that drives the plot forward. It creates tension and obstacles for the characters, forcing them to make difficult choices and, ultimately, evolve or change. Without conflict, there is no drama, no stakes, and no reason for the audience to care about what happens next.

In film, conflict serves several key purposes:

Motivates characters: Conflict forces characters to take action, whether they are pursuing a goal, defending themselves, or overcoming obstacles.

Engages the audience: Conflict creates questions that the audience wants answered—Will the hero succeed? How will they overcome this challenge? These questions keep viewers emotionally invested.

Develops the story: As the characters struggle with conflict, the plot progresses. The conflict propels the story forward, leading to turning points and character growth.

Creates emotional depth: Conflict often reveals a character's fears, desires, and vulnerabilities. By watching how characters navigate conflict, the audience gains insight into their inner world.

Types of Conflict

There are several types of conflict that can occur in a story, each offering different opportunities for drama and character development. Understanding the various types of conflict will help you decide which is most appropriate for your story and characters.

Internal Conflict (Character vs. Self)

Internal conflict is the struggle that occurs within a character's mind or soul. This type of conflict involves a character grappling with their own emotions, desires, fears, or flaws. Internal conflict often revolves around moral dilemmas, personal growth, or the character's inner journey.

For example, in *Black Swan*, Nina's internal conflict is her battle with perfectionism and her descent into madness as she struggles to achieve artistic greatness. This internal struggle drives the narrative and creates emotional depth.

Key Elements of Internal Conflict:

The character is in conflict with themselves, their beliefs, or their desires.

The conflict often involves moral dilemmas, fear, self-doubt, or personal growth.

The resolution typically results in inner change, self-acceptance, or realization.

External Conflict (Character vs. External Forces)

External conflict occurs between a character and outside forces, such as other people, nature, society, or fate. These conflicts are often more visible and tangible, forming the backbone of action-oriented stories.

Character vs. Character: This is the most common type of external conflict, where the protagonist is in direct opposition to another character. For example, in *The Dark Knight*, Batman faces external conflict with the Joker, a chaotic villain whose goals threaten Gotham City.

Character vs. Nature: In this type of conflict, the protagonist struggles against the elements or natural forces. This is often seen in survival stories like *The Revenant*, where Hugh Glass must endure extreme weather, wild animals, and the wilderness itself.

Character vs. Society: This conflict involves a character fighting against societal norms, laws, or systems. In *The Hunger Games*, Katniss Everdeen battles against a dystopian society that forces children into a deadly competition for entertainment.

Character vs. Fate/Supernatural: Here, the protagonist fights against destiny, the gods, or supernatural forces beyond their control. For instance, in *Final Destination*, the characters struggle to cheat death after narrowly escaping a fatal disaster.

Key Elements of External Conflict:

The character is in conflict with an external force (another character, nature, society, or fate).

The conflict is often action-driven, with visible obstacles or adversaries.

The resolution usually involves the character overcoming or succumbing to these external forces.

Relational Conflict

Relational conflict arises from the dynamics between characters, often focusing on emotional or interpersonal struggles. This can include conflicts between friends, lovers, family members, or colleagues, and it often explores themes of trust, betrayal, love, or loyalty.

For example, in *Marriage Story*, the conflict revolves around the emotional struggles and disintegration of a marriage, with both characters experiencing inner turmoil and external tension as they navigate their divorce.

Key Elements of Relational Conflict:

The conflict arises from emotional or interpersonal struggles between characters.

The conflict may involve love, jealousy, betrayal, or loyalty.

The resolution often results in changed relationships, new understanding, or reconciliation.

Structuring Conflict in Film

To create a compelling narrative, it's important to structure your conflict in a way that builds tension and keeps the audience engaged. The structure of conflict often follows a three-act format, with each act representing different stages of the protagonist's journey through the conflict.

Act 1: Introduction of Conflict

In the first act, the protagonist's world is established, and the main conflict is introduced. The inciting incident—an event that disrupts the character's life—sets the story in motion and forces the protagonist to confront the central conflict. This is the moment where the stakes are established, and the character is given a goal or challenge that they must overcome.

Key Elements of Act 1:

The protagonist's world and desires are introduced.

The inciting incident triggers the central conflict.

The protagonist is forced to take action or make a decision that drives them into the story.

Act 2: Escalation of Conflict

The second act is where the conflict intensifies. The protagonist faces obstacles and complications that make their journey more difficult. The stakes are raised, and the character is often tested both physically and emotionally. As the conflict escalates, the protagonist may experience moments of doubt, failure, or inner conflict that push them to their limits.

At the midpoint of the second act, there is often a major turning point—a moment where the conflict takes an unexpected turn, revealing new information or creating a major obstacle that shifts the direction of the story.

Key Elements of Act 2:

The conflict escalates, with increasing obstacles and challenges.

The protagonist is tested and pushed to their limits.

A turning point or revelation shifts the conflict in a new direction.

The stakes are raised, creating tension and urgency.

Act 3: Resolution of Conflict

The third act is the climax and resolution of the conflict. This is where the protagonist faces the final obstacle or confrontation, and the central conflict is resolved. The climax is the most intense moment of the story, where the protagonist either succeeds or fails in their goal. After the climax, the resolution ties up loose ends and shows the consequences of the protagonist's journey.

In this final act, the character's arc is completed—whether they have grown, regressed, or remained steadfast—and the story's themes are brought to a satisfying conclusion.

Key Elements of Act 3:

The climax presents the final confrontation or resolution of the conflict.

The protagonist either succeeds or fails in their goal.

The resolution shows the consequences of the character's choices and journey.

Loose ends are tied up, and the story's themes are reinforced.

Crafting a Satisfying Resolution

The resolution is the payoff for all the tension and conflict built up over the course of the story. A satisfying resolution provides closure and ties together the character arc, themes, and plot. Whether the protagonist wins, loses, or finds a middle ground, the resolution should feel earned and meaningful.

Stay True to the Character Arc

The resolution should reflect the character's growth or transformation. If the protagonist has undergone a positive arc, the resolution should show how they have overcome their flaw or achieved their goal. If it's a negative arc, the resolution might depict the consequences of the character's downfall or moral failure.

For example, in *The Shawshank Redemption*, the resolution shows how Andy Dufresne's perseverance and hope have paid off, leading to his eventual escape and freedom. His arc, from despair to hope, is completed in a way that feels satisfying and true to the character.

Resolve Major Plot Threads

All major plot points and subplots should be resolved in the final act. This doesn't mean that every question needs to be answered, but the primary conflicts and storylines should reach a logical conclusion. Unresolved plot threads can leave the audience feeling unsatisfied unless intentionally left open for thematic or artistic reasons.

For example, in *Inception*, the resolution leaves the spinning top—whether it falls or not—ambiguous, allowing the audience to interpret whether Cobb is in a dream or reality. However, the main conflict of Cobb's emotional journey is resolved, making the ending satisfying despite the open question.

Deliver on the Story's Promises

A satisfying resolution delivers on the promises made in the story. If your story is set up as a mystery, the resolution should offer a meaningful reveal. If it's a love story, the audience expects some form of resolution in the relationship. Avoid abrupt or unearned endings that feel disconnected from the rest of the narrative.

For example, in *The Sixth Sense*, the resolution delivers a shocking twist that ties together the mystery and provides emotional closure for both the protagonist and the audience.

Examples of Conflict and Resolution in Popular Films

The Dark Knight: The central conflict between Batman and the Joker escalates as Gotham falls into chaos. The resolution comes when Batman defeats the Joker but must take the blame for Harvey Dent's actions, solidifying his role as the Dark Knight.

Gladiator: The conflict revolves around Maximus' quest for revenge against Commodus. The resolution occurs when Maximus kills Commodus in the arena, completing his journey and earning him a peaceful afterlife.

A Beautiful Mind: The conflict is John Nash's battle with schizophrenia. The resolution comes when he learns to manage his condition and finds peace, allowing him to continue his academic work and achieve personal fulfillment. Conflict and resolution are the cornerstones of drama, and structuring them effectively is essential to creating a compelling narrative. By introducing a strong central conflict, escalating the stakes, and crafting a satisfying resolution, you can build a film that engages the audience and provides emotional depth. Whether the conflict is internal, external, or relational, it should challenge the characters, drive the story forward, and lead to a resolution that ties the narrative together and reinforces the themes of the film. With these tools, you can craft a dramatic and satisfying story that keeps your audience invested from beginning to end.

The Hero's Journey: Applying Classic Storytelling to Your Film

The Hero's Journey is one of the most enduring and widely recognized storytelling frameworks in literature and film. Popularized by Joseph Campbell in his book *The Hero with a Thousand Faces*, this narrative structure describes the universal pattern that many stories, myths, and legends follow. The Hero's Journey provides a blueprint for crafting compelling stories of growth, challenge, and transformation. By understanding and applying the Hero's Journey to your film, you can create a story that resonates deeply with audiences, offering timeless themes of adventure, self-discovery, and triumph.

In this chapter, we'll explore the stages of the Hero's Journey and how to adapt this classic storytelling structure to your film, whether you're working in action, drama, fantasy, or even more intimate, character-driven narratives.

What is the Hero's Journey?

The Hero's Journey is a three-act narrative structure that follows the protagonist (the "Hero") as they embark on a transformative journey. The Hero leaves their familiar world, faces trials and challenges in an unknown realm, and returns home changed by their experiences. This structure often represents a metaphor for personal growth, with the Hero learning important lessons and overcoming obstacles both external and internal.

The Hero's Journey consists of 12 key stages, although not every story includes all of them, and they can be adapted based on the genre or narrative you're crafting. These stages map out the arc of the Hero, from the ordinary world to the extraordinary and back again.

The 12 Stages of the Hero's Journey

Let's break down the 12 stages of the Hero's Journey and explore how each can be applied to filmmaking.

The Ordinary World

The story begins by introducing the Hero in their everyday, normal life. This world is familiar and comfortable but also lacking something. The Hero may feel incomplete or unfulfilled, and the audience gets to know their background, strengths, weaknesses, and desires.

Example: In *The Matrix*, Neo's ordinary world is his life as a hacker and office worker. He feels something is missing and suspects there is more to the world than he knows.

Application: In your film, use this stage to establish the character's personality and normal environment, setting up the stakes and what the Hero will eventually leave behind. Make sure to introduce any important relationships, flaws, or conflicts that will drive the Hero's motivations.

The Call to Adventure

The Hero is presented with a challenge or opportunity that disrupts their ordinary world. This call to adventure is the catalyst for the journey, pulling the Hero toward the unknown.

Example: In *Star Wars: A New Hope*, Luke Skywalker receives the call to adventure when he discovers the message from Princess Leia in R2-D2, asking for help to fight the Empire.

Application: The call to adventure should be a significant event that shakes the Hero out of their routine and compels them to act. This can be anything from receiving a mysterious message, encountering a dangerous foe, or learning about a great danger or opportunity that needs to be addressed.

Refusal of the Call

Initially, the Hero may be reluctant or afraid to take on the challenge. This refusal comes from fear of the unknown or a sense of inadequacy. The Hero may doubt their abilities or the necessity of leaving their ordinary world.

Example: In *The Lion King*, Simba initially refuses the call to return to Pride Rock and claim his rightful place as king. He's filled with guilt over his father's death and prefers to stay in exile.

Application: Use the refusal to create tension and show the Hero's internal conflict. This makes the eventual acceptance of the journey more impactful, as the Hero overcomes their doubts or fear.

Meeting the Mentor

The Hero encounters a mentor or guide who provides wisdom, training, or tools to help them face the upcoming challenges. The mentor helps prepare the Hero for the journey ahead, offering advice or a push in the right direction.

Example: In *The Lord of the Rings*, Frodo meets Gandalf, who becomes his mentor, guiding him on how to carry the One Ring and navigate the dangerous world of Middle-earth.

Application: The mentor doesn't have to be a traditional figure of wisdom; they could be an ally, a mystical figure, or even a hard-nosed mentor. Their purpose is to provide the Hero with the skills, knowledge, or motivation they need to continue on the journey.

Crossing the Threshold

The Hero commits to the journey and leaves the safety of the ordinary world, entering the unknown. This is a point of no return, where the Hero is fully committed to the adventure ahead.

Example: In *The Matrix*, Neo literally crosses the threshold by taking the red pill, which pulls him out of the simulated reality and into the harsh world of the real.

Application: In your film, this is the moment when the Hero steps into a new, dangerous, or unfamiliar world. It's often accompanied by physical movement—crossing a border, entering a new place, or venturing into the unknown. The stakes should feel raised from this point onward.

Tests, Allies, and Enemies

The Hero faces a series of challenges, meets new allies, and encounters enemies. These trials test the Hero's resolve, abilities, and character, allowing them to grow in strength and knowledge. Along the way, the Hero may form important relationships that will support them later in the journey.

Example: In *Harry Potter and the Sorcerer's Stone*, Harry meets Hermione and Ron, and the trio face various challenges together at Hogwarts, from learning spells to battling a troll.

Application: This stage is great for developing secondary characters and fleshing out the world. The Hero's interactions with allies and enemies will define the journey and shape their character.

Approach to the Inmost Cave

The Hero approaches the central challenge or greatest danger in the story. This stage often represents the Hero preparing for a major confrontation, whether physical, emotional, or moral. The stakes are higher than ever, and failure feels imminent.

Example: In *The Hunger Games*, Katniss prepares for the final deadly showdown in the arena, knowing that only one contestant can survive.

Application: Use this stage to build suspense and tension. The Hero should be preparing themselves, gathering resources, or facing their darkest fears before the ultimate challenge.

The Ordeal

The Hero faces their greatest challenge yet—this is the climax of the journey, where the Hero is tested to their limits. It's a life-or-death moment, either literally or metaphorically, where the Hero must confront their fears, adversaries, or internal flaws.

Example: In *The Lion King*, Simba confronts Scar in a final battle for control of Pride Rock, overcoming his guilt and realizing his rightful place as king.

Application: The ordeal is the story's most intense, high-stakes moment. It's often the emotional and narrative climax where the Hero either triumphs or faces devastating loss. The outcome of the ordeal sets the stage for the resolution.

Reward (Seizing the Sword)

After overcoming the ordeal, the Hero is rewarded with a prize, victory, or newfound knowledge. This reward represents a significant achievement, but the journey is not yet over.

Example: In *Indiana Jones and the Last Crusade*, Indiana retrieves the Holy Grail after overcoming a series of deadly trials.

Application: The reward doesn't always have to be a physical object. It could be knowledge, power, reconciliation, or emotional clarity. It marks a turning point where the Hero is fundamentally changed by the journey.

The Road Back

The Hero begins the journey back to the ordinary world, but the conflict is not fully resolved. There may be one final obstacle or challenge to overcome before the journey is complete.

Example: In *The Dark Knight*, after capturing the Joker, Batman still has to face the aftermath of Harvey Dent's transformation into Two-Face and the consequences of Gotham's corruption.

Application: Use the road back to build toward the final resolution. The Hero may face setbacks or consequences that test their resolve one last time, forcing them to reflect on what they've learned.

Resurrection

The Hero faces a final test, where they must demonstrate the growth and transformation they've undergone. This is a critical moment where the Hero is "reborn" and emerges victorious or changed. Often, this involves sacrificing something or making a selfless choice.

Example: In *The Matrix*, Neo is killed by Agent Smith but is resurrected with newfound powers and self-awareness, fully embracing his role as "The One."

Application: The resurrection is the Hero's final confrontation with the forces that opposed them. This moment often echoes the ordeal but serves as a culmination of the Hero's journey. It's where the Hero proves they have truly transformed.

Return with the Elixir

The Hero returns to the ordinary world, but they are changed by their journey. They bring with them the "elixir"—a metaphor for the knowledge, power, or peace they have gained. The journey concludes with the Hero's reintegration into their world, but they are no longer the same person.

Example: In *The Lord of the Rings*, Frodo returns to the Shire after the defeat of Sauron, but he is forever changed by his journey, unable to fully return to the simple life he once knew.

Application: The return with the elixir symbolizes the Hero's growth and transformation. It brings closure to the story, showing how the Hero has affected the world or been affected by it.

Adapting the Hero's Journey to Your Film

The Hero's Journey is flexible and can be adapted to fit any genre or style of storytelling. You don't have to follow the structure rigidly, but using its framework can help guide your story's progression and ensure that your character undergoes meaningful growth.

Fantasy and Adventure: The Hero's Journey is often used in epic fantasies, where the protagonist embarks on a literal adventure filled with trials and dangers (e.g., *The Hobbit*, *Harry Potter*).

Drama: In more intimate, character-driven dramas, the Hero's Journey can reflect an emotional or psychological journey, where the character must confront internal struggles (e.g., *A Beautiful Mind*, *Good Will Hunting*).

Action: The Hero's Journey is commonly found in action films, where the protagonist faces external obstacles and enemies, but the journey often represents personal growth as well (e.g., *Die Hard*, *Mad Max: Fury Road*).

By understanding the Hero's Journey, you can create a film with universal appeal, tapping into the timeless themes of growth, transformation, and overcoming challenges.

The Hero's Journey is one of the most powerful storytelling structures, providing a blueprint for character growth, conflict, and resolution. By applying this classic framework to your film, you can create a narrative that resonates deeply with audiences, blending adventure, personal growth, and transformation. Whether your story is a grand epic or a small, personal drama, the Hero's Journey can help guide your characters through meaningful arcs, offering audiences a story that feels timeless and emotionally satisfying.

The Art of Dialogue: Writing Conversationally for the Screen

Dialogue is one of the most essential tools in screenwriting, serving as a vehicle for character development, story progression, and emotional resonance. Well-written dialogue can draw audiences into the world of the film, reveal the personalities and motivations of the characters, and subtly communicate important themes. On the other hand, poorly written dialogue can feel stilted, unnatural, or expository, pulling the audience out of the story. Writing dialogue that sounds conversational, flows naturally, and feels authentic to the characters requires skill, practice, and a keen ear for how people speak. In this chapter, we'll explore the art of dialogue, focusing on how to write compelling, natural, and engaging conversations for the screen.

Why Dialogue Matters

Dialogue in film has a dual purpose: it reveals character and drives the story forward. Every line of dialogue should serve a purpose, whether it's to reveal something about a character's personality, convey important information, or create tension between characters. In addition to being functional, good dialogue adds depth and authenticity to the film's world.

Effective dialogue accomplishes the following:

Reveals Character: Through the way a character speaks, their word choices, tone, and style of speech, the audience learns about their background, personality, and motivations.

Advances the Plot: Dialogue can introduce new plot points, explain events, or clarify relationships between characters.

Creates Subtext: What characters don't say is often as important as what they do say. Subtext allows dialogue to operate on multiple levels, revealing hidden emotions, tensions, or motives beneath the surface of the conversation.

Adds Authenticity: Dialogue should feel natural and reflect how real people speak, with all their quirks, pauses, and informalities. Natural dialogue helps immerse the audience in the world of the film.

Builds Conflict: Conversations are a great tool for creating tension, especially when characters have opposing desires or goals. Conflict in dialogue can be direct (through arguments or disagreements) or indirect (through subtle power dynamics or unspoken frustrations).

Elements of Great Dialogue

To write strong, natural dialogue, it's important to focus on several key elements that contribute to its effectiveness:

Character Voice

Each character should have a distinct way of speaking that reflects their background, personality, and worldview. The way they express themselves should feel consistent with who they are and differentiate them from other characters.

For example, a highly educated character may use precise language and formal sentence structures, while a more casual character might use slang or contractions. Dialogue is a reflection of a character's inner world, and their speech patterns should reveal their emotional state, confidence level, or even insecurities.

Example: In *The Big Lebowski*, the Dude's laid-back, rambling speech perfectly reflects his slacker personality, while Walter's more aggressive and forceful dialogue reveals his combative nature.

Tip: When writing dialogue, ask yourself how each character would uniquely say a line. Consider their background, upbringing, and current emotional state. Avoid making all characters sound alike.

Economy of Language

Film dialogue should be concise and to the point. Unlike in novels or plays, where long speeches are more common, film dialogue is usually shorter and more efficient. Every line should have a purpose—whether it's advancing the plot, revealing character, or building tension. Avoid unnecessary dialogue that doesn't serve the story.

Example: In *No Country for Old Men*, the dialogue between characters is often brief but loaded with meaning, leaving much to the imagination and heightening the tension. The characters say only what's necessary, and the silences between them speak volumes.

Tip: Practice cutting down your dialogue to its most essential elements. If a line isn't doing work for the story, character, or conflict, consider removing or reworking it.

Subtext

Subtext refers to the unspoken thoughts, emotions, or motivations behind a character's words. Often, what characters say is not what they truly mean. Writing dialogue with subtext allows you to create layers of meaning, adding depth to the conversation and leaving room for audience interpretation.

Example: In *Casablanca*, Rick's conversation with Ilsa is filled with subtext. They talk about mundane things, but beneath the surface, they're both grappling with unresolved emotions from their past romance.

Tip: Think about what your characters want to say but can't. Is there tension between their spoken words and their true feelings? Use body language, pauses, or indirect statements to convey subtext.

Conflict and Tension

Conflict is the lifeblood of drama, and dialogue is one of the best ways to create it. Tension in dialogue can come from characters who have opposing goals, conflicting beliefs, or unresolved issues. Even in scenes where characters seem to be getting along, there may be an undercurrent of tension, whether from hidden motivations, secrets, or frustrations.

Example: In *The Social Network*, the dialogue between Mark Zuckerberg and his lawyers is filled with tension, as both sides dance around the real issues of betrayal, ambition, and intellectual property.

Tip: In each conversation, think about what each character wants and how they can use the dialogue to achieve their goal. Conflict arises when characters want different things or have different approaches to a situation.

Natural Flow

Good dialogue should feel natural and conversational, even if it's carefully constructed. Real people don't speak in perfectly formed sentences or deliver exposition in a robotic manner. They pause, interrupt each other, change the subject, and sometimes struggle to find the right words. The key to writing natural dialogue is capturing this flow while still keeping the conversation focused and purposeful.

Example: In *Pulp Fiction*, the dialogue between Vincent and Jules during their iconic "Royale with Cheese" conversation feels organic, flowing from topic to topic in a way that mimics how real people talk. Yet, it's also crafted with purpose, revealing character and setting the tone for the film.

Tip: Read your dialogue aloud to see if it sounds like something people would actually say. Does it flow naturally, or does it feel stilted? Listening to real conversations or watching films with great dialogue can also help you develop an ear for natural speech.

Writing Dialogue with Purpose

When crafting dialogue, it's important to ensure that each conversation serves a specific purpose within the scene and the larger story. Here are some ways to ensure your dialogue is focused and purposeful:

Advance the Plot

Every scene should move the story forward, and the dialogue within that scene should contribute to this goal. Whether through revealing important information, introducing new challenges, or setting up future conflicts, dialogue should help drive the plot toward its resolution.

Example: In *Inception*, the dialogue between Cobb and his team explains the mechanics of dream infiltration, which is essential for understanding the film's plot. Yet, it's delivered in a way that feels natural within the context of their mission.

Reveal Character

Dialogue is one of the most direct ways to reveal character traits, values, and desires. How characters speak, what they talk about, and how they respond to others all help define who they are. Use dialogue to show a character's strengths, weaknesses, insecurities, or ambitions.

Example: In *Good Will Hunting*, Will's dialogue reveals his brilliance, but also his deep insecurities and defensive nature. His interactions with the therapist show his reluctance to confront his inner demons, which drives much of the emotional arc of the film.

Build Relationships

Dialogue is the foundation of character relationships. It's how characters connect, argue, bond, or break apart. Whether it's the romantic banter between lovers, the tense exchanges between enemies, or the heartfelt conversations between friends, dialogue defines the nature of these relationships and how they evolve over time.

Example: In *Before Sunrise*, the entire film revolves around the evolving relationship between Jesse and Céline as they walk through Vienna. Their conversations are the heart of the movie, showing how they connect on deeper levels as they share personal stories and philosophical ideas.

Create Subtext

As mentioned earlier, subtext adds depth to dialogue by allowing characters to communicate more than what's on the surface. Dialogue that is layered with subtext creates tension, mystery, and emotional complexity. Think about what your characters are not saying and use that to inform their interactions.

Example: In *Lost in Translation*, much of the relationship between Bob and Charlotte is conveyed through subtext. Their conversations are often simple, but what remains unspoken—about their dissatisfaction with their lives and their deepening connection—gives the dialogue emotional weight.

Use Silence and Pauses

Sometimes, what isn't said in a conversation is more powerful than what is. Silence, pauses, or ellipses can be effective tools in dialogue, allowing space for emotions to simmer or tension to build. Pauses give characters time to reflect, hesitate, or reconsider their words, adding layers of meaning to the exchange.

Example: In *A Quiet Place*, silence is literally a survival mechanism, but it's also used to communicate the tension and fear within the family. The absence of spoken dialogue makes every glance, gesture, and unspoken moment more significant.

Techniques for Writing Authentic Dialogue

Here are some practical techniques you can use to write dialogue that feels authentic, engaging, and purposeful:

Listen to Real Conversations

One of the best ways to write natural dialogue is to listen to how real people speak. Pay attention to the rhythms, word choices, and patterns of everyday conversations. Notice how people interrupt each other, use filler words ("um," "like"), or speak in incomplete sentences. Capturing the nuances of real speech will make your dialogue more believable.

Read Your Dialogue Out Loud

When you read dialogue out loud, it becomes clear whether it sounds natural or forced. If the dialogue feels awkward or unnatural when spoken, it likely needs to be reworked. Reading aloud also helps you spot repetitive words, clunky phrasing, or sentences that are too long for natural conversation.

Avoid Exposition Dumps

Exposition is important for explaining key details of the plot, but dumping too much information into dialogue can feel forced and unnatural. Instead, weave exposition subtly into conversations or use visual storytelling to convey information. Let characters reveal what they know gradually through context rather than reciting long blocks of explanation.

Use Character-Specific Language

Different characters should speak differently based on their background, personality, and circumstances. Avoid giving all characters the same speech patterns or vocabulary. Think about how each character would express themselves based on their education, culture, and emotional state. This will make your dialogue feel more varied and unique.

Embrace Imperfection

People rarely speak in perfect sentences. They stammer, pause, and repeat themselves. Embracing these imperfections in your dialogue will make it feel more authentic. Don't be afraid to let characters stumble over words, get interrupted, or trail off mid-sentence. This adds realism and makes the dialogue more relatable.

Show, Don't Tell

Rather than having characters state their emotions or motivations outright, show these through their dialogue. For example, instead of a character saying, "I'm scared," they might express their fear through hesitation, indirect language, or actions that convey their emotions more subtly. Let the audience infer emotions from how the character speaks rather than having them say everything explicitly.

Writing dialogue for the screen is both an art and a craft. It requires a deep understanding of character, an ear for natural speech, and a sense of purpose behind every word. By focusing on character voice, economy of language, subtext, and conflict, you can craft dialogue that is engaging, meaningful, and cinematic. Through dialogue, you reveal character, drive the plot forward, and create relationships that resonate with the audience. With practice and attention to detail, you can master the art of writing conversationally for the screen, making your film's dialogue a powerful tool for storytelling.

Cinematography with a Smartphone: The Importance of Composition

In filmmaking, composition is one of the most critical aspects of cinematography, and this holds true even when using a smartphone as your camera. How you frame a shot, position your subject, and balance the elements within the frame can greatly impact the visual storytelling of your film. With a smartphone's compact and portable nature, you have unique opportunities to explore creative compositions that may be more challenging with traditional cameras. This chapter will delve into the significance of composition in smartphone cinematography, offering techniques and tips to help you create visually compelling shots that engage your audience and enhance your storytelling.

Why Composition Matters

Composition refers to the arrangement of visual elements within your frame, and it plays a crucial role in how your audience perceives and connects with your story. Good composition can draw attention to important details, convey emotions, and create a sense of balance or tension. Even with the limitations of a smartphone camera, mastering composition allows you to elevate the quality of your shots and make them more cinematic.

Key Benefits of Strong Composition:

Visual Clarity: Clear composition directs the viewer's attention to the most important aspects of the scene, helping to communicate your message more effectively.

Emotional Impact: The way elements are arranged within the frame can evoke specific emotions, whether it's creating a sense of harmony or discomfort.

Professional Look: Well-composed shots give your film a polished, professional feel, even if it's filmed on a smartphone.

Techniques for Strong Composition in Smartphone Filmmaking

To make the most of your smartphone camera, here are some essential composition techniques that will help you create engaging and visually striking shots.

The Rule of Thirds

The rule of thirds is one of the most fundamental principles in visual composition. It involves dividing the frame into nine equal parts by drawing two vertical and two horizontal lines, creating a grid. By placing your subject along these lines or at their intersections, you create a more dynamic and balanced composition.

Why It Works: The human eye naturally gravitates toward these points of intersection, making the composition feel balanced and visually appealing. This rule prevents your subject from being centered, which can sometimes result in a flat or static image.

How to Use It: Most smartphones have a built-in grid feature in their camera settings. Enable the grid and use it to position your subject or key elements along the lines or intersections. This technique works especially well for landscape shots, interviews, and close-ups.

Tip: Experiment with breaking the rule of thirds once you've mastered it, as placing your subject in the center or on the edges can create intentional tension or symmetry, depending on your scene's needs.

Leading Lines

Leading lines are natural or man-made lines within the environment that guide the viewer's eye toward a specific point in the frame, often the subject of your shot. These lines can be anything from roads and fences to shadows and architectural elements.

Why It Works: Leading lines create depth and perspective, drawing the viewer's attention into the frame and giving your shots a more three-dimensional feel. This technique is especially effective in creating a sense of movement or guiding the viewer through a scene.

How to Use It: Look for lines in your environment—such as roads, rivers, or even walls—and position your subject at the end of those lines. This helps direct the viewer's gaze toward the subject in a natural, visually satisfying way.

Tip: Leading lines work well in establishing shots, where you want to give the audience a sense of location, or in action scenes where you need to emphasize movement.

Symmetry and Balance

Symmetry and balance are powerful tools in cinematography that can create visually harmonious compositions. Symmetry involves mirroring elements on both sides of the frame, while balance refers to distributing visual weight equally across the frame.

Why It Works: Symmetry is pleasing to the eye and can create a sense of order and stability, which is useful when you want to convey calmness or control. Balanced compositions help avoid visual distractions by ensuring that no part of the frame feels too heavy or cluttered.

How to Use It: Use symmetry in scenes where you want to highlight the beauty of architecture, landscapes, or portraits. Balance your compositions by ensuring that elements on either side of the frame are visually equal in weight, which can be achieved by placing objects or people at similar distances from the center.

Tip: Asymmetry can also be used intentionally to create unease or tension in a scene, so don't hesitate to break the rules when the story calls for it.

Depth and Layers

Creating a sense of depth in your compositions adds dimension and realism to your shots, helping to immerse the viewer in the scene. Depth is achieved by including elements in the foreground, middle ground, and background of your frame.

Why It Works: Layers within a frame add complexity and keep the viewer engaged by giving them multiple points of interest. Depth also enhances the illusion of three-dimensional space, making your shots feel more dynamic and alive.

How to Use It: Frame your shot with objects or people in the foreground, while your subject remains in the middle ground or background. This layering creates a sense of space and distance, making the shot more visually interesting.

Tip: Use natural elements like trees, doorways, or furniture to create layers in your shots, adding visual complexity without overwhelming the scene.

Framing Within a Frame

Framing within a frame involves using elements within the scene to create a frame around your subject. This technique draws attention to the subject and adds a sense of focus and intimacy to the shot.

Why It Works: By creating a frame around the subject, you naturally direct the viewer's attention to where it matters most. It also adds depth to the shot and can give a sense of voyeurism, as though the viewer is peering into the scene.

How to Use It: Look for natural frames within the environment, such as doorways, windows, or arches. Position your subject within these frames to isolate them and make them the focal point of the composition.

Tip: Framing within a frame works particularly well for close-ups and portraits, where you want to emphasize the subject's emotions or reactions.

Negative Space

Negative space refers to the empty or unoccupied space around your subject. While it may seem counterintuitive, negative space can be just as important as the subject itself, as it helps create balance and gives your composition room to breathe.

Why It Works: Negative space gives the viewer's eyes a place to rest, which can be especially effective in minimalist compositions. It also highlights the subject by isolating it against a clean, uncluttered background.

How to Use It: Place your subject in a small portion of the frame, leaving the rest as negative space. This creates a sense of isolation or contemplation, which can be used to evoke specific emotions or themes.

Tip: Use negative space when you want to convey loneliness, vastness, or simplicity in your scene. It's a subtle but powerful way to influence the emotional tone of your shot.

Making the Most of Smartphone Cinematography

With smartphones, you may not have access to high-end lenses or complex equipment, but mastering composition allows you to create professional-quality shots regardless of your tools. By focusing on how you arrange elements within the frame, you can craft visually compelling scenes that elevate your storytelling.

Experiment with Angles

Smartphones are lightweight and portable, allowing you to easily experiment with different angles. Try low-angle shots to give your subject a sense of power or authority, or high-angle shots to make the subject feel small or vulnerable. The freedom to move your phone around quickly and easily is one of the biggest advantages of smartphone filmmaking.

Consider Movement

With smartphones, you can effortlessly introduce movement into your shots by using handheld techniques. Tracking shots, pans, and tilts can be executed with ease, so don't hesitate to incorporate motion into your compositions to create more dynamic visuals.

Composition is the foundation of cinematic storytelling, and mastering it can significantly improve the quality of your smartphone filmmaking. By applying principles like the rule of thirds, leading lines, and negative space, you can create visually striking shots that draw viewers into your story. With practice and experimentation, you'll discover that even with a smartphone, you can achieve compositions that rival those of traditional cinema, enhancing both the visual and emotional impact of your film.

Using Natural Light: Filming Without Expensive Gear

Lighting is one of the most crucial elements in filmmaking, as it sets the tone, enhances the mood, and draws attention to important details in each scene. While professional film sets often rely on expensive lighting rigs and equipment, many independent filmmakers and smartphone users don't have access to these tools. However, you can achieve beautiful, cinematic lighting by using a resource available to everyone: natural light.

In this chapter, we'll explore how to film effectively using natural light, taking advantage of the sun's positioning, the environment, and simple techniques to make your scenes visually stunning without the need for costly gear. With some planning and creativity, you can use natural light to elevate your smartphone film, giving it a polished, professional look.

Why Natural Light Matters in Filmmaking

Natural light is a versatile and powerful tool in cinematography. When used correctly, it can create dynamic contrasts, enhance the atmosphere, and lend authenticity to your film. Natural light also has a soft, diffused quality that is difficult to replicate with artificial lights, making it ideal for a range of scenes, from soft, intimate moments to dramatic, high-contrast visuals.

Here's why natural light is so valuable for filmmakers:

Cost-Effective: Natural light is free and widely available, making it an ideal solution for filmmakers working with limited budgets.

Realism and Authenticity: Since natural light is how we experience the world, using it in your film can lend an authentic and organic feel to your scenes.

Softness and Warmth: Natural light, especially during certain times of the day (like the golden hour), can create a soft, warm, and flattering light that enhances skin tones and textures.

However, natural light can also be unpredictable, which means you need to understand how to work with its changing qualities to maintain consistent and effective lighting.

The Importance of Time and Weather

One of the biggest advantages of natural light is that it changes throughout the day, offering different moods and tones depending on the time and weather conditions. Knowing when to film and how to adjust to weather changes can make a significant difference in the quality of your shots.

Golden Hour

Golden hour occurs shortly after sunrise and just before sunset, when the sun is low in the sky. The light during this time is soft, warm, and diffused, creating a flattering, cinematic glow. The shadows are longer, and the contrast is gentle, making it ideal for character close-ups, romantic scenes, and establishing shots with a beautiful, atmospheric quality.

Advantages:

Soft, even light with minimal harsh shadows.

Warm, golden tones that add depth and richness to the image.

Longer shadows for more dramatic compositions.

Application: Schedule your outdoor shoots for golden hour to capture the most flattering and cinematic natural light. This is especially useful for scenes with characters in focus, as the light enhances skin tones and creates a beautiful, glowing backdrop.

Midday Light

Midday light, when the sun is high in the sky, tends to be much harsher and more direct. This can create strong, unflattering shadows on faces and objects, especially if the sun is directly overhead. While midday light is not ideal for character close-ups, it can work well for certain genres or moods, such as action scenes or desert landscapes that require a harsher, more intense atmosphere.

Challenges:

Harsh, direct light that creates deep shadows.

Overexposure in certain areas of the frame, especially bright skies or reflective surfaces.

Unflattering light for close-ups, particularly for faces.

Application: If you must shoot during midday, try positioning your actors in the shade or use reflective surfaces (such as white boards or foam) to bounce light back onto your subject. Alternatively, embrace the harsh light for stylized, high-contrast shots, particularly in more dramatic or gritty scenes.

Cloudy or Overcast Days

Cloud cover acts as a natural diffuser, softening the sunlight and eliminating harsh shadows. Overcast days provide even, diffused lighting that is great for shooting scenes with consistent lighting across the frame. It's ideal for character-driven scenes or situations where you want to avoid strong contrasts between light and shadow.

Advantages:

Soft, even lighting without harsh shadows.

More consistent exposure throughout the frame.

Less need for additional lighting tools or reflectors.

Application: Overcast days are perfect for shooting dialogue scenes, close-ups, or any shot where you need soft, flattering light. The consistency of the light makes it easier to shoot long scenes without worrying about dramatic lighting changes.

Magic Hour (Twilight)

Magic hour occurs just after sunset and before darkness fully sets in. The light during this time is soft and muted, with cool, blue tones. Magic hour is perfect for creating a sense of mystery, calm, or emotional reflection in your scenes. While it's similar to golden hour in terms of softness, the color temperature is cooler, adding a more subdued or melancholic tone.

Advantages:

Soft, diffused light with a cool color temperature.

Dreamlike or mystical atmosphere.

Minimal shadows and even lighting.

Application: Magic hour is ideal for quiet, contemplative scenes or moments that require a serene or ethereal quality. Be mindful that magic hour is brief, so you'll need to plan and work quickly to capture this unique lighting.

Practical Techniques for Using Natural Light

While natural light is a fantastic resource, it requires some technique and planning to make the most of it. Here are several practical strategies for using natural light to your advantage in different filmmaking scenarios:

Use Reflectors

Reflectors are one of the simplest and most effective tools for controlling natural light. By bouncing light onto your subject, reflectors allow you to fill in shadows and create more balanced lighting. You can use a variety of reflective surfaces, from professional reflectors to DIY options like white foam boards, aluminum foil, or even a piece of cardboard wrapped in tin foil.

How to Use:

Fill Light: Use a reflector to bounce sunlight onto the shadowed side of your subject's face, creating a more even, flattering look. This is especially helpful during midday when the light is harsh and creates strong shadows.

Backlight Control: If the sun is behind your subject, use a reflector to redirect some of that light onto their face, ensuring they're not completely silhouetted.

Tip: Position the reflector at different angles to achieve the desired fill light. Experiment with different materials for softer or stronger light reflection.

Positioning Your Subject

Where you place your subject in relation to the sun can dramatically affect the mood and clarity of your shot. By understanding how light falls, you can position your subject for the most flattering or dramatic effect.

Types of Lighting:

Front Lighting: When the light source (sun) is in front of the subject, illuminating their face directly. This creates even lighting with minimal shadows, but can sometimes result in a flat, less dramatic look.

Backlighting: When the light source is behind the subject, it creates a rim of light around them, which can be visually striking and add depth to the shot. Be careful with overexposure when using backlighting; a reflector can help bounce light onto the subject's face.

Side Lighting: This type of lighting creates more dramatic shadows and highlights on the subject's face, emphasizing texture and form. It's great for creating a more cinematic, high-contrast look.

Tip: Move your subject or the camera around to find the best position in relation to the sun. Experiment with side or backlighting to add visual interest or enhance the mood of the scene.

Use Natural Diffusion

On bright, sunny days, the light can be too harsh, creating unflattering shadows and hot spots. You can soften the light by using natural diffusers like trees, umbrellas, or translucent curtains. These elements act as a filter between the sunlight and your subject, providing softer, more even lighting.

How to Use:

Shade: Position your subject under a tree or an awning to diffuse the sunlight naturally.

Artificial Diffusers: If you don't have access to natural diffusers, use translucent materials like white sheets, light diffusing panels, or even umbrellas to soften the direct sunlight.

Tip: Be creative with finding or creating diffusion materials. A frosted shower curtain or a translucent fabric stretched over a frame can serve as an effective, low-cost diffuser for outdoor shoots.

Embrace Shadows and Contrast

Natural light can create beautiful shadows and contrast that add depth and drama to your film. Instead of avoiding these shadows, embrace them to create mood, tension, or visual interest. Harsh light and deep shadows can be especially effective in genres like film noir, thrillers, or action films.

Application: In scenes where you want to evoke mystery, tension, or conflict, position your subjects to cast long shadows or allow strong contrasts between light and dark areas of the frame. Play with the interaction between light and shadow to tell a story visually.

Plan for the Light

Since natural light is constantly changing, it's important to plan your shoots around the best lighting conditions. Know when and where the sun will be during your shooting schedule, and anticipate how it will affect your scenes.

How to Plan:

Use apps like *Sun Seeker* or *Sun Surveyor* to track the sun's position throughout the day, helping you time your outdoor shoots for optimal lighting conditions.

Have a plan for what to shoot at different times of the day. For example, film wide landscape shots during golden hour and close-up character moments when the light is softer and more flattering.

Be prepared to adjust your shooting plan if the weather changes unexpectedly. Cloudy days may offer great diffused lighting, but you may need to shoot quickly during moments when the light is ideal.

Tip: Always have a backup plan in case natural light doesn't cooperate. If a scene requires specific lighting conditions that aren't available, try rescheduling for a different time of day or use reflectors and diffusers to control the light as needed.

Indoor Filming with Natural Light

Natural light isn't just for outdoor scenes—you can use it effectively indoors as well. Windows and doors can act as natural light sources, giving you beautiful, soft lighting for intimate, controlled shots.

Window Lighting

Windows are a fantastic source of natural light, offering soft, directional lighting that can illuminate your subject evenly without creating harsh shadows. Position your subject near a window to make use of this light, and adjust their angle to create the desired mood or tone.

Types of Window Light:

Side Window Light: Light coming from the side of the subject creates beautiful, soft shadows on one side of the face, adding depth and dimension.

Front Window Light: Light from a window in front of the subject provides even, flattering light with minimal shadows, ideal for close-ups or dialogue scenes.

Back Window Light: Light coming from behind the subject creates a natural backlight effect, which can add a soft glow around your subject and create a silhouette.

Tip: Use curtains or blinds to diffuse or control the amount of light coming through the window. If the light is too strong, sheer curtains can soften it, creating a more even glow.

Doorways and Skylights

In addition to windows, doorways and skylights can be used to direct natural light into a scene. Skylights provide soft, overhead light that can fill an entire room, while doorways can offer controlled light beams that create contrast and shadows.

Application: Use doorways to frame your subject and allow light to stream in from behind them, creating a dramatic backlight effect. Skylights are ideal for creating soft, natural overhead light that spreads evenly throughout the room.

Natural light is one of the most powerful and accessible tools available to filmmakers, allowing you to create stunning visuals without the need for expensive gear. By understanding the qualities of light at different times of day, using reflectors and diffusers to control light, and positioning your subjects thoughtfully, you can harness the power of natural light to enhance the look and feel of your film. Whether you're shooting indoors or outdoors, using natural light effectively will give your film a cinematic quality that elevates the storytelling and immerses your audience in the world you've created.

Recording Voice-Overs: Using Your Phone for Narration

Voice-overs are a powerful narrative tool in filmmaking, often used to provide context, offer insights into a character's thoughts, or move the story forward in ways that visuals alone cannot. While professional recording studios are ideal for capturing voice-overs, modern smartphones are equipped with surprisingly good microphones that allow you to record high-quality audio right from your phone. Whether you're creating a documentary, a short film, or a fictional narrative, knowing how to effectively record voice-overs using your phone can save you time and money without sacrificing quality.

In this chapter, we'll explore the process of recording voice-overs with your smartphone, including tips on setting up a recording environment, using apps for the best results, and ensuring your voice-over sounds professional and polished.

Why Voice-Overs Matter in Filmmaking

Voice-overs serve a variety of purposes in filmmaking, often bridging gaps in the story, adding depth to characters, or explaining complex ideas. When done well, voice-overs can add layers to your narrative, provide exposition, or create emotional impact by letting the audience hear a character's inner thoughts or a narrator's perspective.

Some common uses of voice-overs in film include:

Character Narration: Offering insight into a character's thoughts or emotions that may not be fully conveyed through visuals.

Exposition: Providing background information or setting up context for the viewer.

Transitioning Between Scenes: Guiding the audience from one scene to another while providing narrative continuity.

Adding Depth to Themes: Using a voice-over to reflect on larger themes or moral questions in the story.

While voice-overs should be used strategically and sparingly to avoid over-reliance, they can be a valuable asset in storytelling when integrated seamlessly into the film.

Setting Up Your Recording Environment

Recording high-quality audio is as much about the environment as it is about the microphone or device you're using. Smartphones are equipped with decent microphones, but to get professional-level results, you need to control the environment in which you're recording.

Find a Quiet Space

The most important factor when recording voice-overs is ensuring that you're in a quiet, controlled environment with minimal background noise. Even the best smartphone microphones will pick up sounds like traffic, air conditioning, or people talking in the background, which can degrade the quality of your recording.

Tips for Quiet Spaces:

Turn off Appliances: Make sure any noisy devices like fans, air conditioners, or refrigerators are turned off during recording.

Choose a Small Room: Smaller rooms tend to have less echo, making them ideal for recording clean audio. Avoid large, open spaces that can cause reverberation.

Record at Off-Hours: If you're in a busy area, try recording early in the morning or late at night when there's less external noise.

Reduce Echo and Reverberation

Echo and reverberation can make voice recordings sound hollow or distant. To minimize these effects, you can add sound-absorbing materials to the recording space. You don't need expensive acoustic panels—household items can work surprisingly well.

DIY Solutions for Reducing Echo:

Blankets and Pillows: Hang blankets on the walls or position pillows around the recording area to absorb sound. Recording in a closet full of clothes is another great option, as the clothing dampens sound reflections.

Rugs and Curtains: Soft materials like rugs and heavy curtains can help absorb sound in rooms with hard surfaces, reducing echo and improving audio quality.

Furniture: A room with furniture (such as couches and bookshelves) naturally absorbs sound better than an empty room, so choose a space that's already filled with soft furnishings.

Consider a Pop Filter

A pop filter is a screen that helps reduce plosive sounds—those harsh bursts of air that occur when pronouncing "p" and "b" sounds. While professional pop filters are inexpensive, you can also create a DIY version by stretching a thin fabric (like a piece of pantyhose) over a circular frame (such as a wire hanger) and placing it in front of your smartphone's microphone.

Tip: Hold the phone a few inches away from your mouth and slightly to the side to avoid recording plosives directly into the microphone.

Best Apps for Recording Voice-Overs on Your Smartphone

While your phone's built-in voice recorder can do the job, there are apps designed to enhance the quality and functionality of your voice-over recordings. These apps offer features such as noise reduction, editing tools, and higher-quality audio formats that can improve the final result.

Ferrite Recording Studio (iOS)

Ferrite is a powerful recording app that combines professional-grade audio recording with intuitive editing tools. It's great for voice-over work because it offers automatic gain control, background noise reduction, and the ability to edit multiple tracks. It also supports high-quality WAV files for crisp, clear audio.

Features:

Multitrack recording and editing

Automatic gain control for consistent volume levels

Built-in noise reduction

Export in high-quality audio formats

Tip: Ferrite's editing tools allow you to cut out mistakes and adjust levels on the go, making it an all-in-one solution for voice-over recording.

Dolby On (iOS/Android)

Dolby On is a free app that automatically optimizes your recordings by reducing background noise and enhancing sound quality. It's ideal for filmmakers looking for a simple, no-fuss recording solution. Dolby On offers real-time effects like compression and EQ, giving your voice-over a polished, studio-quality sound with minimal effort.

Features:

One-touch recording with automatic noise reduction

Built-in effects such as compression, EQ, and reverb

High-quality export options

Tip: Use Dolby On's real-time EQ settings to enhance the clarity of your voice, particularly if you're recording in a less-than-ideal environment.

Voice Recorder Pro (iOS/Android)

Voice Recorder Pro is a straightforward app that offers high-quality audio recording with some essential editing features. It's great for voice-over recordings that need to be exported in a variety of formats, including MP3, WAV, and AAC. The app also allows you to adjust the microphone sensitivity to capture clearer audio depending on your environment.

Features:

Adjustable microphone sensitivity

Export in multiple formats (MP3, WAV, AAC)

Basic editing tools for trimming and adjusting audio

Tip: Adjust the microphone sensitivity depending on your environment. In a quiet space, set it to high to capture more detail, and in a noisier area, reduce the sensitivity to avoid picking up background noise.

Easy Voice Recorder (iOS/Android)

Easy Voice Recorder is a user-friendly app that supports high-quality audio recording and offers basic editing features. It's perfect for filmmakers who want a simple, reliable way to capture voice-overs without a steep learning curve. The app also supports a wide range of file formats and allows you to upload recordings directly to cloud services for easy storage and sharing.

Features:

Record in high-quality PCM or MP3 formats

Easy upload to cloud services like Google Drive or Dropbox

Basic editing features for trimming and adjusting recordings

Tip: Take advantage of cloud storage integration to keep your voice-over files organized and easily accessible, especially if you're working with a team.

Tips for Recording High-Quality Voice-Overs

Recording a voice-over with your phone can yield professional results if you follow a few key tips. Here are some best practices to ensure your narration sounds clear, consistent, and polished.

Use the Right Distance

When recording, you don't want to hold the phone too close to your mouth, as this can lead to distortion and "popping" sounds from plosives. On the other hand, recording from too far away can make your voice sound distant and pick up more background noise.

Tip: Hold the phone about 6 to 8 inches away from your mouth for the best results. Experiment with the distance to find the sweet spot where your voice sounds clear and full, without distortion.

Maintain Consistent Volume

One of the biggest challenges when recording voice-overs is keeping a consistent volume throughout the session. Inconsistent volume can make the voice-over sound uneven and difficult to follow.

Tip: Speak at a natural, even volume and avoid sudden changes in pitch or intensity. If you need to emphasize certain words, do so through tone rather than volume to avoid peaking or distortion.

Warm Up Your Voice

Just like actors warm up before performing, warming up your voice before recording a voice-over can help you deliver a clearer, more confident performance. Vocal warm-ups can help reduce strain and ensure that your voice sounds natural.

Tip: Do some simple vocal exercises like humming or lip trills before you start recording. Drink water to stay hydrated and avoid dairy products, as they can coat your throat and affect vocal clarity.

Record Multiple Takes

Don't be afraid to record several takes of the same lines to ensure you get the best possible version. Each take may bring out different nuances or emotions that could improve the final product.

Tip: Record multiple takes with slight variations in tone, pace, and delivery. This gives you more options in post-production to choose the best performance for the scene.

Watch Out for Background Noise

Even in a relatively quiet room, subtle background noises can sneak into your recording. Pay attention to things like distant traffic, footsteps, or even the hum of your refrigerator.

Tip: Pause for a moment before recording to listen for any sounds that might interfere with your voice-over. If possible, unplug any electronic devices that might create unwanted noise, and make sure doors and windows are closed.

Editing and Enhancing Your Voice-Over

Once you've recorded your voice-over, the next step is to edit and enhance the audio to ensure it sounds polished and professional. This can involve removing mistakes, cleaning up background noise, and adjusting levels for consistency.

Noise Reduction

Even with careful planning, some background noise might make its way into your recording. Fortunately, many audio editing apps and software programs offer noise reduction tools that can help clean up your audio.

Tip: Apps like *Audacity* (a free desktop app) or *Ferrite* (mobile) offer noise reduction features that allow you to isolate and reduce background noise without affecting the quality of your voice.

Trimming and Splicing

Editing tools allow you to trim the beginning and end of your voice-over to remove any unwanted sounds, like coughs, clicks, or long pauses. You can also splice together multiple takes to create a seamless final track.

Tip: In Ferrite or other audio editing apps, use the trim and splice features to create a clean, fluid voice-over track. Make sure to crossfade or smooth the transitions between clips to avoid harsh cuts.

Adjusting Levels

To ensure your voice-over is consistent throughout, you may need to adjust the levels of your recording. This involves normalizing the audio so that all parts of the track are at a similar volume, making it easier for the audience to follow along.

Tip: Use automatic gain control or manual level adjustments in your editing app to ensure that no part of the recording is too loud or too quiet. Avoid boosting the levels too much, as this can introduce distortion.

Recording voice-overs using your smartphone is an accessible and cost-effective way to add narration to your film. By carefully selecting your recording environment, using the right apps, and following best practices for audio capture, you can achieve professional-sounding results. With the right technique, even a simple smartphone recording can enhance your film's narrative, giving it greater depth and clarity. Whether you're narrating a documentary, voicing a character's thoughts, or providing exposition, mastering voice-over recording will add a powerful storytelling tool to your filmmaking repertoire.

Developing a Storyboard: Planning Your Shots on a Budget

Storyboarding is one of the most crucial steps in pre-production, allowing filmmakers to visualize their film before they even start shooting. It involves creating a series of sketches or images that represent each shot of your film, helping you plan camera angles, composition, movement, and transitions. For filmmakers working with a tight budget, developing a storyboard is especially important because it helps you save time, avoid costly mistakes, and make the most of your resources.

In this chapter, we'll explore the process of developing a storyboard for your film, focusing on how to plan your shots efficiently and creatively, even if you're working with limited resources. Whether you're using simple hand-drawn sketches or digital tools, storyboarding is essential for organizing your ideas, communicating with your team, and staying on track during production.

Why Storyboarding is Essential for Budget Filmmakers

For filmmakers on a budget, time and resources are often limited. Every shot counts, and wasting time on set trying to figure out camera angles or blocking can lead to delays and overspending. Storyboarding helps you pre-visualize your film, so when you get to set, you know exactly what shots you need, how they'll look, and how they'll flow together. Here's why storyboarding is especially important for low-budget filmmaking:

Saves Time on Set: With a clear plan in place, you'll spend less time setting up shots and making decisions on the fly. This means more efficient shooting days and fewer wasted resources.

Minimizes Mistakes: Storyboarding allows you to spot potential problems, such as awkward camera angles or continuity issues, before they happen, reducing the need for reshoots.

Maximizes Resources: By planning your shots in advance, you can better allocate your budget, ensuring that you use your time, equipment, and crew efficiently.

Improves Communication: A storyboard helps you clearly communicate your vision to your crew, actors, and anyone else involved in the production, ensuring everyone is on the same page.

How to Develop a Storyboard

Developing a storyboard doesn't have to be a complicated or expensive process. Even simple, hand-drawn sketches can effectively communicate your ideas. The key is to break down your script into individual shots, plan out the visual flow of each scene, and consider how your shots will contribute to the overall story.

Break Down Your Script

The first step in storyboarding is breaking down your script into individual scenes and shots. Look at each scene and decide how you want to visually represent it. Ask yourself the following questions:

What is the key action in this scene?

What emotions or themes do I want to convey?

How can I use the camera to enhance the story?

For each scene, break it down further into specific shots. For example, you might have a wide establishing shot to introduce a location, followed by a close-up to focus on a character's reaction, and then a medium shot for dialogue.

Tip: Go through your script and highlight key moments that require special attention—such as an important reveal, a character's emotional shift, or a dramatic action sequence. These moments will be the focus of your storyboard.

Decide on Shot Types

Each shot in your storyboard should have a specific purpose, whether it's to introduce a new location, reveal a character's emotions, or show the relationship between characters. Think about the different types of shots you'll use and how they'll contribute to the scene.

Common shot types include:

Wide Shots: Establish the setting or show the overall action happening in a scene.

Medium Shots: Focus on characters, often used for dialogue or interactions.

Close-Ups: Highlight important details, like a character's facial expression or a key object in the scene.

Over-the-Shoulder Shots: Show the interaction between two characters by framing one in the foreground and the other in the background.

POV Shots: Put the camera in the position of a character, allowing the audience to see through their eyes.

Tip: Vary your shot types to create visual interest and help guide the audience's emotional journey. For example, wide shots can create a sense of distance or loneliness, while close-ups can build intimacy and tension.

Create Simple Sketches or Use Digital Tools

Once you've broken down your script and decided on shot types, it's time to start sketching out your storyboard. You don't need to be an artist to create a functional storyboard—simple stick figures and basic shapes can effectively communicate your ideas. The goal is to provide a clear visual guide for each shot, including key elements like the position of characters, objects, and camera angles.

For each shot, sketch the following:

Character Positions: Where the characters are located in the frame.

Camera Angle: The angle from which the scene is shot (e.g., low angle, high angle, eye level).

Camera Movement: If the camera is moving (e.g., panning, tracking, zooming), indicate this in the sketch.

Key Action or Emotion: What is happening in the shot? Is a character reacting to something? Is there an important object being shown?

If you prefer digital tools, there are several apps and software programs designed to help filmmakers create storyboards:

Storyboarder: A free, open-source app that allows you to quickly create simple storyboards. It includes drawing tools and the ability to add notes and descriptions for each shot.

Canva: While primarily a graphic design tool, Canva offers templates that can be adapted for storyboarding. You can easily create visual layouts and export them as PDFs or images.

ShotPro: A 3D storyboarding app that allows you to create detailed, interactive storyboards with virtual sets and characters. It's ideal for filmmakers who want more detailed visual planning.

Tip: If drawing isn't your strength, you can also use photos as placeholders. Take snapshots of your locations or use images from online sources to stand in for your storyboard shots.

Add Notes and Descriptions

Alongside your sketches, it's helpful to add notes and descriptions for each shot. These can include information about camera movement, lighting, sound cues, or any other technical details that are important for the scene. For example, you might note that a particular shot involves a slow zoom, or that the lighting should be warm and soft to reflect the mood of the scene.

Important Details to Include:

Shot Duration: How long will the shot last?

Camera Movement: Is the camera stationary or moving? If moving, how?

Lighting Notes: What kind of lighting is needed (e.g., natural, low-key, high contrast)?

Sound: Are there any important sound elements (e.g., voice-over, background noise, music) to consider?

Transitions: If the shot transitions into the next one in a specific way (e.g., fade, cut, dissolve), make a note of it.

Tip: Use arrows to indicate movement within the frame, such as where characters are walking or how the camera should move. This makes the storyboard more dynamic and easy to interpret for others.

Plan for Camera Movement

Camera movement can add energy, emotion, and fluidity to a scene. As you create your storyboard, think about how the camera will move through each shot. Even with a smartphone, there are plenty of ways to introduce dynamic camera movement, such as panning, tracking, or handheld shots.

Common camera movements include:

Panning: Moving the camera horizontally from one side to another.

Tilting: Moving the camera vertically (up or down).

Tracking: Moving the camera along with the action, often following a character or object.

Zooming: Adjusting the lens to zoom in or out on a subject.

Handheld: Holding the camera without a stabilizer, creating a more spontaneous, raw feel.

Tip: If you're on a tight budget, use simple tools like a tripod for smooth pans and tilts, or handheld shots for more dynamic movement. You can also DIY a dolly using wheels or sliders for more complex tracking shots.

Think About Transitions

Transitions between shots are an important part of the visual flow of your film. Storyboarding helps you plan how each shot will connect to the next, whether through a smooth cut, a fade, or a more creative transition like a wipe or match cut. These transitions are crucial for maintaining pacing and mood.

Types of Transitions:

Cut: A simple, immediate change from one shot to the next.

Fade In/Out: Gradually transitioning from black to the image (fade in) or from the image to black (fade out).

Dissolve: One image gradually transitions into another, often used to indicate the passage of time.

Match Cut: A cut where two visually similar scenes are matched together, creating a seamless transition.

Tip: Consider using match cuts or dissolves for transitions between similar scenes, or abrupt cuts for dramatic moments. Planning your transitions in advance ensures smooth pacing and consistency.

Test Your Storyboard with Animatics

Once you've created your storyboard, you can take it one step further by turning it into an animatic—a rough, animated version of your storyboard that simulates the timing and flow of the film. This helps you test the pacing and visual rhythm of your scenes before shooting.

How to Create an Animatic:

Import your storyboard sketches into a video editing program like *iMovie*, *Adobe Premiere*, or *DaVinci Resolve*.

Add each image to the timeline and adjust the duration to match the planned shot length.

Add temporary sound effects, dialogue, or music to simulate the final product.

Tip: Animatics are especially useful for action sequences or complex scenes with multiple camera movements, as they allow you to visualize the timing and flow of the scene before committing to the shoot.

Storyboarding on a Budget: Tips and Tricks

While big-budget productions often have teams dedicated to storyboarding, independent filmmakers can still create effective storyboards without breaking the bank. Here are some tips for storyboarding on a budget:

Use Index Cards: If you prefer a tactile approach, use index cards to sketch out each shot. You can lay them out on a table or pin them to a board to visualize the sequence of your shots.

Photograph Your Shots: If drawing isn't your strength, use your phone to take photos of potential locations or setups. These can act as placeholders for your storyboard images.

Involve Your Team: Collaborate with your crew, actors, or friends to act out scenes and help you visualize the shots. This can give you a better sense of how the scene will play out.

Start Simple: Don't worry about making your storyboard perfect or overly detailed. The goal is to have a clear visual plan that helps guide your shoot, so focus on the essentials.

Developing a storyboard is an essential step in planning your shots and organizing your film, especially when working on a budget. By breaking down your script, choosing your shot types, and sketching out each scene, you can visualize your film and create a roadmap for production. Whether you're using simple hand-drawn sketches or digital tools, storyboarding helps you stay on track, avoid costly mistakes, and maximize your resources. With a clear storyboard in hand, you'll be better equipped to execute your vision efficiently and creatively, ensuring a smooth and successful shoot.

Mastering Transitions: Fluid Cuts in Mobile Editing

Transitions in film are more than just the bridge between two scenes—they are a powerful storytelling tool that can enhance the rhythm, mood, and continuity of your film. When used effectively, transitions create a fluid flow from one shot to the next, helping to guide the audience's attention, create tension or excitement, or subtly shift between moments in time or space. For mobile filmmakers, mastering transitions is especially important, as it can elevate the production quality of your film, making it feel more polished and professional. In this chapter, we'll explore how to achieve smooth, fluid transitions using mobile editing tools, focusing on both simple cuts and creative techniques that work well with limited resources.

Why Transitions Matter

Transitions serve several key functions in filmmaking:

Guide the Viewer: Transitions help orient the audience, showing them where the story is going and providing visual continuity between scenes.

Set the Mood: Different transitions can evoke different emotions. For instance, a fast, sharp cut can create a sense of urgency, while a slow dissolve might evoke reflection or passage of time.

Control the Rhythm: Transitions can speed up or slow down the pacing of your film, allowing you to control the flow and rhythm of the story.

Signify Time and Space: Transitions help indicate shifts in time, location, or even emotional state, making the storytelling clearer and more dynamic.

For mobile filmmakers, learning to master transitions—whether through simple cuts or more complex techniques—will make your film feel more cohesive and fluid, even if you're working with basic editing apps.

Basic Types of Transitions

There are several basic types of transitions used in film, each with its own unique effect. As a mobile filmmaker, you'll want to focus on mastering these before experimenting with more advanced techniques.

The Standard Cut

The standard cut is the most basic and common type of transition. It simply jumps from one shot to the next without any visual effects. While it may seem plain, the standard cut is incredibly versatile and should be your go-to transition for most edits. A well-timed cut can feel seamless and natural, keeping the audience engaged without drawing attention to the transition itself.

Example: A cut from a wide shot of a room to a close-up of a character's face during a conversation. The cut allows the audience to focus on the dialogue while keeping the flow of the scene smooth.

When to Use: Use standard cuts for most scene changes or within a scene when you want to maintain a natural, uninterrupted flow. It's perfect for dialogue, action sequences, or any situation where you don't want the transition to be distracting.

The Jump Cut

A jump cut occurs when two shots of the same subject are taken from slightly different angles or times, creating a "jump" in the action. This technique can be used to speed up time, show a progression, or create a disorienting effect.

Example: In *Run Lola Run*, jump cuts are used to show the passage of time as the protagonist runs through the city. The effect creates a sense of urgency and fragmented reality.

When to Use: Use jump cuts to speed up time, compress long actions (such as someone walking across a room), or create a stylistic, jarring effect.

Fade In/Fade Out

Fades transition the screen from black to the image (fade in) or from the image to black (fade out). This transition is often used to indicate the beginning or end of a scene or to signify the passage of time.

Example: A film might fade to black at the end of a scene to signal the conclusion of an emotional moment, giving the audience time to absorb what happened before moving to the next scene.

When to Use: Fades are ideal for introducing or concluding a scene. They are often used for dramatic effect, such as transitioning between major narrative shifts, or when you want to suggest the passage of time between two events.

Dissolve (Crossfade)

A dissolve, or crossfade, occurs when one image fades into another. This type of transition is typically used to show the passage of time, blend two scenes together, or create a dreamlike or reflective atmosphere.

Example: In *The Godfather*, dissolves are often used to transition between scenes that are connected by theme or emotion, such as dissolving from a character's contemplation to a memory or related event.

When to Use: Use dissolves when you want to create a gentle, flowing transition between two scenes. This technique is ideal for montages, emotional reflections, or to indicate a passage of time.

Wipe

A wipe is a transition where one shot pushes another off the screen, often from one side to the other. This can be a straight wipe, a circular wipe, or any shape that moves across the screen. Wipes were commonly used in early cinema and are still a fun, stylistic choice for certain genres.

Example: The *Star Wars* films famously use wipes to transition between locations or scenes in the galaxy, adding a sense of momentum and adventure.

When to Use: Wipes work well in more stylized or genre-specific films, such as comedies, action-adventure films, or retro-inspired projects. They can be playful and help move the story along in a dynamic way.

Creative Transition Techniques for Mobile Filmmakers

Once you've mastered the basics, you can experiment with more creative transitions that add flair and visual interest to your film. These techniques can be achieved with mobile editing apps and require a bit of ingenuity but can elevate your film's production value.

Match Cut

A match cut is a transition where two scenes are linked by a similar visual element or action. The camera may cut from one object to another that looks similar, creating a smooth and often clever transition between two seemingly unrelated scenes.

Example: In *2001: A Space Odyssey*, there's a famous match cut where a bone thrown into the air by a prehistoric human cuts to a similarly shaped spaceship floating in space. This iconic cut signifies the passage of time and the evolution of human technology.

How to Do It on Mobile: Look for visual similarities between two shots and use a cut to connect them. For instance, you could cut from a close-up of a character's hand gripping an object to a similarly shaped object in a different location. Use mobile editing apps like *iMovie* or *KineMaster* to align the two images seamlessly.

When to Use: Use match cuts to create a clever, seamless transition between two scenes that are thematically or visually linked. They are ideal for showing connections between locations, objects, or time periods.

Whip Pan

A whip pan transition involves rapidly moving the camera from one side to another, creating a blur that can be used to transition between two scenes. This dynamic technique can inject energy into your film, especially in action sequences.

Example: In *Hot Fuzz*, Edgar Wright uses whip pans to transition between fast-paced scenes, adding to the film's frenetic energy and comedic timing.

How to Do It on Mobile: To create a whip pan, move your camera quickly from one side to the other while filming. In post-production, cut between the two clips during the blur to create a seamless transition. Apps like *LumaFusion* or *FilmoraGo* allow you to align and trim clips for a smooth whip pan effect.

When to Use: Use whip pans for action scenes, chase sequences, or any moment where you want to inject high energy and keep the audience engaged.

Invisible Cut

An invisible cut is designed to look seamless, as if the camera never stops rolling, even though you're transitioning between shots. This technique is often used to create the illusion of a continuous shot and is great for maintaining visual continuity without drawing attention to the cut.

Example: In *Birdman*, the film uses invisible cuts to create the illusion of a single continuous take, immersing the audience in the characters' world without obvious breaks in time or space.

How to Do It on Mobile: To achieve an invisible cut, you can use objects or motion to hide the transition. For instance, you could cut as the camera passes behind a character's back, using their body as a natural wipe to cover the cut. Mobile apps like *InShot* or *PowerDirector* allow you to trim clips precisely for this effect.

When to Use: Use invisible cuts when you want to create a continuous, uninterrupted flow between scenes. This technique is perfect for long takes, dialogue-heavy scenes, or sequences where you want to maintain immersion.

L-Cut and J-Cut

L-cuts and J-cuts involve overlapping the audio from one scene with the visuals from another. In an L-cut, the audio from the current scene continues to play as the next scene begins visually. In a J-cut, the audio from the upcoming scene starts playing before the visuals change, creating a more seamless transition between the two scenes.

Example: In *Arrival*, J-cuts are frequently used to transition between the present and flashbacks, with the sound from one scene leading into the next, helping to blur the lines between past and present.

How to Do It on Mobile: In apps like *Adobe Premiere Rush* or *KineMaster*, you can split your audio from the video track, allowing you to overlap the audio between two scenes. Drag the audio clip to extend it across both scenes, creating a smooth, fluid transition.

When to Use: Use L-cuts and J-cuts for dialogue scenes, flashbacks, or moments where you want the audio to guide the viewer through the transition. These cuts are great for maintaining narrative flow without drawing attention to the visual cut.

Best Mobile Editing Apps for Smooth Transitions

There are several mobile editing apps that offer powerful tools for creating smooth transitions, even if you're working with limited resources. Here are some of the best apps for mastering transitions on a smartphone:

Adobe Premiere Rush

Adobe Premiere Rush is a mobile-friendly version of Adobe's powerful video editing software. It offers a range of transitions, including dissolves, fades, and slides, as well as more advanced tools like keyframe animation, which can help you create custom transitions. Premiere Rush is great for creating professional-level transitions with minimal effort.

Tip: Use the keyframe tool to animate transitions like zoom-ins or pans, creating dynamic shifts between scenes.

LumaFusion

LumaFusion is a feature-rich mobile editing app designed for more advanced users. It offers a wide range of professional-grade transitions, from simple cuts and fades to more creative options like wipes, slides, and match cuts. The app also allows for multi-track editing, making it easy to overlap audio and video for L-cuts and J-cuts.

Tip: LumaFusion's multi-track timeline allows you to experiment with creative transitions, like layering video clips to create custom dissolves or fades.

KineMaster

KineMaster is one of the most popular mobile editing apps and offers an intuitive interface with a variety of transition options. You can apply classic transitions like cuts and fades, or use more stylized transitions like wipes and spins. KineMaster also supports audio adjustments, making it ideal for creating L-cuts and J-cuts.

Tip: Experiment with KineMaster's blending modes to create unique transitions, such as dissolving one image into another using opacity shifts.

InShot

InShot is a simple, beginner-friendly app that's great for quick edits and basic transitions. It offers a selection of transitions, including standard cuts, fades, and zooms, as well as more playful transitions like spins and wipes. InShot is ideal for filmmakers who want to create smooth transitions without getting bogged down by complex tools.

Tip: Use InShot's zoom transitions to create dynamic shifts between scenes, adding energy and visual interest to your film.

Mastering transitions is an essential skill for any filmmaker, especially when working on mobile. By learning how to effectively use cuts, fades, dissolves, and creative techniques like match cuts and whip pans, you can create fluid, engaging transitions that elevate the quality of your film. With the right mobile editing apps and a bit of creativity, you can achieve professional-level transitions that guide your audience smoothly through your story, enhancing the visual and emotional impact of your film. Whether you're working with simple tools or experimenting with more complex techniques, mastering transitions will make your film feel polished and cohesive.

Making a Movie in One Take: Challenges and Strategies

Creating a film in a single, continuous take is an ambitious and captivating approach to storytelling. This technique, where the camera follows the action without cuts or interruptions, brings a unique intensity and realism to the film, immersing viewers in a seamless flow of events. However, making a one-take movie requires meticulous planning, coordination, and skill. It presents significant challenges but also opens up creative opportunities to explore storytelling in new and exciting ways.

This chapter delves into the complexities of shooting a one-take movie, covering the technical, logistical, and creative strategies needed to pull off this remarkable feat. With the right preparation, teamwork, and problem-solving skills, you can create a memorable, one-of-a-kind film that leaves a lasting impact.

Why a One-Take Movie?

One-take movies are visually striking, heightening the sense of realism and immediacy by eliminating cuts that might disrupt the viewer's connection to the story. This technique can amplify suspense, emotional impact, or the feeling of "being there" alongside the characters. Films like *Birdman* and *1917* have demonstrated how effective one-take (or "simulated" one-take) movies can be in drawing the audience deeper into the story.

Benefits of a One-Take Movie:

Enhanced Immersion: The continuous shot feels like real time, making viewers feel like part of the action.

Heightened Tension: Without cuts, there's no escape from the unfolding events, which can build suspense and emotional intensity.

Innovative Storytelling: It challenges traditional cinematic conventions, allowing filmmakers to experiment with narrative flow and audience engagement.

Key Challenges in Filming a One-Take Movie

Creating a one-take film isn't easy, as every moment has to be precisely executed. From choreography to lighting, even the smallest misstep can disrupt the entire sequence, requiring a restart. Let's look at the primary challenges and how to address them.

1. Meticulous Choreography

In a one-take movie, actors, the camera operator, and often the entire crew must move in perfect harmony. Since there are no cuts, every movement and interaction needs to be choreographed down to the smallest detail to avoid accidental overlaps or delays.

Solution: Work with your actors and crew to plan every movement. Rehearse extensively, just as you would for a live stage production, so everyone knows exactly where to be at each moment. Block out each scene, marking where actors should stand and where the camera will move.

Tip: Break down the choreography into smaller, manageable sections during rehearsals to ensure everyone is comfortable with the sequence before doing full-length takes.

2. Consistent Performance

With no breaks between scenes, actors must maintain the intensity and continuity of their performance throughout the entire film. Any hesitation, missed line, or emotional shift could throw off the flow.

Solution: Encourage actors to stay "in character" even during brief transitions or silent moments. Extended rehearsals can help them understand the emotional pacing and develop endurance, so they deliver a consistent performance across the entire sequence.

Tip: Emphasize character backstory and motivation during rehearsals to help actors stay immersed, even in challenging scenes where emotions fluctuate quickly.

3. Technical Precision

Capturing a one-take movie requires reliable equipment and flawless execution from the camera operator. This includes maintaining focus, keeping shots stable, and ensuring the audio is clear throughout.

Solution: Use stabilizing equipment, such as gimbals or steadicams, to reduce camera shake and ensure smooth movement. Additionally, practice handling focus and exposure changes in real-time, especially if you're moving through different lighting environments.

Tip: Invest in a lightweight, high-quality camera setup that won't strain the camera operator during long takes. Use manual focus or lock focus on key scenes to avoid sudden shifts.

4. Lighting Continuity

One of the most difficult aspects of a one-take movie is managing lighting. As the camera moves, you may encounter different lighting needs, and adjusting lights on the fly without interrupting the shot requires careful planning.

Solution: Plan your lighting to allow for natural transitions. Use ambient or existing light sources, like windows or lamps, and place lights where they won't be seen but will still illuminate the scene effectively. Consider using LED lights that can be controlled remotely for minor adjustments during filming.

Tip: Use shadow and darkness strategically. Not every part of the set needs to be fully lit, and darker areas can add atmosphere and intrigue to the scene.

5. Sound Management

Achieving clear audio without cuts is challenging, especially in scenes with complex action or movement. Every footstep, line of dialogue, and background sound must be captured seamlessly.

Solution: Use wireless microphones on actors and strategically place boom mics in different locations, moving them subtly as needed. Ensure that all sound sources, from dialogue to ambient noise, are balanced and won't overpower each other during the take.

Tip: Conduct sound checks at every location within the set to identify potential issues and adjust mic placements accordingly. If some sounds need to be added in post-production, use ADR (Automated Dialogue Replacement) to maintain continuity.

Strategies for Successfully Filming a One-Take Movie

While the challenges are significant, the rewards of successfully executing a one-take movie are worth the effort. Here are some strategies to help you prepare and carry out your vision.

1. Extensive Rehearsals

Rehearsals are essential for mastering timing, performance, and technical elements. Think of each rehearsal as a live performance—aim for precision in movement, delivery, and camera positioning until everyone is confident**Use Camera Rehearsals**: During rehearsals, bring the camera into the mix so the crew and actors get comfortable with the actual flow of the shot. This helps identify potential issues with framing or blocking early on.

Run Full-Length Takes: Once individual scenes are perfected, move to full-length takes. Doing so will test endurance and help everyone adjust to the continuous flow of a one-take film.

2. Breaking down the Sequence

Approach your one-take film as a series of "mini scenes" rather than a single, overwhelming take. By focusing on one section at a time, you can address specific challenges and make adjustments as needed before attempting the full shot.

Visual Cues: Use visual cues on set to help actors and crew remember where they need to be at specific moments, especially during transitions.

Mark Key Moments: Identify pivotal moments in the sequence, such as scene transitions or emotional beats, so that everyone knows when they'll be shifting or adjusting.

3. Pre-Plan for Adaptability

While every detail is choreographed, it's wise to anticipate the unexpected. An actor might miss a line, or a light might go out, and everyone involved needs to be prepared to adapt.

Plan for Small Adjustments: Prepare your actors to stay in character and improvise if something minor goes wrong. Encourage them to adjust naturally if an obstacle arises.

Designate Roles: Assign specific crew members to monitor technical elements, like sound and lighting, so they can make quick adjustments as needed without disrupting the flow.

4. Choose the Right Environment

The setting of your one-take movie can either enhance or complicate your shot. A controlled environment is typically easier to manage, while unpredictable locations, like outdoors, require more adjustments.

Consider Closed Sets: Using an indoor location can give you more control over sound, lighting, and camera movement.

Scout Locations Thoroughly: If filming outdoors or in a public space, scout the area at different times of the day to identify lighting changes, noise levels, and other factors that could impact filming.

5. Prepare for Post-Production Touch-Ups

Even with a one-take film, post-production is still important. Minor adjustments in color grading, audio balancing, and visual effects can enhance the final product and smooth out any imperfections.

Sound Editing: Clean up audio inconsistencies or add sound effects to improve the overall quality.

Color Grading: Uniform color grading can help blend transitions between areas with different lighting, creating a more cohesive look.

Tip: While one-take movies are designed to feel raw and uncut, don't hesitate to use subtle post-production techniques to polish the final product.

Making a movie in one take is a formidable challenge that requires coordination, precision, and creative problem-solving. By focusing on choreography, practicing extensive rehearsals, and preparing for the unexpected, you can create a seamless and immersive viewing experience. With dedication and teamwork, a one-take film can be an extraordinary way to tell a story, captivating audiences with its intensity and artistry.

Filming Action Sequences: Capturing Dynamic Scenes on a Phone

Filming action sequences is one of the most exciting aspects of filmmaking, but it also comes with unique challenges—especially when shooting with a smartphone. Action scenes require energy, fluidity, and precision to keep the audience engaged, and smartphone filmmakers need to be strategic to capture dynamic, high-impact shots without access to the high-end equipment often used in professional productions. However, with the right techniques, you can create thrilling action sequences that feel polished and cinematic, even on a budget.

In this chapter, we'll explore how to film action scenes using a smartphone, focusing on techniques for capturing dynamic movement, coordinating stunts safely, and using simple tools to elevate the quality of your shots. Whether you're shooting a fight scene, chase sequence, or dramatic stunt, these strategies will help you bring your action scenes to life.

Why Action Sequences Matter

Action sequences serve as the adrenaline-pumping moments in a film, heightening the drama, conflict, and stakes of the story. Well-executed action can keep the audience on the edge of their seat, creating a sense of urgency, danger, or excitement. They are also key to defining a film's tone—whether it's gritty realism, high-octane spectacle, or intense suspense.

To make action sequences impactful, you need to focus on:

Clarity: Ensuring the audience can follow the action and understand what's happening, despite fast movement or complex choreography.

Energy: Maintaining a sense of speed, tension, and excitement.

Safety: Coordinating stunts and movements in a way that looks dangerous without putting anyone at risk.

Key Challenges of Filming Action on a Phone

Smartphones offer portability and ease of use, but they come with limitations that can make capturing dynamic action difficult:

Limited Lens Options: Most smartphones don't have the zoom or wide-angle capabilities of professional cameras, which can limit the types of shots you can achieve.

Image Stabilization: While some smartphones offer built-in stabilization, it's not as powerful as the systems found in professional cameras, which can make handheld action shots shaky or jittery.

Lighting: Action scenes are often filmed in a variety of lighting conditions, and smartphones typically struggle in low-light situations or high-contrast environments.

Despite these limitations, smartphones are still capable of producing high-quality action scenes if you use the right techniques and plan your shots carefully.

Strategies for Capturing Dynamic Action on a Smartphone

Plan and Choreograph the Scene

Action sequences rely heavily on choreography. Whether it's a fight scene, a car chase, or an intense foot pursuit, every movement needs to be carefully planned and timed to create smooth, cohesive action that makes sense to the viewer.

Challenge: Without a clear plan, action scenes can feel chaotic and disjointed, leaving the audience confused or disengaged.

Solution: Choreograph the scene in advance and rehearse it multiple times before filming. Break down the sequence into smaller, manageable segments, focusing on the most important beats—such as a punch, a fall, or a sudden turn. Each action should flow into the next to maintain continuity and energy.

Tip: Use wide shots during rehearsal to capture the full choreography and see how the movements fit together. Once you're comfortable with the timing, you can switch to tighter shots that highlight the action's intensity.

Use Multiple Camera Angles

Action scenes benefit from being shot from multiple angles, as it gives the editor more footage to work with when cutting the sequence. Different angles can also enhance the intensity of a moment by showing the action from various perspectives, keeping the audience engaged.

Challenge: It's hard to capture the entire action in one continuous take, especially when using a smartphone's limited field of view.

Solution: Film the same action sequence multiple times from different angles—wide shots, close-ups, and medium shots. This allows you to piece together a dynamic sequence during editing. For example, you can start with a wide shot to establish the scene, cut to a close-up during an intense moment, and then transition to a medium shot to capture the reaction of the characters.

Tip: Experiment with high-angle and low-angle shots to emphasize the power dynamics between characters. For instance, shooting from a low angle can make a character appear dominant or intimidating, while a high angle can make them seem vulnerable.

Shoot in Slow Motion

Many smartphones have built-in slow-motion capabilities, which can be incredibly useful for filming action scenes. Slow motion adds drama to fast-paced movements, allowing the audience to see every detail of a punch, jump, or crash.

Challenge: Overusing slow motion can reduce the energy of an action scene, making it feel sluggish.

Solution: Use slow motion selectively. Focus on key moments in the action sequence that benefit from being slowed down, such as a character narrowly dodging an obstacle or a dramatic leap through the air. Balance slow-motion shots with fast-paced cuts to maintain the momentum of the scene.

Tip: Practice using your smartphone's slow-motion feature in different lighting conditions. Slow-motion video often requires more light than regular video, so you may need to adjust your lighting setup to avoid underexposure.

Utilize Handheld Shots for Energy

Handheld shots can add a raw, gritty feel to an action sequence, making the audience feel like they're in the middle of the chaos. Smartphone cameras are ideal for handheld shots due to their small size and portability, but it's important to maintain some level of control to avoid overly shaky footage.

Challenge: Too much shake can make the footage difficult to watch, reducing the clarity of the action.

Solution: Use a handheld gimbal to stabilize the camera while still maintaining the dynamic energy of handheld footage. This allows you to capture smooth movement without losing the raw intensity that handheld shots provide. If you don't have access to a gimbal, try using your body as a stabilizer—keep your arms close to your chest and move your whole body, not just your hands, to reduce shake.

Tip: Use handheld shots for moments of heightened intensity, such as during fight sequences or chase scenes, to convey a sense of immediacy and urgency.

Create Motion with Camera Movement

Dynamic camera movement is key to capturing exciting action sequences. Even if the actors aren't moving at high speeds, moving the camera can create the illusion of fast-paced action.

Challenge: Poorly executed camera movement can be distracting or disorienting to the audience.

Solution: Plan your camera movements in advance. Use tracking shots to follow characters as they run, fight, or drive, giving the audience a sense of forward momentum. You can also use panning or tilting to reveal action as it happens, keeping the camera in motion to match the intensity of the scene.

Tip: Practice tracking shots using simple objects to get comfortable moving with your smartphone. If you're filming a chase, consider using a bicycle or skateboard to follow the action smoothly.

Focus on Impact

Action sequences are all about impact—whether it's a punch, a crash, or an explosion, the audience needs to feel the weight and force of the action. Using sound effects, quick cuts, and visual cues, you can create the illusion of powerful impacts without needing elaborate stunts or special effects.

Challenge: Capturing real, high-impact stunts can be dangerous and difficult to film.

Solution: Use a combination of close-up shots and sound effects to imply impact without actually showing it. For example, in a fight scene, you can cut to a close-up of a fist swinging toward the camera, followed by a reaction shot of the person being hit. By timing the punch with a well-placed sound effect, you can create the illusion of a hard hit without anyone getting hurt.

Tip: Experiment with quick, rapid cuts during moments of impact to heighten the intensity. This can create a sense of disorientation that makes the action feel more chaotic and realistic.

Use Props and Practical Effects

Practical effects and props can add a layer of realism to your action scenes, making the environment feel more immersive. Objects like breakaway glass, smoke, or even simple items like dirt or water can be used to enhance the action and make the stakes feel higher.

Challenge: It can be difficult to find or afford expensive props and effects on a tight budget.

Solution: Use DIY practical effects. For instance, throw dirt into the air during a fight scene to simulate debris, or use simple squibs (like water balloons filled with red-dyed water) to simulate blood splatter. Props like fake weapons or destructible objects can also add to the realism without putting anyone at risk.

Tip: Test your props and effects beforehand to make sure they work on camera. Some effects may look good in person but may not translate well on screen, so do a few trial runs before filming the actual scene.

Editing Your Action Sequence

After you've captured your action scene, the real magic happens in the editing room. Editing is crucial for creating the pacing, tension, and clarity that makes an action scene truly engaging.

Cut on Action

Cutting on action is a technique where you edit the footage to match the movement of the characters or objects, making the transition between shots feel seamless. For example, if a character throws a punch, you can cut to a different angle as the punch is mid-swing, creating a smooth flow between shots.

Tip: Look for natural points of movement to make your cuts, such as when a character is turning, punching, or jumping. This keeps the action fluid and prevents the audience from noticing the cuts.

Use Fast Cuts

Fast cuts can increase the intensity and pace of an action sequence. By rapidly cutting between different angles or moments of action, you create a sense of speed and urgency.

Tip: Use fast cuts for moments of high intensity, like a fight or a chase. However, avoid overusing this technique, as too many rapid cuts can disorient the viewer. Balance fast cuts with longer, wider shots to give the audience a chance to process the action.

Add Sound Effects and Music

Sound effects play a vital role in making action scenes feel impactful. The sound of punches landing, tires screeching, or explosions can make the action feel more immersive. Music can also be used to heighten the tension, guiding the audience's emotions throughout the scene.

Tip: Use high-quality sound effects and layer them in your editing software to give the action more depth. Add music that matches the pacing of the scene, increasing the tempo during high-stakes moments and slowing it down during moments of suspense or buildup.

Best Apps for Editing Action Sequences on a Phone

Several mobile apps can help you edit action sequences and add the finishing touches to your scene:

Adobe Premiere Rush

Adobe Premiere Rush is a versatile mobile editing app that allows for multi-track editing, advanced color correction, and audio mixing. It's perfect for editing complex action scenes, giving you the flexibility to layer sound effects, add transitions, and make precise cuts.

KineMaster

KineMaster offers a range of tools for mobile filmmakers, including chroma key (for green screen effects), keyframe animation, and blending modes. It's a great app for adding dynamic effects to your action sequences.

LumaFusion

LumaFusion is a professional-grade mobile editing app that supports multi-track editing, advanced transitions, and audio mixing. It's ideal for filmmakers who need more control over their editing process and want to create a polished, cinematic action scene.

Filming action sequences on a smartphone may seem challenging, but with the right techniques, you can capture dynamic, exciting scenes that feel cinematic and engaging. By carefully planning your choreography, using multiple angles, and enhancing the action with smart editing, you can create high-energy sequences that keep your audience on the edge of their seat. Whether you're filming a fight scene, a chase, or a stunt, the key is to maintain clarity, intensity, and fluidity—making the most of your smartphone's capabilities to deliver thrilling action that stands out.

Building Suspense: How to Create Tension with Simple Tools

Building suspense is an essential skill in filmmaking, especially when you're working with limited resources. Suspense draws the audience in, keeps them engaged, and creates an emotional connection to the story. The beauty of suspense lies in its simplicity—it doesn't require high-end equipment or expensive sets to be effective. With careful planning, strategic pacing, and a few simple tools, you can create tension that keeps viewers on the edge of their seats.

In this chapter, we'll explore techniques for building suspense using basic filmmaking tools, focusing on how to manipulate camera angles, sound, pacing, and lighting to create tension. Whether you're working on a thriller, horror film, or any scene that demands a sense of unease, these methods will help you craft a suspenseful atmosphere that captivates your audience.

Why Suspense is Crucial in Filmmaking

Suspense is the art of making the audience feel anticipation, fear, or anxiety about what might happen next. It's about holding back just enough information to keep viewers guessing and then delivering the payoff in a satisfying or shocking way. The key to effective suspense is controlling what the audience knows versus what the characters know. When used correctly, suspense can:

Create Emotional Investment: Suspense hooks the audience emotionally, making them care about the outcome of a scene or the fate of a character.

Build Anticipation: By delaying certain events or reveals, you make the audience anticipate what's going to happen, increasing tension with each passing moment.

Enhance Conflict: Whether it's between characters or an internal struggle, suspense heightens conflict, making every decision and action feel more critical.

Core Elements of Suspense

To build suspense, you need to combine several elements in a way that works for your story. While suspense often relies on visual techniques, sound, and editing, it's important to keep in mind that the most powerful tool you have is timing. Here are some key elements of suspense:

Pacing: Slow down key moments to allow the tension to build. Delaying action or a key reveal can make the audience feel like something big is just around the corner.

Uncertainty: Keep the audience in the dark about crucial details, or give them limited information that raises questions and creates mystery.

Danger: Even the suggestion of danger—whether physical, emotional, or psychological—adds stakes to the scene, making the audience worry about the characters' fate.

Atmosphere: The setting, lighting, and sound design all contribute to a suspenseful atmosphere. You can turn a seemingly ordinary environment into something menacing with the right techniques.

Techniques for Building Suspense

Slow Pacing and Deliberate Timing

One of the most effective ways to build suspense is by controlling the pacing of your scene. Suspense thrives in the moments when nothing seems to be happening but the audience knows something is coming. By slowing down the action, you create space for the viewer's imagination to run wild, building anticipation for what's to come.

Challenge: Moving too slowly can make a scene feel boring rather than tense, so you need to find the right balance between suspenseful pacing and keeping the story moving.

Solution: Use long, drawn-out shots or moments of silence to stretch out time. This works particularly well when the audience knows something the character doesn't—like an unseen threat approaching. Keep the pacing slow but not stagnant, allowing tension to gradually rise.

Tip: In dialogue-heavy scenes, insert pauses between lines to heighten the tension. A character pausing before delivering an important or ominous line can make the moment feel more impactful.

Camera Movement and Angles

The way you position and move the camera can dramatically affect the level of suspense in a scene. Strategic camera angles, subtle movements, and shifts in focus can manipulate the audience's perception, guiding them to feel unease or fear without directly showing the danger.

Low-Angle Shots: Shooting from a low angle can make a character or object appear more menacing or powerful. This can create a sense of dread, as though the audience is looking up at something overwhelming or dangerous.

Tight Close-Ups: Close-ups that focus on a character's face, eyes, or hands can build intimacy and tension, especially when the audience is waiting for a reaction or reveal.

Tracking Shots: Slow tracking shots following a character from behind can create suspense by suggesting they are being watched or pursued.

Dutch Angles: Tilting the camera slightly (also known as a Dutch angle) can create a sense of imbalance or disorientation, signaling to the audience that something is off or wrong.

Tip: When filming on a smartphone, use a handheld gimbal to create smooth tracking shots, or experiment with handheld movements for a more unsettling, shaky effect. Even slight, intentional instability in the camera work can increase tension.

Lighting and Shadows

Lighting is a powerful tool for creating suspense. Shadows, dim lighting, and strategic use of light sources can make an ordinary setting feel ominous. Darkness itself is often associated with fear because it represents the unknown, so you can use lighting to hide or reveal just enough to keep the audience on edge.

Challenge: Overusing darkness can make the scene too visually unclear, frustrating the viewer.

Solution: Use contrast between light and shadow to create pockets of darkness where threats could be hiding. Low-key lighting, which emphasizes shadows and selective lighting, is ideal for suspenseful scenes. You can also use practical lights—such as lamps, candles, or flashlights—to create a more immersive, tense atmosphere.

Tip: When filming with a smartphone, make the most of available light sources by positioning them to cast long shadows or silhouette characters. For an extra layer of tension, consider using flickering lights or lighting that changes over the course of the scene.

Sound and Silence

Sound is one of the most effective ways to build suspense. Often, the anticipation of a sound (or the sudden absence of sound) can create more tension than the sound itself. The strategic use of silence, quiet ambient noise, and sound effects can make the audience feel like something is about to happen, even if the visuals remain static.

Challenge: Overuse of sound effects or loud noises can make the suspense feel forced or melodramatic.

Solution: Use silence to your advantage. Silence creates unease, as it suggests something is about to break the quiet. Slowly building ambient noise—such as a faint creak, a distant footstep, or an eerie hum—can raise the tension before the eventual payoff. Sudden loud sounds, like a door slamming or an unexpected scream, work best after long moments of quiet.

Tip: Record subtle ambient sounds with your smartphone's built-in microphone, such as wind, creaking wood, or rustling fabric. These small sounds can be layered in during editing to add depth to the suspense.

Red Herrings and Misdirection

Misdirection is a classic suspense technique that keeps the audience guessing. By leading the viewer to believe something is going to happen—only to have it not happen—you can build tension and prolong the suspense. Red herrings (false clues or distractions) are another great way to keep the audience on edge, as they think they've figured something out, only to be proven wrong.

Challenge: Overusing red herrings can frustrate the audience if they feel misled too often without a payoff.

Solution: Use misdirection sparingly to heighten suspense, but always deliver a payoff afterward. For example, you might have a character hear a noise and slowly approach a door, only for it to be a false alarm. However, immediately afterward, the real threat could appear from a different direction, catching both the character and the audience off guard.

Tip: Visual misdirection—such as focusing the camera on a seemingly important object while the real threat approaches from out of frame—can be highly effective in building suspense.

Revealing Information Gradually

Suspense often comes from the audience knowing just enough to sense that something bad is about to happen, but not having all the information yet. By revealing information in small, deliberate increments, you can build tension and keep the viewer engaged.

Challenge: Revealing too much information too soon can break the suspense, while revealing too little can leave the audience confused.

Solution: Gradually reveal details through dialogue, camera movements, or sound cues. For example, you might hint at the presence of a threat by showing a character reacting to an unseen noise or by briefly focusing on a suspicious object. Let the audience piece together the clues, but don't reveal everything at once.

Tip: Use tight framing to show only part of the scene, keeping key details hidden until the right moment. For example, a character could open a door, but the camera only shows their face reacting to what they see, delaying the reveal of what's inside.

Building to a Payoff

Suspense isn't just about creating tension—it's about delivering on that tension with a satisfying or shocking payoff. Whether it's a sudden scare, a shocking reveal, or a dramatic resolution, the payoff must feel earned and proportional to the buildup.

Challenge: If the payoff doesn't match the tension that's been built, the audience will feel let down or frustrated.

Solution: Pay off the suspense with a moment that justifies the buildup. This could be a sudden action, a key piece of information, or a major plot twist. Make sure the payoff is visually and emotionally impactful, using sound, lighting, and camera angles to emphasize the moment.

Tip: For more psychological suspense, consider leaving certain questions unresolved, allowing the tension to linger in the audience's mind even after the scene ends.

Best Tools and Apps for Creating Suspense on a Phone

While professional filmmakers use high-end equipment to create suspenseful scenes, you can achieve similar effects with your smartphone by using the right tools and apps.

Filmic Pro

Filmic Pro is one of the most powerful video recording apps for smartphones, offering manual control over focus, exposure, and frame rate. These features allow you to capture more cinematic footage, which is crucial for controlling the mood and tension of a suspenseful scene.

Adobe Premiere Rush

For editing suspenseful scenes, Adobe Premiere Rush allows you to add sound effects, music, and adjust pacing with ease. You can manipulate your footage to create tension through careful cuts, layering sound effects, and adjusting the color and lighting of each shot.

KineMaster

KineMaster is a versatile editing app that includes advanced features like keyframe animation, audio mixing, and transitions. You can use it to add tension-building music, adjust the timing of your shots, and enhance the atmosphere of your film.

Ferrite Recording Studio

For recording and editing suspenseful sound design, Ferrite Recording Studio is a great app that allows you to capture ambient noise, layer sound effects, and manipulate audio to create eerie or unsettling atmospheres.

Building suspense doesn't require a big budget or high-end equipment—what matters most is your ability to manipulate the audience's emotions through pacing, camera work, sound, and timing. By using the tools and techniques outlined in this chapter, you can create tension-filled scenes that keep viewers on the edge of their seats, even when filming with a smartphone. With careful planning, clever use of visual and audio cues, and a strong understanding of pacing, you can craft suspense that elevates your film and engages your audience at every turn.

The Importance of Storyboarding: Planning Your Film's Flow

Storyboarding is one of the most critical steps in the pre-production process of filmmaking. It serves as the blueprint for your film, allowing you to visualize how the scenes will unfold, how the camera will move, and how each shot will transition into the next. Whether you're working on a large-scale production or a simple project filmed on a smartphone, storyboarding helps you plan your shots in detail, making the actual filming process smoother and more efficient. More than just a series of sketches, storyboards are vital tools that help you establish the flow, pacing, and visual narrative of your film.

In this chapter, we'll explore the importance of storyboarding in filmmaking, focusing on how it enhances the planning process, saves time and money, and helps ensure that your final product matches your creative vision. We'll also provide tips on how to create effective storyboards, even if you're working on a budget or have limited drawing skills.

Why Storyboarding is Crucial for Filmmaking

Storyboarding isn't just about drawing out each scene; it's about organizing your film in a way that ensures visual continuity and narrative flow. Here's why storyboarding is so important for the filmmaking process:

Visualizing Your Film

One of the most significant advantages of storyboarding is that it allows you to see your film before you shoot it. You can visualize how each shot will look, how characters and objects will be positioned in the frame, and how the camera will move. This pre-visualization is crucial for identifying potential issues with the composition, pacing, or flow before you're on set.

Benefit: By sketching out each shot, you can experiment with different angles, framing, and compositions to see what works best for your film. This also helps ensure that your creative vision is fully realized in the final product.

Planning Camera Movement

Storyboards allow you to plan complex camera movements in advance. Whether you're doing a simple pan or a complex tracking shot, having a visual guide helps you figure out where the camera needs to be, how it will move, and how that movement will transition from one shot to the next.

Benefit: This level of planning helps you avoid costly mistakes on set, where redoing a camera movement could take up valuable time and resources. Storyboarding also ensures that each camera movement serves the story rather than being done for the sake of style alone.

Establishing Shot Composition

The composition of each shot—the arrangement of characters, objects, and background elements within the frame—plays a crucial role in storytelling. Storyboarding allows you to carefully plan your compositions in advance, ensuring that each shot effectively conveys the intended mood, theme, or message.

Benefit: Pre-planning your compositions helps you make the most of your locations, props, and lighting setups. It ensures that every shot is visually compelling and contributes to the overall narrative flow of the film.

Maintaining Continuity

Storyboards help maintain visual continuity across scenes, ensuring that the transitions between shots are smooth and consistent. This is especially important in films with complex narratives, multiple locations, or scenes that take place at different times but need to appear cohesive on screen.

Benefit: Storyboards help you track key visual elements—such as character positioning, props, and lighting—across different shots and scenes. This reduces the risk of continuity errors that can break the immersion for viewers.

Saving Time and Money

By planning your shots in advance, storyboarding saves you time on set. With a clear visual guide, you and your crew know exactly what shots you need, how they should look, and how they will be framed. This reduces the amount of time spent setting up shots or making decisions during filming.

Benefit: Time is money in filmmaking, especially if you're working with a limited budget. Storyboarding helps streamline the filming process, allowing you to shoot more efficiently and avoid unnecessary reshoots.

Enhancing Communication

A storyboard is a valuable tool for communicating your vision to the rest of your team. Whether you're working with a cinematographer, production designer, or actors, storyboards provide a clear visual reference that helps everyone understand how the film should look and feel.

Benefit: Storyboards eliminate confusion and ensure that everyone is on the same page during production. This is particularly useful when explaining complex shots, camera movements, or visual effects to your crew.

The Storyboarding Process

Now that we've established why storyboarding is so important, let's dive into how you can create an effective storyboard for your film. The good news is that you don't need to be an expert artist to create useful storyboards—simple sketches or even digital tools can help you communicate your ideas effectively.

Breaking Down Your Script

The first step in storyboarding is breaking down your script into individual shots. Look at each scene in the script and decide how it will be visually represented on screen. Think about what the most important moments in each scene are and how you want to frame them.

Tip: For each scene, ask yourself the following questions: What's the primary action or emotion? How will the characters be positioned in the frame? Will the camera move, and if so, how? How will this shot transition into the next?

Sketching Each Shot

Once you've broken down the script, it's time to start sketching. Don't worry if you're not a great artist—the purpose of storyboarding is to convey ideas, not create polished drawings. Focus on showing the composition, movement, and key elements of each shot.

Key Elements to Include:

Character Positions: Where are the characters located in the frame? Are they moving?

Camera Angles: Is the camera at eye level, or are you using a high or low angle to create a specific effect?

Camera Movements: Is the camera panning, tilting, or tracking the action? If so, use arrows to indicate the movement.

Props and Backgrounds: Are there key objects or environmental elements that need to be in the shot?

Shot Duration: Is it a quick cut, or does the shot linger for effect?

Using Digital Storyboarding Tools

If you're not comfortable drawing by hand, there are several digital tools that can help you create storyboards. These apps and programs often come with pre-made templates or 3D models that allow you to build your storyboard without needing advanced drawing skills.

Storyboarder: A free, open-source storyboarding app that allows you to create simple sketches and add annotations for each shot.

Canva: While typically used for graphic design, Canva has templates that can be adapted for storyboarding. You can create digital storyboards and export them as PDFs or images.

ShotPro: A 3D storyboarding app that lets you design complex scenes using 3D models of characters, props, and sets.

Incorporating Transitions

One of the most important functions of a storyboard is to plan how each shot will transition into the next. Whether you're using simple cuts or more elaborate transitions like dissolves, fades, or wipes, storyboarding helps you visualize the flow of your film and ensure smooth transitions.

Tip: Use arrows to show where the camera will move or how the scene will transition. For example, if you're planning a match cut (where two similar shots transition smoothly into one another), make sure both shots are framed similarly in the storyboard to maintain visual continuity.

Adding Notes and Descriptions

Alongside your sketches, it's a good idea to add notes or descriptions that provide additional context for each shot. These notes can include details about camera settings, lighting, sound cues, or any special effects you're planning to use.

Tip: If you're using practical effects, stunts, or complex choreography, be sure to add detailed instructions in the notes to ensure everything is clear to the cast and crew.

Practical Storyboarding Tips for Low-Budget Filmmakers

Storyboarding doesn't have to be expensive or time-consuming. Here are some practical tips for filmmakers working on a budget:

Use Index Cards: If you prefer a more hands-on approach, use index cards to sketch out each shot. This allows you to rearrange the shots easily and see the overall flow of the film.

Photograph Your Shots: If drawing isn't your strong suit, consider taking photos of your locations or stand-ins for characters to use as placeholders in your storyboard. You can arrange these photos in order to visualize your shot sequence.

Storyboard Only Key Scenes: If you don't have time to storyboard the entire film, focus on the most complex or important scenes. Action sequences, dialogue-heavy scenes, and scenes with significant camera movement or visual effects benefit the most from detailed storyboards.

Collaborate with Your Team: If you're working with a cinematographer, production designer, or other creative professionals, involve them in the storyboarding process. Their input can help you refine your ideas and identify potential technical challenges.

How Storyboarding Helps with Editing

Storyboarding isn't just useful during the pre-production and filming stages—it also plays a key role in post-production. By planning out your shots in advance, you'll have a clearer idea of how each scene will come together during editing. Storyboards help you:

Ensure Continuity: Because you've already planned the transitions and shot sequences, storyboards help you maintain continuity during editing, ensuring that each shot flows smoothly into the next.

Save Time in the Editing Room: With a clear plan in place, you'll spend less time trying to piece together scenes in the editing room. You'll know exactly what shots you need, how long they should be, and how they should be arranged.

Visualize the Final Product: Storyboarding allows you to see the "big picture" of your film, giving you a sense of how each scene contributes to the overall story arc. This makes it easier to make decisions during editing that align with your original vision.

Storyboarding is an essential part of the filmmaking process, providing a roadmap for your film and helping you visualize how each shot will unfold. By planning your camera movements, compositions, and transitions in advance, you can ensure that your film has a smooth flow, cohesive pacing, and clear visual storytelling. Whether you're working with hand-drawn sketches, digital tools, or photographs, storyboarding is a powerful tool that will save you time, money, and frustration during production and post-production.

Syncing Multiple Devices: Using Multiple Phones for Your Film

Filmmaking with smartphones has opened up creative possibilities that were once limited to high-budget productions. One particularly powerful technique is using multiple phones simultaneously to capture different angles, perspectives, or even entirely separate scenes at the same time. This allows filmmakers to achieve a more dynamic and professional look while also maximizing efficiency on set. However, syncing multiple devices presents challenges, especially when it comes to maintaining visual continuity, managing audio, and ensuring everything can be easily pieced together in post-production.

This chapter will explore the benefits of using multiple smartphones for filmmaking, the challenges you may face when syncing footage and audio across multiple devices, and practical strategies to streamline the process. Whether you're capturing a scene from various angles or shooting in different locations simultaneously, these techniques will help you stay organized and produce high-quality results.

Why Use Multiple Phones in Your Film?

Using multiple phones for a film can significantly improve both the visual storytelling and production process, particularly for low-budget or independent filmmakers.

Benefits:

Multiple Angles: Shooting with more than one phone allows you to capture the same scene from different perspectives simultaneously, giving you more editing options and flexibility.

Efficiency: Filming different scenes or sections of the same scene with multiple phones can speed up production, reducing the need for reshoots or waiting to capture another angle.

Creative Opportunities: With multiple devices, you can experiment with split screens, simultaneous actions, or diverse points of view, enriching the visual complexity of your film.

Challenges of Syncing Multiple Devices

While using multiple phones for filmmaking offers clear advantages, syncing footage, audio, and camera settings between devices can be a complex process. Some of the key challenges include:

Maintaining Continuity: Ensuring that lighting, color balance, and framing remain consistent across different devices is essential for visual continuity.

Syncing Audio and Video: Matching audio from one phone with video from another, or syncing video footage from different devices, can be time-consuming during post-production.

Managing File Formats and Frame Rates: Different phones may use different file formats or frame rates, which could complicate the syncing process if they aren't aligned.

How to Sync Multiple Phones for Filmmaking

Match Frame Rates and Resolution

Before you start shooting, it's essential to ensure that all phones are recording at the same frame rate and resolution. Consistent frame rates and resolution across devices ensure that the footage will look uniform and be easier to sync in post-production.

Solution: Adjust the settings on each phone manually to ensure they match. For a cinematic feel, use a frame rate of 24 frames per second (fps). Common resolutions include 1080p or 4K, depending on the quality you want and the storage space available.

Tip: Use an app like *Filmic Pro* on all devices, which allows manual control over frame rates, resolution, and other key settings.

Use a Clapperboard or Clap for Syncing

One of the simplest and most effective ways to sync footage from multiple phones is to use a clapperboard (or just clap your hands if you don't have one) at the start of each take. The clapperboard provides a clear visual and audio cue that can be used to sync the video and sound in post-production.

Solution: At the beginning of each take, make sure all phones are rolling and clearly record the clapperboard in the frame. The sound of the clap and the visual snap of the board closing provide an easy point for aligning multiple videos and audio tracks later.

Tip: If you don't have a traditional clapperboard, simply have someone clap loudly in view of all cameras. The sudden spike in audio will make syncing easier in editing.

Wireless Audio Syncing with External Microphones

Capturing high-quality audio can be tricky when using multiple phones, as each device may pick up different levels of sound or background noise. To ensure consistent and professional sound, use external microphones that can be synced across devices.

Solution: Use wireless lavalier mics or directional microphones connected to an external audio recorder or a single phone designated for sound. Record the audio separately from the footage, and sync it with your video during post-production. Alternatively, if all phones are equipped with microphones, ensure they capture sound simultaneously to use as backup reference audio.

Tip: In post-production, you can use audio from the external recorder or phone as the master track and sync the other phones' video to it.

Maintain Lighting and Color Consistency

Smartphones have different camera sensors, and even slight variations in lighting or white balance can lead to noticeable differences in footage from multiple phones. To ensure continuity, it's important to maintain consistent lighting and color profiles across all devices.

Solution: Lock the exposure and white balance on each phone before shooting. Apps like *Filmic Pro* allow you to manually control exposure and white balance settings, preventing the cameras from automatically adjusting and causing inconsistencies.

Tip: Use the same lighting setups for each camera to reduce discrepancies. In post-production, use color grading tools to match the footage from different devices if there are still slight variations.

Cloud Storage and File Management

Managing multiple phones means dealing with a large amount of footage, often stored in different formats or locations. Keeping everything organized is essential for a smooth editing process.

Solution: Use cloud storage services like Google Drive, iCloud, or Dropbox to upload all footage from each phone into organized folders. Label the clips with clear names based on scene, angle, or take number, so they're easy to find during editing.

Tip: Sync the phones' clocks before shooting to help match the timecode on each file, making it easier to organize footage by the time it was shot.

Post-Production Syncing

Once the footage has been captured, the next challenge is syncing everything in post-production. There are several ways to do this depending on your editing software:

Manual Syncing: Using the visual and audio cues from the clapperboard or hand clap, manually align the video and audio tracks in editing software like *Adobe Premiere Pro*, *Final Cut Pro*, or *DaVinci Resolve*. This involves matching the sound of the clap or snap with the frame where the clapper closes.

Auto Syncing: Some software, like *Final Cut Pro* or *Premiere Pro*, has auto-sync features that use audio tracks to automatically align footage from different devices. This method works best if each phone captures clear sound that can be used for synchronization.

Tip: To make post-production easier, label each camera angle or perspective as "Cam A," "Cam B," etc., when importing footage. This allows you to easily track which phone was capturing which part of the scene.

Creative Uses of Multiple Phones

Shooting with multiple phones unlocks a range of creative opportunities, allowing you to experiment with dynamic storytelling techniques that are difficult to achieve with a single camera.

Simultaneous Multi-Angle Coverage

Capture a scene from different angles at the same time, providing more options during editing. For instance, in a dialogue scene, you can film over-the-shoulder shots of both characters simultaneously, reducing the need to reshoot the same scene from multiple angles.

Split-Screen Storytelling

Using footage from multiple phones, you can create split-screen scenes that show two or more perspectives simultaneously. This is useful for showing parallel action, phone conversations, or contrasting viewpoints in real time.

Choreographing Complex Action

If you're filming an action scene, you can use multiple phones to cover different parts of the action from various perspectives. One phone could follow a character running, while another films the environment they are moving through, creating a dynamic, multi-layered narrative.

Creative POV Shots

Attach smartphones to objects, props, or even actors to create unique POV (point of view) shots. For instance, a phone strapped to a bicycle could capture fast-moving action, or a phone attached to an actor's chest could give an immersive, first-person view of their experience.

Best Tools for Syncing Multiple Phones

Several apps and tools can make syncing multiple phones easier and more efficient, both during filming and in post-production:

Filmic Pro: This app gives you manual control over frame rate, resolution, white balance, and more, making it easier to ensure consistency across multiple devices.

Adobe Premiere Pro: Premiere's auto-sync feature can match audio tracks from different phones, helping you align footage easily.

Final Cut Pro: Final Cut's multi-camera editing feature allows you to sync multiple angles automatically, creating a seamless editing process for multi-phone setups.

LumaFusion: This mobile editing app supports multi-track editing, making it easier to sync and edit footage directly on a smartphone or tablet.

Using multiple smartphones for filmmaking opens up a world of creative possibilities, from capturing dynamic multi-angle shots to streamlining production by filming different scenes simultaneously. However, syncing multiple devices comes with challenges—especially when it comes to matching frame rates, managing audio, and maintaining visual continuity. By following the strategies outlined in this chapter, you can effectively sync footage from multiple phones and create a cohesive, high-quality final product. With the right planning and tools, you can harness the power of multiple devices to elevate your film and achieve a professional look, even on a tight budget.

Filming in Public: How to Navigate Permits and Permissions

Filming in public spaces offers exciting opportunities for your film, adding depth, realism, and atmosphere that can be difficult to replicate on a set. Public locations like city streets, parks, and busy marketplaces provide a dynamic, lived-in backdrop that can elevate the authenticity of your project. However, filming in public comes with logistical challenges, including navigating permits, securing permissions, and ensuring you're complying with local laws. Understanding the rules and regulations around filming in public is crucial to avoiding fines, legal complications, or disruptions to your shoot.

This chapter will guide you through the process of obtaining permits, gaining necessary permissions, and managing your crew and equipment in public spaces. Whether you're working on a small independent project or a larger production, knowing how to navigate these challenges will make your public filming experience smoother and more efficient.

Why Permits and Permissions Matter

Permits and permissions are required for several important reasons:

Legal Compliance: Many cities and municipalities require filmmakers to obtain permits before shooting in public spaces to ensure that the production does not disrupt public order or safety.

Public Safety: Filming, especially with large equipment or stunts, can pose risks to public safety. Permits help local authorities coordinate with filmmakers to ensure safety measures are in place.

Avoiding Fines: Filming without proper permits can lead to costly fines, legal action, or even the shutdown of your production.

Respect for Privacy: Filming in public places may involve capturing people or private property unintentionally. Proper permissions help you avoid legal issues related to privacy violations.

Key Considerations for Filming in Public

Before diving into the specifics of obtaining permits and permissions, it's important to understand the main factors that will affect your public shoot:

Location: Different cities, towns, and countries have varying laws and regulations regarding filming in public. Some may require permits for even small, low-impact shoots, while others may only require permits for large-scale productions.

Size of Your Crew: Larger productions with more equipment, vehicles, or personnel will typically require more complex permits and coordination with local authorities. Smaller productions may have fewer restrictions but should still be aware of local rules.

Equipment: If you're using tripods, lights, or large rigs, you'll likely need a permit. Handheld or smartphone filming may not require permits in some locations, but it's essential to check.

Impact on the Environment: Consider how your shoot will affect the location. If you're filming in a busy area, blocking pedestrian traffic, or creating noise, a permit will likely be required.

Filming People and Private Property: Even in public spaces, individuals and businesses have a right to privacy. You may need to obtain permission or release forms if people or recognizable private properties are prominently featured in your film.

Steps for Obtaining Filming Permits

The process for obtaining permits varies depending on your location, but the general steps are fairly similar across different regions. Here's how to approach getting the necessary permits for your shoot:

Research Local Requirements

The first step is to research the specific rules and regulations in the location where you plan to film. Local film offices, city websites, or government offices are good places to start. Many cities have a dedicated film office or permit office that provides detailed guidelines for filmmakers.

Tip: Check if the location has any special regulations for filming at historical landmarks, public parks, or city streets, as these may require additional permits or permissions.

Apply for the Permit in Advance

Permits usually need to be applied for well in advance of your shoot, as processing can take anywhere from a few days to several weeks, depending on the location and the scope of your production.

Tip: Apply as early as possible to avoid delays in your production schedule. Be prepared to provide details such as your production dates, times, the size of your crew, equipment you'll be using, and the specific locations where you'll be filming.

Provide a Detailed Production Plan

When applying for a permit, you'll often need to submit a production plan. This includes information about your crew, equipment, filming schedule, and any potential disruptions to public spaces (such as blocking sidewalks or using loud equipment). You may also need to provide proof of insurance that covers any potential damage or liability during the shoot.

Tip: Be as specific as possible in your production plan. If you'll be using drones, special effects, or stunts, make sure to include these details in your application.

Budget for Permit Costs

Depending on the location, there may be fees associated with obtaining a permit. These can range from nominal fees for small productions to more substantial costs for larger shoots that require road closures, security, or other city services.

Tip: Include permit fees in your production budget. Some locations may also require you to hire police officers or security personnel for crowd control or safety, which can increase costs.

Be Prepared for Location-Specific Conditions

Certain locations may have specific rules or conditions attached to your permit. For example, you may only be allowed to film at certain times of the day, or you may be required to avoid certain areas during peak hours.

Tip: Review all conditions carefully before your shoot to ensure you're complying with the terms of your permit. If any conditions seem unclear, contact the permit office for clarification.

Securing Permissions for Private Property and People

In addition to permits for public spaces, you may need to obtain permission from property owners or individuals if they are featured prominently in your film.

Filming on Private Property

If you're filming on or near private property—such as a restaurant, office building, or residential home—you'll need to obtain permission from the property owner. This is particularly important if your film shows recognizable features of the property, such as logos, signage, or the interior.

Solution: Draft a location release form that outlines the terms of the agreement between you and the property owner. The release form should include details about the shoot, the intended use of the footage, and any compensation (if applicable).

Tip: Even if you're filming on public land but capturing a private property in the background, it's a good idea to get permission, especially if the property is prominently featured.

Obtaining Releases from Individuals

If you're filming in a public space where people are visible in the background, you generally don't need permission, as they have no reasonable expectation of privacy in a public area. However, if someone becomes a focus of the shot, or if their face is clearly identifiable, you should obtain a signed release form from them.

Solution: Keep a stack of release forms with you on set, especially if you plan to interact with or feature members of the public in your film. These forms grant you permission to use their likeness in your project.

Tip: If you're filming in a crowded area and can't obtain individual releases from everyone in the background, consider blurring faces or filming in such a way that individuals are not identifiable.

Filming Without Permits: Risks and Alternatives

Sometimes, filmmakers may choose to film without permits, especially for small, guerrilla-style productions. However, this comes with significant risks:

Legal Penalties: Filming without a permit in areas that require one can result in fines, equipment confiscation, or the shutdown of your production.

Public Disruptions: If your shoot creates a public disturbance (such as blocking foot traffic or causing noise), authorities may intervene and halt filming.

Insurance Issues: Without a permit, your film may not be covered by insurance, which can lead to financial losses if something goes wrong.

Alternatives:

Low-Impact Filming: If your production is small and doesn't require much equipment, you may be able to film without a permit in areas where local laws allow low-impact filming, such as handheld or smartphone shoots.

Private Locations: Consider filming on private property with the owner's permission to avoid the need for a public permit. This can offer more control and fewer restrictions.

Managing Your Crew and Equipment in Public Spaces

Once you've secured the necessary permits and permissions, it's important to manage your crew and equipment effectively to avoid disrupting the public or attracting unwanted attention.

Minimize Your Footprint

Even with a permit, it's good practice to minimize your impact on public spaces. This includes keeping equipment neatly organized, avoiding unnecessary noise, and being respectful of pedestrians and local businesses.

Tip: Use a small, mobile crew whenever possible, and rely on portable or handheld equipment to keep your setup flexible.

Communicate with Local Authorities

If your shoot requires street closures, large equipment setups, or any significant public disruption, work closely with local authorities to ensure a smooth process. This may include hiring police officers for crowd control or working with local security.

Tip: Keep an open line of communication with the local permit office and law enforcement to ensure your shoot runs smoothly without unexpected interruptions.

Embracing Minimalism: Working with What You Have

In filmmaking, minimalism isn't just a stylistic choice—it's often a necessity, especially for independent filmmakers working with limited resources. Embracing minimalism means stripping your production down to its essentials and making the most of what you have, rather than relying on expensive equipment, elaborate sets, or a large crew. With careful planning, creativity, and resourcefulness, you can produce a high-quality film that's visually engaging and emotionally compelling, even on a tight budget.

This chapter will explore the principles of minimalist filmmaking, focusing on how to maximize your resources, simplify your production process, and find creative solutions to common filmmaking challenges. Whether you're working with a smartphone, a small cast, or limited access to locations, these strategies will help you create a film that feels intentional and polished without the need for elaborate tools or setups.

The Power of Minimalist Filmmaking

Minimalism in filmmaking isn't about cutting corners—it's about focusing on the core elements of storytelling and using your constraints to fuel creativity. By embracing a minimalist approach, you can:

Enhance Creativity: Working with fewer resources forces you to think outside the box, finding innovative solutions to problems and discovering new ways to tell your story.

Focus on Storytelling: Without the distractions of complex setups or special effects, you can concentrate on the most important aspects of your film: the story, characters, and emotions.

Streamline Production: A minimalist approach simplifies your workflow, making it easier to stay organized, meet deadlines, and manage your budget. Fewer moving parts mean fewer opportunities for things to go wrong.

Highlight the Essentials: Minimalism forces you to strip away anything unnecessary, ensuring that every shot, line of dialogue, and camera movement serves a purpose in your story.

Key Elements of Minimalist Filmmaking

To successfully embrace minimalism in filmmaking, focus on these key elements:

Simple and Strong Storytelling

At the heart of every great film is a compelling story. In minimalist filmmaking, the story becomes even more important because you don't have big-budget effects, set pieces, or large-scale action to fall back on. The emotional depth and narrative structure must carry the film.

Solution: Focus on telling a simple, yet powerful, story. Minimalist films often revolve around a single location, a small cast, or a simple concept that explores complex themes. Films like *Locke* (2013) or *Buried* (2010) are prime examples of minimalist storytelling, with both films confined to a single space and driven almost entirely by character and dialogue.

Tip: Start with a core idea that can be explored deeply within a limited setting or timeframe. Short, self-contained stories work particularly well in minimalist filmmaking.

Use Available Locations

Instead of trying to secure expensive locations or sets, work with what you already have. Your home, a local park, or a public space can become the setting for your film if you frame and light the location creatively. Minimalist filmmakers excel at turning ordinary spaces into compelling settings for their stories.

Solution: Scout locations that are easily accessible and offer versatility. For example, a single apartment could serve as multiple different locations if you change the angle, lighting, and set dressing. When filming in public spaces, keep the crew small and equipment minimal to avoid drawing too much attention or needing costly permits.

Tip: Think about how to use a single location creatively by dividing it into different zones or using different areas at different times of day to create variety.

Natural Light and Minimal Lighting Setups

Lighting can transform even the simplest location into a visually compelling environment. In minimalist filmmaking, natural light or simple lighting setups are often used to achieve professional results without the need for expensive lighting equipment.

Solution: Take advantage of natural light as much as possible, especially if you're filming outdoors or near large windows. You can use reflectors to bounce light onto your subjects, or inexpensive softboxes or LED lights to enhance lighting in low-light conditions.

Tip: Plan your shooting schedule around the best natural light conditions. For example, the golden hour (shortly after sunrise or before sunset) provides soft, diffused light that's perfect for cinematic shots.

Small Cast and Crew

Keeping your cast and crew small is not only a practical decision in minimalist filmmaking but can also create a more intimate working environment. Smaller teams are more agile, flexible, and easier to manage, especially when shooting on location or with limited resources.

Solution: Focus on a small cast of strong actors who can carry the story. You don't need dozens of characters or extras to create a compelling film; a few well-developed characters and strong performances can provide all the emotional weight you need.

Tip: If possible, have crew members take on multiple roles. For example, your cinematographer might also handle lighting, or your director might double as the editor. This can streamline production and keep the team small and efficient.

Minimal Equipment

You don't need a lot of equipment to make a great film. In fact, minimalist filmmaking often calls for keeping your gear to the essentials. This not only reduces costs but also makes it easier to stay mobile and adaptable during shooting.

Solution: Use lightweight, portable gear, like a smartphone or DSLR camera, to capture your footage. Stabilizers, handheld gimbals, and portable tripods can help you achieve smooth shots without the need for large rigs. For sound, consider using a high-quality external microphone that connects to your camera or smartphone.

Tip: If you're shooting with a smartphone, use apps like *Filmic Pro* to gain manual control over exposure, focus, and frame rate, giving you more creative flexibility without the need for advanced equipment.

Creative Use of Sound

Sound design is a crucial aspect of minimalist filmmaking, especially when you're working with fewer visual elements. Even with simple visuals, great sound can enhance the mood, tension, or emotion of a scene, making it feel more immersive.

Solution: Focus on capturing clean, high-quality dialogue and ambient sound. Use a combination of well-placed microphones, minimal background noise, and careful post-production sound editing to create a rich soundscape. Foley effects (recording everyday sounds) can also be used to add depth and texture to your film.

Tip: Silence can be as powerful as sound in minimalist films. Don't be afraid to use quiet moments or long pauses to build tension or emotion.

Focus on Performance and Emotion

In minimalist filmmaking, the actors' performances often carry the weight of the story. Without elaborate visuals or special effects, the emotional depth and complexity of your characters become even more important.

Solution: Spend time working with your actors to create authentic, emotionally resonant performances. Rehearse scenes until the actors are comfortable with the material and can deliver nuanced, powerful performances that captivate the audience.

Tip: Use close-up shots to focus on subtle facial expressions, allowing the actors' emotions to take center stage. In a minimalist setting, these small moments can have a significant impact.

Strategies for Minimalist Filmmaking

Work Within Constraints

Rather than seeing your limitations as obstacles, view them as creative opportunities. Constraints often lead to innovation, forcing you to come up with inventive solutions that can make your film more unique.

Example: Instead of thinking about what you *can't* do because of budget or equipment limitations, focus on what you *can* do with the resources at hand. Many successful minimalist films, like *The Blair Witch Project* (1999) and *Tangerine* (2015), turned their constraints into strengths, using handheld cameras or smartphones to create a raw, authentic feel.

Prioritize the Essentials

When working with limited resources, it's important to prioritize the elements that will have the greatest impact on your film. This means focusing on storytelling, performance, and visual composition rather than elaborate sets, costumes, or effects.

Example: In *Roma* (2018), director Alfonso Cuarón used long, static shots and minimal camera movement to draw attention to the characters and the story, rather than relying on flashy editing or special effects.

Use Editing to Enhance Minimalism

Post-production can be a powerful tool in minimalist filmmaking. Even if you've shot with minimal resources, thoughtful editing can transform your footage into a polished final product. Focus on pacing, rhythm, and visual continuity to create a cohesive and engaging story.

Solution: Use simple editing techniques to enhance your film. Clean cuts, crossfades, and well-timed pauses can create tension, build atmosphere, or guide the audience's emotional journey. Avoid over-editing or using excessive effects, as this can distract from the story's core message.

Tip: If you're editing on a smartphone or tablet, apps like *LumaFusion* or *Adobe Premiere Rush* offer professional-level editing tools that are easy to use on the go.

Embracing minimalism in filmmaking is about focusing on what truly matters: the story, the performances, and the emotions that drive the narrative. By working with what you have—whether it's limited equipment, a small cast, or a single location—you can create a powerful and engaging film that connects with audiences on a deep level. Minimalism forces you to be resourceful and creative, making every decision count and pushing you to tell your story in the most impactful way possible. With the right mindset and strategies, you can produce a film that feels intentional, polished, and rich in substance, even with limited resources.

Mobile Cinematography: Enhancing Shots with Simple Gear

With the rapid advancements in smartphone technology, mobile cinematography has become an accessible and powerful tool for filmmakers. However, while smartphones offer convenience and portability, the quality of your shots can still be significantly enhanced with the right accessories and techniques. Simple, affordable gear can elevate your mobile filmmaking, helping you achieve cinematic-quality visuals that rival more traditional setups.

This chapter will explore the key techniques and gear that can help you enhance your shots using just a smartphone, focusing on tools like stabilizers, lenses, lights, and audio equipment. Whether you're filming a short scene or an entire feature, these tips will help you create professional-looking footage using minimal gear.

The Power of Mobile Cinematography

Smartphone cameras have evolved dramatically in recent years, with high-resolution sensors, advanced image stabilization, and manual control over exposure and focus. These advancements make mobile devices powerful tools for filmmakers, particularly for those working on a budget or in locations where larger camera setups aren't feasible.

Why Embrace Mobile Cinematography?

Portability: Smartphones are lightweight and easy to carry, allowing you to shoot in various environments with minimal setup time.

Affordability: Filming with a smartphone eliminates the need for expensive cameras and accessories, making high-quality cinematography accessible to more filmmakers.

Flexibility: With the right apps and gear, you can have full manual control over your smartphone's camera settings, enabling you to create professional-level shots.

Discreet Filming: Shooting with a smartphone can be less intrusive than using a traditional camera, allowing you to capture more natural moments in public spaces.

Essential Gear for Mobile Cinematography

While your smartphone's built-in camera can produce impressive results, adding a few key accessories can significantly enhance your shots. Here are some of the most useful tools to consider for mobile cinematography:

Stabilizers and Gimbals

One of the most common challenges with mobile filmmaking is keeping your shots steady. Handheld footage can often appear shaky, especially when you're moving the camera. A stabilizer or gimbal is an essential tool for creating smooth, professional-looking footage.

Gimbals: Gimbals are motorized stabilizers that keep your smartphone steady while you move. They allow you to shoot smooth tracking shots, pans, and tilts without the shake typically associated with handheld shooting. Popular options include the DJI Osmo Mobile and Zhiyun Smooth series.

Tripods: For static shots, a small, lightweight tripod is an excellent investment. Many mobile tripods are portable and easy to set up, allowing you to lock your camera in place for interviews, still shots, or time-lapses. Look for tripods with adjustable legs and ball heads for maximum flexibility.

Tip: If you don't have a gimbal, you can use a handheld rig or create stability by holding your phone with both hands and tucking your elbows in to minimize shake.

External Lenses

Smartphone cameras are equipped with fixed lenses that provide a wide field of view, but adding external lenses can expand your creative options. These lenses are easy to attach and can dramatically change the look of your footage.

Wide-Angle Lenses: A wide-angle lens allows you to capture more of the scene, making it ideal for landscapes, establishing shots, or cramped locations where you can't physically move the camera further back.

Telephoto Lenses: A telephoto lens provides zoom capability without sacrificing image quality, allowing you to shoot from a distance or achieve tighter close-ups.

Anamorphic Lenses: Anamorphic lenses are a popular choice for filmmakers because they create the cinematic widescreen aspect ratio with subtle lens flares and distortion, giving your footage a filmic look. Moment and Moondog Labs are two brands that offer high-quality anamorphic lenses for smartphones.

Tip: When using external lenses, ensure they are compatible with your smartphone model and that they attach securely to avoid any shifts during filming.

Lighting Gear

Lighting is a critical element of cinematography, and even the best smartphone camera can struggle in low-light conditions. Portable lighting gear can help you achieve professional lighting setups without needing large, expensive lights.

LED Panels: Compact LED lights are ideal for mobile filmmaking. They are lightweight, battery-operated, and often come with adjustable color temperatures and brightness levels. You can attach LED panels to your smartphone rig or place them off-camera to light your subject.

Ring Lights: For soft, even lighting on a subject's face, a ring light is a simple but effective tool. Ring lights are often used for interviews, vlogging, or close-ups, and they reduce shadows while creating a flattering, even glow.

Clip-On Lights: For quick, portable lighting, consider using clip-on lights that attach directly to your smartphone. These small, rechargeable lights are easy to carry and can brighten up dark scenes without bulky equipment.

Tip: Use natural light whenever possible. Shooting during golden hour (the hour after sunrise or before sunset) provides soft, diffused light that adds warmth and depth to your footage. When using artificial lights, try to diffuse them with softboxes or reflectors for a more natural look.

Audio Accessories

Clear, high-quality audio is essential for professional filmmaking. While smartphone microphones have improved, they still struggle to capture clear dialogue or ambient sound in noisy environments. Adding external audio gear can dramatically enhance the quality of your film's sound.

Lavalier Microphones: Lavalier mics (clip-on mics) are ideal for capturing clear dialogue in interviews or scenes with minimal background noise. They connect directly to your smartphone or an external audio recorder, allowing you to capture crisp, isolated audio.

Shotgun Microphones: For capturing directional sound, a shotgun mic is a great option. These mics focus on the sound in front of them while minimizing background noise, making them ideal for filming in noisy environments or capturing clean audio from a distance.

External Recorders: For even more control over your sound, consider using an external audio recorder like the Zoom H1n or Tascam DR-40. These devices allow you to record high-quality audio independently from your smartphone and sync it with your footage during post-production.

Tip: Always monitor your audio levels during filming, especially if you're in a noisy environment. Use headphones to ensure the audio is clear and free of distortion or interference.

Techniques for Enhancing Shots with Minimal Gear

Along with using the right gear, there are several key techniques you can employ to enhance the quality of your shots and make the most of your mobile setup.

Mastering Composition

Good composition is critical to creating visually appealing shots, regardless of the equipment you're using. Applying basic composition principles can make even a simple shot look cinematic.

Rule of Thirds: This guideline involves dividing the frame into a 3x3 grid and positioning your subject along the grid lines or at their intersections. This creates a balanced and aesthetically pleasing composition.

Leading Lines: Use natural or architectural lines in your environment to draw the viewer's eye toward your subject. Leading lines can be roads, fences, hallways, or even shadows.

Depth of Field: While smartphones typically have deep focus, you can create a sense of depth by placing objects in the foreground, middle ground, and background. This adds dimension to your shots and makes them feel more dynamic.

Tip: Use the grid feature on your smartphone's camera app to help you apply the rule of thirds and ensure your compositions are balanced.

Utilizing Slow Motion and Time-Lapse

Many smartphones come equipped with slow-motion and time-lapse features, which can add dramatic effect to your footage.

Slow Motion: Slow motion is great for highlighting fast action, like a person running or an object falling. Use it to capture intricate details that would be missed at regular speed.

Time-Lapse: Time-lapse is ideal for showing the passage of time, like clouds moving across the sky or a busy street. It compresses hours into seconds, creating a visually engaging effect that can enhance the storytelling in your film.

Tip: Plan your slow-motion and time-lapse shots carefully. For slow motion, make sure there's enough light, as lower frame rates typically require more exposure. For time-lapse, stabilize your phone with a tripod to avoid camera shake over long periods.

Incorporating Movement

Smooth camera movement can instantly make your shots feel more professional and cinematic. Simple movements like pans, tilts, or tracking shots can add dynamism to otherwise static scenes.

Solution: Use a gimbal for smooth, controlled movement, or rely on natural handheld techniques for a more intimate, documentary-style feel. Start with slow, deliberate camera movements to maintain stability and ensure the audience can follow the action.

Tip: Practice your camera movements before filming to ensure they are smooth and match the pacing of the scene. If you're using handheld techniques, stabilize your shots by moving with your whole body rather than just your hands.

Manual Controls for Cinematic Effects

Using apps like *Filmic Pro* allows you to take full manual control of your smartphone's camera, enabling you to adjust settings like ISO, shutter speed, white balance, and focus. This level of control lets you achieve more professional, cinematic effects.

ISO and Shutter Speed: Control your exposure by adjusting ISO and shutter speed. Lower ISO values create cleaner images with less noise, while the right shutter speed ensures motion is captured without blur.

Focus Pulling: Manual focus control lets you execute focus pulls, a popular cinematic technique where you shift focus from one subject to another in a single shot. This technique can add drama and guide the viewer's attention.

Tip: Use the app's focus peaking feature (if available) to ensure sharp focus on your subject, especially in low-light conditions or during complex focus pulls.

Enhancing your mobile cinematography is about finding the right balance between creativity and practical tools. With the addition of simple gear like stabilizers, lenses, lights, and audio equipment, you can elevate your smartphone footage to a professional level without breaking the bank. Combining these tools with thoughtful composition, camera movement, and manual control will allow you to produce stunning visuals that rival traditional film setups.

Whether you're shooting a short film, documentary, or music video, these techniques will help you make the most of your mobile device and create compelling, cinematic footage.

Choosing the Right Smartphone: Best Phones for Filmmaking

With the growing popularity of mobile filmmaking, the smartphone has become a powerful tool for creators. Thanks to advanced cameras, sophisticated image processing, and features like manual controls, some smartphones are capable of delivering near-professional quality video footage. However, not all smartphones are created equal when it comes to filmmaking, and choosing the right device is crucial to achieving the best possible results for your project. In this chapter, we'll explore the key features to look for when choosing a smartphone for filmmaking, focusing on camera quality, video capabilities, and other critical features that enhance your mobile filmmaking experience. We'll also review some of the best smartphones currently available for filmmakers, giving you a guide to selecting the right device for your creative needs.

Key Features to Look for in a Filmmaking Smartphone

When choosing a smartphone for filmmaking, there are several key factors to consider. These features will determine the quality of your video footage and the ease with which you can shoot, edit, and manage your film.

Camera Quality

The camera is the heart of your smartphone's filmmaking capabilities, and it's essential to select a phone with a high-quality camera system.

Resolution: Look for phones that shoot in at least 4K resolution. Higher resolution provides more detail and flexibility in post-production, allowing you to crop, zoom, or stabilize your footage without losing quality.

Sensor Size: Larger camera sensors generally perform better in low light and capture more detail, leading to sharper, more dynamic images.

Aperture: A wider aperture (lower f-number) lets in more light, improving low-light performance and creating a shallow depth of field for more cinematic shots.

Video Recording Capabilities

While camera quality is important, it's also crucial to consider the video-specific features of the smartphone.

Frame Rates: Look for phones that offer multiple frame rate options, such as 24fps (for a cinematic look), 30fps (standard for TV), and 60fps (for smooth motion or slow-motion effects).

Slow Motion: If you plan to capture fast action or want to add dramatic slow-motion shots to your film, ensure the phone supports high frame rates for slow-motion video (e.g., 120fps or 240fps).

Stabilization: Optical image stabilization (OIS) or electronic image stabilization (EIS) helps reduce camera shake, especially in handheld or moving shots, providing smoother, more professional-looking footage.

Manual Controls

Manual controls give you greater creative freedom and control over your shots, allowing you to adjust settings like exposure, focus, ISO, and shutter speed, much like you would with a DSLR or mirrorless camera.

Solution: Choose a smartphone with a built-in "Pro" mode for video or install a third-party app like *Filmic Pro* to gain access to manual controls, enabling you to fine-tune your shots for the desired cinematic effect.

Dynamic Range and HDR

Dynamic range refers to the smartphone's ability to capture details in both the brightest and darkest parts of an image. High Dynamic Range (HDR) video enhances this capability by balancing out the contrast between light and dark areas, resulting in more visually striking footage.

Solution: Look for smartphones with HDR video recording or Dolby Vision support for more vivid and detailed footage, especially in challenging lighting conditions.

Audio Capabilities

Clear audio is just as important as high-quality visuals in filmmaking. Many smartphones come with built-in microphones, but they may not provide professional-level audio.

Solution: Choose a phone that supports external microphones through USB-C, Lightning, or a 3.5mm headphone jack adapter. This allows you to use lavalier or shotgun mics to capture clean, high-quality sound.

Battery Life

Filming, especially in 4K or high frame rates, drains battery life quickly. A smartphone with a large battery or fast charging capability will help ensure you don't run out of power in the middle of an important scene.

Solution: Opt for a smartphone with a robust battery and carry a portable charger or extra battery packs during extended shooting sessions.

Storage Capacity

Video files, especially in 4K, can take up a significant amount of storage space. Look for a phone with ample internal storage or the ability to expand storage via microSD cards.

Solution: Choose a phone with at least 128GB of storage, or ensure it supports cloud storage solutions or external drives to store large video files.

Best Smartphones for Filmmaking

Here's a look at some of the top smartphones available today that are ideal for filmmaking, each offering unique strengths for mobile cinematography.

iPhone 15 Pro Max

The iPhone 15 Pro Max is considered one of the best smartphones for filmmakers, thanks to its powerful camera system, robust video features, and seamless integration with editing software.

Key Features:

48MP primary camera with ProRAW and ProRes recording capabilities

4K video recording at 24fps, 30fps, and 60fps

Dolby Vision HDR video

Cinematic Mode with shallow depth of field at 4K

Excellent low-light performance and color accuracy

Supports external microphones through the Lightning port

The iPhone 15 Pro Max also supports ProRes video recording, making it ideal for filmmakers who want more control over color grading and editing in post-production. Its combination of hardware and software makes it one of the most versatile phones for both amateur and professional filmmakers.

Samsung Galaxy S23 Ultra

The Samsung Galaxy S23 Ultra is another top contender for filmmakers, offering one of the most advanced camera systems available on a smartphone, with excellent low-light performance and manual control features.

Key Features:

200MP main camera with ultra-high resolution

8K video recording at 30fps, 4K at 60fps

Super Steady mode for ultra-smooth footage

Pro Video mode with full manual controls

HDR10+ support for dynamic range

Compatible with a range of external microphones via USB-C

The S23 Ultra's impressive zoom capabilities, wide range of frame rates, and manual controls make it an excellent choice for filmmakers who want versatility and power in a smartphone.

Google Pixel 8 Pro

Known for its software-based photography and videography enhancements, the Google Pixel 8 Pro excels in computational filmmaking, making it a great option for those who want top-notch video without needing a complicated setup.

Key Features:

50MP primary camera with outstanding HDR capabilities

4K video at 30fps and 60fps

Impressive Night Sight for low-light filmmaking

Active stabilization for smooth handheld shots

Cinematic Blur for shallow depth of field effects

Supports external mics via USB-C

The Pixel 8 Pro's software-driven features, including its excellent HDR and low-light performance, make it ideal for filmmakers working in challenging lighting conditions.

Sony Xperia 1 V

Sony's Xperia 1 V is designed with creators in mind, offering a wealth of manual controls and video-centric features that make it stand out for filmmakers who prefer precise control over their footage.

Key Features:

4K HDR OLED display for accurate monitoring

4K video recording at 120fps for slow-motion

Full manual control over ISO, shutter speed, and white balance

Cinematography Pro app for advanced video settings

High-quality Zeiss optics and real-time eye autofocus

Supports external audio through a 3.5mm headphone jack

The Xperia 1 V's focus on manual control and professional-level features make it ideal for filmmakers who want a smartphone with DSLR-like capabilities.

OnePlus 11

OnePlus continues to push the boundaries of smartphone video quality with the OnePlus 11, which offers a powerful camera system, smooth stabilization, and detailed 4K video.

Key Features:

50MP main camera with 4K video at 30fps and 60fps

Excellent image stabilization for handheld shots

Hasselblad camera tuning for accurate color reproduction

Pro mode with manual controls for video

Ultra-fast charging to keep you filming longer

For filmmakers looking for a more affordable option without compromising on features, the OnePlus 11 is a strong contender, offering a good balance of high-quality video, stability, and battery life.

Additional Tips for Choosing a Smartphone for Filmmaking

Third-Party Apps: Consider whether the smartphone supports professional filmmaking apps like *Filmic Pro*, which offers advanced manual controls and shooting features beyond what is available in the native camera app.

Ecosystem: If you plan to edit your footage on the same device or within a specific ecosystem (such as Apple's iOS or Google's Android), choose a smartphone that integrates well with your preferred editing software, like *iMovie*, *Final Cut Pro*, or *Adobe Premiere Rush*.

Build Quality: Filmmaking often involves shooting in various conditions, so a durable phone with water resistance and strong build quality is ideal for outdoor shoots or travel-heavy projects.

Choosing the right smartphone for filmmaking depends on your specific needs, budget, and the type of films you plan to create. Whether you're looking for top-tier image quality, manual controls, or advanced video features like HDR and high frame rates, the smartphones listed above offer some of the best options for mobile cinematography. By selecting a smartphone that excels in camera performance, video recording

Distribution on a Budget: Getting Your Film to Audiences

Creating a film is a monumental achievement, but the next step—getting your film in front of an audience—can be just as challenging, especially when you're working with a limited budget. Fortunately, digital platforms and DIY distribution methods have made it easier than ever to reach a wide audience without the need for traditional film distribution deals. With careful planning, creativity, and the right strategy, you can successfully distribute your film to the masses without breaking the bank.

In this chapter, we'll explore various cost-effective ways to distribute your film, including digital platforms, self-distribution strategies, and marketing techniques that will help you build an audience. Whether you're an independent filmmaker releasing your first short film or a seasoned creator looking for budget-friendly options, these tips will guide you through the distribution process.

Why Distribution Matters

Distribution is essential because it allows your film to reach its audience. After investing time, effort, and resources into production, you want to make sure your work is seen by as many people as possible. Distribution also opens doors to future opportunities, such as funding for your next project, connections with industry professionals, and potential income from sales or licensing.

Benefits of Strategic Distribution:

Audience Reach: Getting your film to the right platforms ensures it reaches your target audience, whether that's niche film fans or a wider demographic.

Monetization: Proper distribution allows you to generate revenue, whether through direct sales, streaming royalties, or digital rentals.

Recognition and Networking: Successful distribution can boost your profile in the industry, leading to more opportunities, collaborations, and exposure for future projects.

Low-Cost Distribution Options

When distributing on a budget, the key is to leverage cost-effective platforms and DIY strategies. Here are some of the most accessible and affordable ways to distribute your film:

Self-Distribution on Digital Platforms

With the rise of digital streaming, filmmakers now have direct access to audiences through a variety of platforms. These platforms allow you to upload, promote, and monetize your film with minimal upfront costs.

YouTube: YouTube is one of the most accessible platforms for self-distribution, especially if you're looking to build an audience or showcase your work for free. With over two billion users, it offers a huge potential reach. While monetization through ads is possible, success often comes from building a subscriber base and using YouTube as a launchpad for other opportunities.

Vimeo On Demand: Vimeo allows filmmakers to sell their films directly to viewers through its Vimeo On Demand service. You can set your own price for rentals or purchases and retain up to 90% of the revenue after transaction fees. Vimeo also provides options for high-quality video hosting and has a more niche, film-focused audience.

Amazon Prime Video Direct: Amazon Prime Video Direct enables filmmakers to upload their films directly to the platform, making them available to Prime subscribers or for rent and purchase. While the payout per view is modest, Amazon's vast user base provides broad exposure, and filmmakers keep a portion of sales revenue.

Tip: Use these platforms to test your film's appeal and build a fan base. Combine multiple platforms to diversify your audience and revenue streams.

Film Festivals

Film festivals are a great way to gain exposure and potentially connect with distributors, industry professionals, or even streaming platforms. However, festival submission fees can add up, so it's important to be strategic when selecting which festivals to enter.

Local and Regional Festivals: Smaller, local festivals often have lower entry fees and provide an excellent opportunity to showcase your film to a targeted, engaged audience. These festivals are more likely to accept independent and low-budget films, offering you a better chance of getting noticed.

Online Festivals: Virtual film festivals, such as those hosted on platforms like FilmFreeway, are becoming increasingly popular and often have lower fees. These festivals allow your film to be seen by audiences around the world without the cost of travel or physical marketing materials.

Niche Festivals: If your film fits into a specific genre (e.g., horror, documentary, animation), consider submitting to niche festivals that cater to those audiences. Specialized festivals often have passionate fans and industry insiders who are more likely to appreciate and promote your work.

Tip: Before submitting to festivals, research their audience, past selections, and submission fees. Create a festival strategy based on your film's strengths and genre.

Crowdfunding for Distribution

If you need additional funds to cover distribution costs, consider launching a crowdfunding campaign. Platforms like Kickstarter and Indiegogo allow you to raise money directly from your audience to help with marketing, festival submissions, or digital platform fees.

Perks and Rewards: Offer incentives such as exclusive behind-the-scenes footage, early access to the film, or merchandise like posters and t-shirts to encourage people to contribute.

Social Media Campaigns: Use your crowdfunding campaign as a way to build an audience before the film is released. Regular updates, videos, and social media engagement can help drum up excitement and bring in more backers.

Tip: Create a compelling campaign video and outline how the funds will be used. Be transparent about your distribution goals and what contributors will get in return.

Distribution Aggregators

If you're looking to distribute your film on multiple streaming platforms but don't want to deal with each individually, a distribution aggregator can help. Aggregators act as middlemen, helping you get your film onto platforms like iTunes, Google Play, and Netflix.

Filmhub: Filmhub is a free-to-use platform that connects independent filmmakers with streaming services and platforms. Filmhub earns a percentage of the revenue once your film starts making money, but there are no upfront fees.

Distribber (or similar services): Some aggregators charge a flat fee to distribute your film to multiple platforms. While this can be more expensive upfront, it streamlines the process and ensures your film is available in a wide range of marketplaces.

Tip: Research aggregators to find the right fit for your film. Some offer marketing support, while others focus purely on distribution, so choose based on your needs.

Direct Sales via Your Website

Selling your film directly through your own website gives you complete control over pricing, distribution, and audience interaction. It also allows you to keep a larger share of the profits since you won't have to split revenue with platforms or aggregators.

Build a Website: Create a professional-looking website with a dedicated page for your film. You can use platforms like Squarespace, WordPress, or Wix to easily build a site without needing advanced technical skills.

E-Commerce Tools: Use e-commerce plugins or services like Gumroad to handle digital downloads or rentals directly from your site. You can set your own prices and even offer tiered pricing options for different formats or bonus content.

Tip: Use your website as a hub for all things related to your film—trailers, behind-the-scenes content, director's notes, and a blog to keep audiences engaged.

Budget-Friendly Marketing for Your Film

In addition to distributing your film, it's important to invest time and effort in marketing to ensure people know about it. Even with limited funds, there are several effective ways to promote your film and build a following.

Leverage Social Media

Social media platforms are powerful tools for building buzz around your film, reaching potential viewers, and keeping your audience engaged. Best of all, they're free to use.

Create Dedicated Pages: Set up official accounts for your film on Instagram, Facebook, Twitter, and TikTok. Share trailers, behind-the-scenes footage, cast and crew interviews, and updates to keep your followers excited.

Hashtag Strategy: Use relevant hashtags to increase the visibility of your posts. Research popular hashtags in the filmmaking or genre-specific communities to reach more people.

Tip: Run low-cost social media ads to target specific demographics who are most likely to be interested in your film. Platforms like Facebook and Instagram allow you to create highly targeted ads based on interests, location, and behavior.

Create a Press Kit

A press kit is a collection of materials designed to help journalists, bloggers, and media outlets promote your film. It typically includes a synopsis, high-resolution images, a director's statement, cast bios, and links to trailers.

Send to Bloggers and Film Websites: Reach out to film bloggers, online magazines, and industry websites that review independent films. Provide them with your press kit and invite them to review your film or interview you about the project.

Share with Influencers: Influencers, especially those in the film or entertainment niche, can help promote your movie to a larger audience. Send them your press kit or offer early access to your film in exchange for social media promotion.

Tip: Keep your press kit concise and professional. Provide easy access to all materials by creating a downloadable PDF or hosting it on your film's website.

Collaborate with Other Filmmakers

Working with other independent filmmakers can help expand your network and increase your film's visibility. By promoting each other's work, you can reach new audiences and benefit from shared resources.

Cross-Promotions: Partner with filmmakers who are also distributing their work to promote each other's films. Share their trailers or clips on your social media and ask them to do the same.

Collaborative Screenings: Host joint screenings with other indie filmmakers. Whether in-person or virtual, these events can help draw a larger audience and provide an opportunity for Q&A sessions or panel discussions with the filmmakers.

Tip: Attend local filmmaker meetups, workshops, or virtual events to build relationships and explore opportunities for collaboration.

Distributing your film on a budget doesn't have to limit your reach or impact. By leveraging digital platforms, self-distribution strategies, and low-cost marketing techniques, you can get your film in front of a wide audience while keeping costs down. Whether you're submitting to festivals, uploading to Vimeo, or selling directly through your website, the key is to stay organized, be creative, and engage with your audience at every step. With the right approach, you can successfully distribute your film and build a dedicated fan base for future projects.

Releasing Your Film: Festivals, YouTube, and Other Platforms

Once you've completed your film, the next challenge is getting it in front of an audience. Releasing your film strategically can mean the difference between it being seen by a handful of viewers and reaching a broad, engaged audience. There are many ways to release your film, from film festivals to digital platforms like YouTube, and each option has its benefits depending on your goals. Whether you're looking for recognition, monetization, or to build a fanbase, choosing the right release strategy is key to your film's success.

In this chapter, we'll explore various platforms and methods for releasing your film, focusing on film festivals, YouTube, streaming services, and other digital platforms. We'll discuss the pros and cons of each approach and provide tips for creating a release plan that aligns with your objectives.

Why Your Release Strategy Matters

Your film's release strategy can influence its overall success, from the number of viewers to potential financial returns and opportunities for future projects. A well-planned release helps build anticipation, attract press coverage, and gain the attention of industry professionals. On the other hand, a poorly timed or unfocused release can result in your film getting lost in the sea of content.

Considerations for Your Release:

Audience Reach: Some platforms have broad, global audiences, while others may focus on niche markets. Understanding where your target audience spends their time is crucial.

Monetization: Certain platforms allow you to earn revenue through rentals, purchases, or ads, while others focus more on visibility and building an audience.

Recognition: Film festivals and awards can provide critical recognition and credibility, which can lead to distribution deals or funding for future projects.

Engagement: Releasing your film on platforms with active communities allows you to interact directly with your audience, fostering fan engagement and loyalty.

Releasing Your Film at Festivals

Film festivals are one of the most traditional ways to release a film and can offer invaluable exposure. They provide an opportunity to showcase your work to industry professionals, critics, and potential distributors. Festivals also create buzz around your film, especially if it receives awards or positive reviews.

Benefits of Festival Releases:

Recognition and Credibility: Winning awards or even being accepted into a prestigious festival can boost your film's profile. Festivals often serve as launching pads for independent films, providing a pathway to wider distribution.

Industry Connections: Festivals attract distributors, producers, and industry professionals who may take an interest in your work and offer opportunities for future projects.

Audience Feedback: Screening your film in front of a live audience gives you the chance to see how viewers react and to gather feedback that could be valuable for future projects.

Types of Festivals to Consider:

Major Festivals: Events like the Sundance Film Festival, Cannes, Venice, and Toronto are highly competitive but offer the most exposure. If your film is accepted, it can dramatically raise your profile in the industry.

Regional and Local Festivals: Smaller festivals may have lower entry fees and less competition, making them more accessible to independent filmmakers. These festivals often have dedicated, passionate audiences.

Niche Festivals: Specialized festivals that focus on particular genres (e.g., horror, documentary, mobile filmmaking) provide a targeted audience that's more likely to appreciate and support your work.

Tip: Be strategic when submitting to festivals. Research each festival's history, audience, and submission guidelines to ensure your film is a good fit. Use platforms like *FilmFreeway* to streamline the submission process.

Releasing Your Film on YouTube

YouTube is one of the most popular and accessible platforms for releasing a film. With over two billion active users, YouTube offers a vast audience and the potential for viral success. Releasing your film on YouTube allows you to reach viewers worldwide, engage directly with your audience, and build a community around your work.

Benefits of YouTube Releases:

Global Audience: YouTube's reach is unmatched, providing instant access to viewers from around the world. This is especially beneficial for filmmakers without large distribution budgets.

Free Platform: Unlike some streaming services, YouTube allows you to upload your film for free, making it an ideal option for independent filmmakers with limited resources.

Monetization Opportunities: Through YouTube's Partner Program, you can earn ad revenue based on views. While the earnings per view can be modest, large viewership can generate significant income over time.

Audience Engagement: YouTube's comment section and community features allow you to interact directly with viewers, fostering a loyal audience.

Strategies for Success on YouTube:

Optimize Your Title and Thumbnail: A catchy title and visually engaging thumbnail are critical for attracting viewers. Your thumbnail should be bold, clear, and reflective of your film's content.

Use YouTube SEO: Research relevant keywords for your film's genre and use them in your title, description, and tags to increase visibility. This helps your film appear in search results and recommended videos.

Promote Your Film: Leverage social media, email lists, and collaborations with other YouTubers or filmmakers to drive traffic to your video. Engaging with communities and forums related to your film's theme or genre can also help increase visibility.

Tip: Consider creating additional content for YouTube, such as behind-the-scenes footage, trailers, or director's commentary, to engage your audience further and encourage them to share your work.

Releasing Your Film on Other Digital Platforms

In addition to YouTube, there are several other digital platforms that can help you reach your target audience and monetize your film. Each platform offers different features, audiences, and opportunities for independent filmmakers.

Vimeo On Demand

Vimeo is a popular platform among filmmakers due to its high-quality video playback and community of creative professionals. Vimeo On Demand allows you to sell or rent your film directly to viewers, keeping more control over pricing and distribution.

Pros:

High-quality streaming and professional presentation.

Flexible monetization options, including rentals, purchases, and subscriptions.

You keep up to 90% of the revenue after fees, making it a profitable option for filmmakers.

Cons:

Vimeo has a smaller audience compared to YouTube, so you'll need to put more effort into driving traffic to your film.

The platform may not be as familiar to casual viewers as YouTube.

Tip: If you choose Vimeo, consider bundling your film with additional content (e.g., bonus scenes, commentary) to provide more value to viewers.

Amazon Prime Video Direct

Amazon Prime Video Direct allows you to upload your film to the Amazon marketplace, where viewers can rent, purchase, or stream it as part of their Prime membership. This platform offers access to a massive audience and the potential for royalties based on views.

Pros:

Access to Amazon's global audience and Prime members.

Flexible pricing options for rentals, purchases, and streaming.

You retain control over distribution and monetization.

Cons:

Royalties can be relatively low unless your film garners significant views.

Navigating the Amazon Video Direct platform can be more complex than YouTube or Vimeo.

Tip: Promote your film through Amazon's built-in marketing tools or pair it with physical products (e.g., DVDs or merchandise) sold on Amazon to increase visibility.

Streaming Services (Netflix, Hulu, etc.)

Getting your film onto a major streaming platform like Netflix, Hulu, or HBO Max is a coveted goal for many filmmakers. These platforms offer wide exposure and, in some cases, substantial licensing fees. However, they are highly competitive, and not all films are accepted.

Pros:

Massive audience reach and credibility boost if accepted.

Potential for lucrative licensing deals or exclusive distribution agreements.

Cons:

Difficult to secure without prior festival success or a distribution deal.

Requires negotiations, legal agreements, and sometimes exclusivity, limiting your ability to distribute the film elsewhere.

Tip: To increase your chances of being picked up by a streaming service, focus on festival submissions, winning awards, and generating buzz through media coverage or social media.

Hybrid Release Strategy

Many filmmakers choose to combine different platforms to maximize their film's reach and revenue potential. For example, you might start with a festival run to build buzz and attract attention from distributors, then release the film on Vimeo or Amazon for paid rentals or purchases, and eventually make it available on YouTube for free to grow your audience.

Benefits of a Hybrid Strategy:

Wider Reach: By releasing your film on multiple platforms, you reach different audiences, from festival-goers to casual viewers online.

Monetization Options: You can combine revenue from rentals, purchases, ads, and sponsorships across platforms.

Maximized Impact: A staggered release can keep your film in the public eye for a longer period, creating ongoing opportunities for exposure.

Promoting Your Film

No matter where you release your film, promotion is essential to its success. Here are some key strategies to help you build anticipation and attract viewers:

Leverage Social Media

Create dedicated social media accounts for your film and start promoting it early. Share trailers, behind-the-scenes content, and updates to generate excitement. Engage with your followers and use targeted ads to reach a broader audience.

Use Email Marketing

Build an email list of people interested in your film, including those who supported your crowdfunding campaign or attended your festival screenings. Keep them updated on release dates, exclusive content, and special offers.

Partner with Influencers

Collaborate with bloggers, YouTubers, or social media influencers in your film's niche. Offer them early access to your film in exchange for reviews, interviews, or social media promotion.

Press and Media Coverage

Send press releases to film blogs, entertainment websites, and local media outlets. Coverage from reputable sources can help boost your film's visibility and attract more viewers.

Releasing your film successfully requires a well-thought-out strategy that aligns with your goals, whether that's earning revenue, building an audience, or gaining recognition. By considering different platforms—such as festivals, YouTube, Vimeo, and Amazon—you can tailor your release plan to suit your film's strengths and reach the widest possible audience. Combining multiple platforms and promotional techniques will ensure that your film gets the attention it deserves, turning your hard work into a successful release.

Monetizing Your Smartphone Film: Turning a Hobby into Income

Creating a film with your smartphone is an accessible and creative way to tell stories, but beyond artistic expression, it can also become a source of income. With digital platforms and the rise of independent filmmaking, even low-budget smartphone films can generate revenue through various channels, including streaming, festivals, crowdfunding, and licensing deals. With the right approach, you can turn your passion for mobile filmmaking into a profitable venture. This chapter explores the different ways to monetize your smartphone film, from selling or renting it online to leveraging crowdfunding and securing distribution deals. Whether you're an aspiring filmmaker looking to make your first dollars from your film or a seasoned creator aiming to expand revenue streams, these strategies will help you maximize the financial potential of your smartphone film.

Why Monetizing Your Smartphone Film is Possible

Smartphone filmmaking is no longer seen as amateur or low-quality. With examples like *Tangerine* (2015) and *High Flying Bird* (2019), both shot on iPhones, the filmmaking world has embraced mobile technology as a viable medium for professional-quality storytelling. This acceptance opens the door for monetization, providing filmmakers with numerous opportunities to profit from their work.

Key Advantages of Monetizing Smartphone Films:

Low Production Costs: Filming with a smartphone often involves lower costs, allowing filmmakers to keep more of the profits.

Access to Digital Platforms: The rise of online streaming and distribution platforms has made it easier for filmmakers to directly reach and monetize global audiences.

Wide Audience Appeal: With proper marketing and distribution, even small-budget films can find an audience that's willing to pay for content.

Strategies for Monetizing Your Smartphone Film

Successful filmmakers often combine multiple revenue streams to maximize their earning potential. Below are some of the most effective strategies to monetize your smartphone film.

Sell or Rent Your Film on Digital Platforms

One of the simplest ways to monetize your film is by selling or renting it on digital platforms. These services let filmmakers upload their films and set a price for viewers to rent or purchase the content.

Amazon Prime Video Direct: Amazon allows filmmakers to distribute their films on Prime Video, offering rental, purchase, or streaming options. Filmmakers can earn royalties based on how many times their film is streamed by Prime members or purchased by other users.

Vimeo On Demand: Vimeo offers a filmmaker-friendly platform that allows you to sell or rent your film directly to viewers, keeping up to 90% of the revenue after transaction fees. Vimeo is known for its high-quality video hosting and professional-looking presentation.

YouTube Rentals: While YouTube is best known as a free platform, you can use its rental service to charge viewers for access to your film. YouTube also offers ad revenue through its Partner Program, allowing you to monetize free-to-watch content.

Tip: Consider offering both rental and purchase options to cater to different audience preferences. Rentals can attract casual viewers, while purchases offer a higher return per transaction.

Leverage Crowdfunding

Crowdfunding is not only a great way to raise funds for production, but it can also help you finance distribution, marketing, and festival submissions. Platforms like Kickstarter and Indiegogo let filmmakers engage directly with their audience, offering rewards in exchange for financial support.

Kickstarter: A popular choice for filmmakers, Kickstarter requires you to meet your funding goal to receive any money, which encourages backers to contribute until the goal is reached. Offer unique rewards, such as early access to the film, behind-the-scenes content, or exclusive Q&A sessions.

Indiegogo: Indiegogo offers a more flexible funding model, allowing you to keep the funds raised even if you don't reach your full goal. This is ideal for filmmakers who need partial funding for festival entries, marketing, or post-production.

Patreon: While typically used for ongoing projects, Patreon can be a good option for filmmakers who want to build a dedicated fanbase. Supporters pledge monthly contributions in exchange for access to exclusive content, early film releases, and other perks.

Tip: Make sure your crowdfunding campaign includes a compelling video, an engaging story, and attractive rewards to inspire potential backers to contribute.

Monetize Through Ad Revenue and Sponsorships

If you plan to release your film for free on platforms like YouTube or Vimeo, you can still generate income through ads and sponsorships. This model is particularly effective if your film has viral potential or targets a niche audience that brands want to reach.

YouTube AdSense: You can enable ads on your YouTube videos and earn revenue based on views and clicks. While the earnings per view can be modest, viral content or large audiences can generate significant income over time.

Brand Sponsorships: Depending on your film's content and target audience, brands may be interested in sponsoring your film or paying for product placement. This is a particularly effective option for genre-specific or niche films, where brands can reach highly targeted viewers.

Tip: Approach brands or companies that align with the themes or target demographic of your film. For example, an outdoor adventure film might partner with a sports or gear brand.

Submit to Festivals and Competitions

Film festivals not only provide exposure but can also be a source of income through prize money or the attention of distributors. Many festivals offer awards and cash prizes for winning films, and festivals with a strong industry presence may help you secure distribution deals.

Mobile Film Festivals: Festivals dedicated to mobile filmmaking, like the International Mobile Film Festival or Mobile Motion Film Festival, cater specifically to filmmakers using smartphones. These festivals can help you stand out in a growing niche and often offer cash prizes.

General Film Festivals: Traditional festivals may also accept smartphone films, especially in categories focused on innovation or new media. Success at major festivals like Sundance or Tribeca can lead to lucrative distribution deals or increased visibility.

Tip: Before submitting to a festival, research its audience, previous selections, and submission fees to ensure it aligns with your film's goals and genre.

License Your Film for Streaming or Distribution

Licensing your film to streaming services or other distribution platforms can be a lucrative way to monetize your work, especially if it has gained traction at festivals or online. Licensing deals allow streaming services, TV networks, or even airlines to show your film for a fee.

Streaming Platforms: Services like Netflix, Hulu, and niche streaming platforms may license independent films, providing a one-time fee or royalty based on viewership. While competitive, gaining entry to these platforms can dramatically boost your film's exposure and income potential.

Airlines and Hotels: Many airlines and hotel chains license independent films to offer as in-flight or in-room entertainment. This market is competitive, but it can be a steady source of revenue if you secure a deal.

Tip: Use a distribution aggregator like Filmhub to submit your film to multiple streaming services and other platforms, streamlining the process of licensing your film.

Create and Sell Merchandise or Digital Extras

If your film builds a dedicated fanbase, you can monetize that audience by offering merchandise or digital extras related to your film. Fans are often willing to buy physical or digital items that enhance their connection to your film.

Merchandise: Offer branded merchandise like t-shirts, posters, or memorabilia related to your film. Platforms like Teespring or Redbubble make it easy to create and sell merchandise without upfront costs.

Digital Extras: Sell digital products like behind-the-scenes footage, director's commentary, or exclusive interviews with cast and crew. Offering these extras as part of a premium package can increase your film's overall revenue.

Tip: Bundle digital extras or merchandise with your film as part of a deluxe edition to increase the perceived value and encourage larger purchases.

Building a Monetization Strategy

To successfully monetize your smartphone film, it's essential to develop a clear strategy that combines multiple revenue streams. Here's how to approach the process:

Understand Your Audience

Identify your target audience and consider where they consume content. For example, if your film appeals to younger viewers, YouTube or social media-based promotion may be your best bet. For niche genres, festivals or platforms like Vimeo could be more effective.

Choose the Right Platforms

Select platforms that align with your monetization goals. If you're seeking direct sales, platforms like Vimeo On Demand or Amazon Prime may be ideal. If you're focused on building an audience, YouTube might be a better fit.

Diversify Revenue Streams

Use a combination of revenue sources, such as digital sales, ads, sponsorships, and merchandise, to maximize your income. By spreading your film across multiple platforms, you can reach different audiences and increase your overall earnings.

Promote Effectively

Effective marketing is key to successful monetization. Use social media, email campaigns, and press coverage to build anticipation for your film's release and ensure it reaches as many viewers as possible.

Monetizing your smartphone film is achievable through a combination of digital platforms, crowdfunding, festivals, licensing deals, and merchandise. By choosing the right strategies and diversifying your revenue streams, you can turn your passion for filmmaking into a sustainable source of income. With the growing acceptance of smartphone films in the industry, the potential to profit from your creative efforts has never been greater.

Building a Brand: Creating an Online Presence as a Filmmaker

In today's digital world, building a brand and establishing a strong online presence is essential for filmmakers. It's no longer enough to simply create great films—you also need to make sure people know who you are, what you do, and where to find your work. By cultivating an online identity, you can engage with your audience, network with industry professionals, and ultimately promote your films more effectively. Your brand represents your style, vision, and professional identity, helping you stand out in an increasingly crowded field.

This chapter will explore how to build a personal brand as a filmmaker, focusing on creating a website, leveraging social media, engaging with your audience, and using digital platforms to promote your work. Whether you're an emerging filmmaker or an established professional looking to strengthen your online presence, these strategies will help you build a recognizable brand that resonates with audiences and industry professionals alike.

Why Building a Brand as a Filmmaker Matters

Your brand is the identity you present to the world. As a filmmaker, your brand communicates your style, values, and the kind of stories you tell. A strong brand helps potential viewers, collaborators, and industry insiders recognize your work, remember your name, and understand what sets you apart from others.

Benefits of Building a Filmmaker Brand:

Audience Engagement: A recognizable brand helps you connect with your audience more effectively. They know what to expect from your work and can follow your journey from project to project.

Industry Recognition: By building a strong online presence, you increase your visibility in the industry, opening doors to networking opportunities, collaborations, and professional growth.

Career Longevity: A solid brand keeps you relevant, even between projects. It helps you stay in the public eye and maintains interest in your work over time.

Steps to Building Your Filmmaker Brand

Building a brand is not just about creating a logo or a catchy tagline—it's about defining your identity as a filmmaker and consistently presenting that identity across all your online platforms. Here are the key steps to building your filmmaker brand:

Define Your Brand Identity

Before you start building your online presence, take some time to define your brand. What kind of filmmaker are you? What themes, genres, or styles do you focus on? Your brand identity should reflect your artistic vision, personal style, and professional goals.

Your Filmmaking Style: Consider what makes your films unique. Do you specialize in a particular genre, like horror, comedy, or documentary? Do you have a distinct visual style, tone, or message? Defining these elements will help you communicate your brand more clearly.

Your Storytelling Focus: Think about the stories you tell and the audiences you want to reach. Are you drawn to character-driven narratives, experimental films, or socially conscious documentaries? Your brand should reflect the types of stories you're passionate about and want to be known for.

Your Personal Values: Your brand is also a reflection of who you are as an individual. Consider how your values, beliefs, and perspectives influence your filmmaking. Incorporating personal values into your brand can make it more authentic and relatable.

Tip: Write a brief personal statement or tagline that captures your identity as a filmmaker. This could be something like "Telling human stories through the lens of sci-fi" or "Exploring the complexity of identity through experimental film." Use this statement to guide the rest of your branding efforts.

Create a Professional Website

A website serves as your online hub, where people can learn about you, view your work, and contact you for opportunities. It's a crucial part of your brand because it gives you control over how you present yourself and your films.

Portfolio of Work: Your website should showcase your filmography, including trailers, full films (if applicable), behind-the-scenes content, and any related press coverage. Make sure your films are easy to access, either embedded from Vimeo, YouTube, or another video platform.

Biography and Personal Story: Include a well-written bio that shares your journey as a filmmaker. Highlight key milestones, awards, and experiences that shape your creative vision.

Contact Information: Make it easy for people to contact you, whether they're potential collaborators, industry professionals, or media outlets. Include a contact form or an email address.

Blog or Updates Section: Consider including a blog or news section where you share updates on your latest projects, film festival submissions, and insights into your creative process. Regular updates keep your site fresh and engaging for visitors.

Tip: Use a clean, professional design that reflects your filmmaking style. If your films are visually dark and moody, choose a sleek design that matches that aesthetic. If your work is bright and colorful, reflect that in your website's color scheme and layout.

Leverage Social Media

Social media platforms are powerful tools for filmmakers looking to build an online presence. They allow you to share your work, connect with fans, and engage with the filmmaking community in real-time. The key to effective social media use is consistency and engagement.

Instagram: Instagram is a visual platform that's perfect for filmmakers. You can share behind-the-scenes photos, stills from your films, short clips, and promotional materials. Use Instagram Stories and Reels to engage with your audience in a more dynamic way.

Twitter/X: Twitter is great for networking, sharing industry news, and participating in discussions about filmmaking. Use it to promote your films, announce project updates, and engage with other filmmakers and audiences in the film community.

Facebook: Facebook is useful for creating a dedicated page for your filmmaking career, where you can share updates, trailers, and events related to your films. It's also a good platform for promoting crowdfunding campaigns or hosting live Q&A sessions.

YouTube/Vimeo: If you regularly create short films, trailers, or other video content, YouTube or Vimeo should be a key part of your social media strategy. Both platforms allow you to build a subscriber base and reach a global audience.

Tip: Use a consistent handle or username across all your social media accounts to make it easier for people to find and follow you. Keep your profile bios aligned with your filmmaker brand and include links to your website.

Engage with Your Audience

Engaging with your audience is one of the most important aspects of building a successful brand. Your online presence should not be one-sided; instead, it should be a conversation between you and your viewers.

Respond to Comments: Whether it's on social media or your website, make sure to respond to comments from your audience. Thank them for their feedback, answer questions, and acknowledge their support. This creates a sense of connection and loyalty.

Host Live Q&As or Watch Parties: Platforms like Instagram Live, Facebook Live, and YouTube allow you to host live Q&A sessions or watch parties for your films. This is a great way to connect directly with your audience, answer their questions, and offer insights into your creative process.

Encourage User-Generated Content: Get your audience involved by encouraging them to create and share content related to your film. For example, you could host a fan art contest, ask viewers to share their thoughts on your film, or invite them to remix clips.

Tip: Create a content schedule to ensure you're consistently posting and engaging with your audience. This could include regular updates on new projects, behind-the-scenes content, and curated posts about filmmaking.

Collaborate with Other Filmmakers

Networking with other filmmakers is not only great for personal growth, but it also helps build your brand within the industry. Collaboration can introduce your work to new audiences and create valuable professional connections.

Guest Blogging: Offer to write guest posts for other filmmakers' blogs or websites, sharing insights from your filmmaking journey or lessons learned on set. This will increase your visibility and establish your authority as a filmmaker.

Collaborative Projects: Partner with other filmmakers on joint projects, like short films, web series, or film festivals. Cross-promoting each other's work helps you reach a broader audience and builds relationships within the film community.

Interviews and Podcasts: Participate in interviews or guest spots on filmmaking podcasts, YouTube channels, or Instagram Lives. This is a great way to share your expertise and promote your work.

Tip: Join online filmmaking communities like Facebook groups, Reddit forums, or filmmaking Slack channels to connect with other creators and share resources.

Promote Your Films on Digital Platforms

Once you've built an online presence, it's essential to use it to promote your films effectively. Whether you're releasing a short film, feature, or web series, you need to get your work in front of the right audience.

Use Targeted Ads: Platforms like Facebook, Instagram, and YouTube allow you to run targeted ads that reach specific demographics. This can be a cost-effective way to promote your film to the right audience, especially around release dates or festival screenings.

Create Trailers and Teasers: Tease your upcoming projects with short trailers or sneak peeks. These help build anticipation and give your audience something to look forward to.

Run a Crowdfunding Campaign: If you're raising funds for a new project, use your online presence to promote your crowdfunding campaign. Share regular updates, thank your backers, and keep them engaged with behind-the-scenes content.

Tip: When promoting your film, highlight what makes it unique. Whether it's the storytelling, genre, or a special message, emphasize the elements that will resonate most with your target audience.

Building a brand as a filmmaker is about more than just creating a logo or a website—it's about crafting a cohesive online identity that reflects your creative vision and professional values. By defining your brand, creating a professional website, leveraging social media, engaging with your audience, and collaborating with other filmmakers, you can establish a strong online presence that enhances your career. Your brand will not only help promote your films but also make you stand out in the competitive world of filmmaking, ensuring that your work reaches a wider audience and opens doors to new opportunities.

Voice Acting and ADR: Overcoming Audio Challenges

Audio is a critical component of any film, and poor sound quality can distract your audience, no matter how visually stunning your film is. Whether it's dialogue that wasn't recorded clearly on set, environmental noise, or the need to re-record specific lines, filmmakers often turn to ADR (Automated Dialogue Replacement) and voice acting to fix audio issues and enhance the overall sound of a film.

This chapter explores the importance of voice acting and ADR in filmmaking, the common audio challenges they help address, and how to execute effective ADR sessions. By understanding how to use these techniques, you can overcome sound problems and improve the auditory quality of your project, ensuring that your film sounds as polished as it looks.

What is ADR?

ADR stands for Automated Dialogue Replacement, a process in which actors re-record their dialogue in a controlled studio environment after the film has been shot. This allows for cleaner, more precise audio that can replace or supplement the original on-set recording. ADR is used to fix poorly captured dialogue, replace unwanted background noise, and even add new lines or alternate takes to enhance the story.

Why ADR is Necessary:

Audio Quality Issues: On-set audio can be compromised by external noise (wind, traffic, crowds), faulty equipment, or poor microphone placement. ADR allows you to re-record dialogue in a controlled environment, resulting in cleaner sound.

Creative Flexibility: ADR gives filmmakers the flexibility to tweak performances, add lines, or adjust delivery after filming. This can be essential for refining a character's voice or addressing pacing and tone issues in the edit.

Localization and Dubbing: ADR is also used for dubbing films in different languages, allowing international audiences to enjoy the film in their native language.

Common Audio Challenges in Filmmaking

Audio issues can arise from several sources, especially in independent and low-budget filmmaking where controlled environments are hard to come by. Here are some common audio challenges that can be resolved with ADR and voice acting:

Environmental Noise

Outdoor locations, busy streets, or open areas can introduce unwanted background noise that overpowers dialogue or creates distracting sounds. While location sound teams do their best to minimize interference, it's often impossible to capture clean dialogue in such conditions.

Solution: ADR allows actors to re-record their lines in a quiet studio, replacing the noisy on-set dialogue. In post-production, the new audio is synced with the visuals to create a seamless final product.

Inconsistent Audio Levels

On set, the placement of microphones or the movement of actors can cause inconsistent audio levels, with some lines being too quiet or too loud compared to others.

Solution: ADR provides consistent sound levels since all dialogue is recorded in a controlled studio environment with proper mic placement and levels. This ensures a uniform audio track for the entire scene.

Muffled or Unclear Dialogue

Sometimes actors' dialogue is unclear due to low microphone quality, poor acoustics, or physical barriers (like masks or heavy costumes) that muffle their voices. In addition, outdoor scenes may feature dialogue drowned out by natural elements like wind or water.

Solution: By using ADR, actors can re-record unclear lines to improve clarity, tone, and delivery. This ensures the audience hears every line of dialogue clearly, even in challenging environments.

Performance Adjustments

Filmmakers may realize in post-production that certain lines could be delivered better, with more emotion, or with different inflection to improve the overall performance.

Solution: ADR allows you to direct actors to adjust their performances. Whether it's more intensity, a different pace, or even changing the script slightly, ADR lets you refine performances after principal photography has wrapped.

How to Execute Effective ADR

Effective ADR requires planning, precision, and careful attention to detail. Here are the key steps for ensuring successful ADR sessions:

Prepare for ADR Early

Plan for the possibility of ADR during pre-production, knowing that certain scenes may require dialogue replacement due to difficult shooting environments. Preparing actors for ADR as part of the process can help them perform better when it's time to re-record lines.

Tip: Keep track of problematic audio during filming. Note which scenes, locations, or specific lines may need ADR so you can schedule the appropriate sessions later on.

Create a Comfortable Studio Environment

The recording environment is critical to successful ADR. Choose a quiet, acoustically treated space where you can control sound and minimize background noise. Ensure actors feel comfortable, as ADR can require multiple takes to get the perfect match for both performance and sync.

Tip: Provide actors with the visual cues they need by showing the scenes they're dubbing over. This helps them match their performance to the original on-screen timing and emotion.

Match Vocal Tone and Performance

One of the biggest challenges of ADR is making sure the newly recorded dialogue matches the tone and delivery of the original performance. If the actor sounds too different in the studio compared to how they performed on set, it will feel out of place.

Tip: Have the actor watch their original performance while re-recording lines so they can sync their vocal tone, energy, and pace with the visuals.

Sync Dialogue Perfectly

Precise synchronization is crucial in ADR. The re-recorded dialogue must match the actors' lip movements and timing exactly, or it will appear unnatural. Modern editing software makes it easier to fine-tune sync, but it still requires attention to detail.

Tip: Use a "beep" or countdown system before recording to help the actor time their delivery accurately. This gives them a cue for when to start speaking, making it easier to sync with the on-screen action.

Blend ADR with On-Set Audio

To make ADR seamless, it's important to blend the newly recorded dialogue with the on-set sound. This can involve adjusting reverb, equalization, and ambient noise to match the new dialogue with the original environment.

Tip: Add room tone and background noise from the original location to the ADR track. This helps blend the new audio with the on-set sound, making the ADR less noticeable.

Voice Acting in Film

Voice acting plays a crucial role in ADR, especially when it comes to adding characters that weren't present during filming, dubbing for animated sequences, or re-recording lines for narrative purposes. Professional voice actors can bring depth, emotion, and realism to characters who exist only as voices.

Applications of Voice Acting in Film:

Narration: Films often use voice-over narration to provide background information or inner monologues. Good voice acting can make the narration feel natural and engaging, while poor narration can take the audience out of the story.

Dubbing for Animated Films: In animation, all character voices are recorded by voice actors. The success of animated characters often hinges on the quality of the voice acting.

Voice for Special Effects or Creatures: In many genres, especially fantasy and science fiction, voice actors are used to create the sounds or dialogue of creatures, robots, or otherworldly beings.

Tip: When casting voice actors, make sure they match the emotional tone and personality of the characters. A good voice actor should be able to bring a character to life using just their voice, enhancing the audience's connection to the film.

Tools and Software for ADR

Several tools and software programs are designed to make the ADR process smoother, helping filmmakers sync dialogue, adjust audio, and blend tracks seamlessly.

Popular ADR Tools:

Pro Tools: One of the industry standards for audio post-production, Pro Tools offers advanced features for recording, editing, and syncing ADR.

Adobe Audition: This user-friendly software allows for precise audio editing and has features specifically designed for dialogue replacement, making it a great option for filmmakers working on a budget.

Avid Media Composer: Known for its video editing capabilities, Avid also offers ADR features that allow filmmakers to sync re-recorded dialogue to their film with precision.

Tip: Whichever software you choose, practice syncing and editing techniques to ensure your ADR sounds natural and is integrated smoothly with your film's audio.

ADR and voice acting are vital tools for overcoming audio challenges in filmmaking. Whether it's fixing dialogue muddied by background noise, enhancing a performance, or adding entirely new vocal elements, these techniques allow filmmakers to ensure their audio matches the quality of their visuals. By planning ahead, creating a comfortable recording environment, and blending ADR seamlessly with on-set sound, you can deliver a film that sounds professional and polished, no matter the challenges faced during production.

Marketing Your Film: Using Your Phone to Build a Buzz

Creating a film is just the first step—getting people to watch it is the next major challenge. In today's digital age, filmmakers have more tools than ever to market their films, and surprisingly, many of those tools are available right on your smartphone. With a well-planned marketing strategy, you can create excitement, engage with audiences, and build anticipation for your film, all from the convenience of your phone.

This chapter explores how you can use your smartphone to build buzz around your film, leveraging social media, video apps, photography tools, and other digital resources. Whether you're releasing an indie short or a full-length feature, these strategies will help you promote your film effectively on a budget.

Why Marketing is Essential for Your Film

No matter how great your film is, it won't gain traction unless people know about it. Marketing creates awareness, builds excitement, and helps your film reach its target audience. In the competitive world of filmmaking, building a buzz is crucial to gaining attention from potential viewers, industry professionals, and distributors. With your smartphone, you have access to powerful marketing tools that allow you to connect with audiences directly.

Key Benefits of Marketing Your Film:

Audience Reach: Strategic marketing ensures that your film reaches its intended audience. A strong marketing campaign helps your film stand out in the crowded digital landscape.

Engagement: Marketing keeps your audience engaged before, during, and after the film's release. Building a community around your film fosters loyalty and excitement.

Building a Fanbase: Successful marketing can help you build a fanbase that will support your current film and follow your future projects. Loyal fans can become advocates for your work, sharing it with their networks.

Key Steps to Marketing Your Film Using Your Smartphone

With the power of social media, video editing apps, and instant communication, you can market your film effectively without expensive tools or a large budget. Here are some key steps to building a successful film marketing campaign using your smartphone.

Create a Social Media Strategy

Social media is one of the most powerful tools for marketing your film. Platforms like Instagram, Twitter, Facebook, and TikTok allow you to reach a global audience and build excitement around your project. The key to success on social media is consistent, engaging content that tells the story of your film and invites your audience to be part of the journey.

Instagram: Use Instagram to share visually engaging content like stills from the film, behind-the-scenes photos, and short clips. Instagram Stories and Reels are great tools for sharing quick updates, teasers, or sneak peeks of the film. You can also run polls and Q&A sessions to engage with your followers.

Twitter/X: Twitter is perfect for sharing quick updates, industry news, and engaging with other filmmakers or fans. Use relevant hashtags, tag cast and crew members, and participate in conversations about your film's genre or topic.

Facebook: Facebook allows you to create a dedicated page for your film, where you can post trailers, event updates, and interact with fans. Facebook Live is a great tool for hosting virtual events like Q&As or film discussions.

TikTok: With its focus on short, viral videos, TikTok is an ideal platform for sharing creative content like behind-the-scenes moments, character introductions, or fun challenges related to your film's theme. TikTok trends can help your content go viral and reach new audiences.

Tip: Use a consistent handle across all social media platforms, and create a unified aesthetic and voice for your film's marketing. This builds brand recognition and makes it easier for people to find and follow you.

Shoot and Share Behind-the-Scenes Content

Audiences love to see what goes on behind the scenes of a film production. It makes them feel more connected to the process and invested in the final product. Use your phone's camera to capture candid moments, interviews with cast and crew, or clips from the set. Behind-the-scenes content helps build a sense of anticipation and gives viewers a deeper understanding of the effort behind the film.

BTS Videos: Use short, informal videos to show how certain scenes were filmed, how props were made, or how actors prepared for their roles. You can edit these clips directly on your phone using apps like *iMovie, Kinemaster*, or *InShot*.

Time-Lapses: Create time-lapse videos of set construction, costume design, or other production elements. Time-lapse videos are visually engaging and provide a fast-paced look at the making of your film.

Interviews: Conduct quick interviews with your cast and crew, asking them to share their thoughts about the film or discuss their favorite scenes. This personal content humanizes the production and gives viewers a chance to connect with the people behind the film.

Tip: Post behind-the-scenes content regularly during production to keep your audience engaged and excited for the film's release.

Release Trailers and Teasers

Trailers and teasers are essential marketing tools that give your audience a taste of what's to come. Use your phone to create short, engaging videos that highlight key moments from your film, set the tone, and leave viewers wanting more.

Teasers: These are short videos (15–30 seconds) that offer a brief glimpse of your film. Use teasers to build anticipation during the early stages of your marketing campaign, releasing small snippets to generate curiosity.

Trailers: A full trailer (1–2 minutes) should highlight your film's plot, characters, and key visual moments without giving too much away. Use a video editing app on your phone to cut together dynamic clips and add music for dramatic effect.

Tip: Release your teaser and trailer on multiple platforms—Instagram, Twitter, Facebook, YouTube—to reach a wider audience. Encourage your cast, crew, and supporters to share them with their networks.

Engage with Your Audience Through Polls, Q&As, and Livestreams

Your phone makes it easy to engage directly with your audience in real-time. Use interactive tools to foster connection, answer questions, and keep your audience involved in the journey of your film.

Polls: Platforms like Instagram Stories and Twitter allow you to create polls. Ask your audience fun questions related to your film, such as what character they're most excited to see or what genre twist they love most. Polls are a quick way to engage your followers while keeping them thinking about your project.

Q&A Sessions: Host Q&A sessions on Instagram Live, Facebook Live, or Twitter Spaces, where fans can ask you and your cast questions about the film. This builds a personal connection and keeps your film top of mind as you answer questions and share insights.

Livestreams: Livestream events like the premiere, festival screenings, or special behind-the-scenes tours of the set. Livestreaming brings your audience into the moment, making them feel like part of the experience.

Tip: Announce your livestreams or Q&A sessions in advance to give your audience time to tune in. Use engaging visuals and countdowns to remind them as the event approaches.

Collaborate with Influencers and Film Bloggers

Film bloggers, influencers, and content creators can help amplify your marketing efforts by sharing your film with their established audiences. Reach out to influencers who align with your film's genre or message and invite them to view and promote your work.

Influencer Collaborations: Film influencers or genre-specific creators (e.g., horror vloggers, documentary reviewers) can help bring your film to the attention of new audiences. Offer them early access to your film, exclusive interviews, or behind-the-scenes content in exchange for promotion.

Guest Blogs or Podcasts: Reach out to film bloggers or podcast hosts who cover independent films. Offer to write a guest post, participate in an interview, or share insights about your filmmaking process. This can help you gain exposure in niche film communities.

Tip: When contacting influencers or bloggers, personalize your outreach. Explain why your film fits their audience and offer them something unique that will make their collaboration worthwhile.

Run Targeted Ads on Social Media

Social media platforms like Facebook, Instagram, and YouTube offer paid advertising options that allow you to target specific demographics. Running ads can help you reach a broader audience, especially around key moments like the release of your film, festival screenings, or crowdfunding campaigns.

Facebook and Instagram Ads: Use Facebook's ad manager to target specific demographics based on age, location, interests, and behaviors. You can run ads promoting your trailer, directing viewers to your website, or encouraging them to attend an event.

YouTube Ads: You can run video ads on YouTube that appear before other videos, helping you reach viewers who are already interested in films or related topics. This is a great way to promote your film's trailer or teaser to a targeted audience.

Tip: Start with a small budget for your ads and adjust based on the results. Monitor the performance of your campaigns to see which platforms and ad formats are most effective for your film.

Tools and Apps for Film Marketing on Your Phone

Your smartphone comes equipped with powerful tools for creating and sharing marketing content. Here are some apps and tools that can help you design, edit, and distribute your promotional materials:

Canva: Create professional-looking posters, social media graphics, and promotional materials directly from your phone using Canva's design templates.

iMovie/Kinemaster: Edit trailers, teasers, and behind-the-scenes clips with these user-friendly mobile video editing apps.

Later/Buffer: Plan and schedule your social media posts ahead of time using tools like Later or Buffer, ensuring a consistent presence across platforms.

Filmic Pro: For filmmakers who want more control over their phone's camera, Filmic Pro allows you to shoot high-quality video with professional-level settings.

Hootsuite: Manage multiple social media accounts and schedule posts from one central dashboard, making it easier to stay organized across platforms.

Marketing your film is essential to building excitement and ensuring that it reaches your audience, and with your smartphone, you have all the tools you need right in your pocket. By leveraging social media, creating engaging content, and connecting with your audience through interactive tools, you can build buzz around your film and create a loyal following. With strategic use of apps, social media ads, and collaborations with influencers, you can market your film effectively, even on a limited budget. Your smartphone is your gateway to building a brand, promoting your work, and ensuring your film gets the attention it deserves.

Finding Your Audience: Using Online Platforms to Distribute Your Film

Creating a film is a major accomplishment, but finding the right audience is what transforms it into a success. In the age of digital media, filmmakers no longer need to rely solely on traditional distribution channels. With the rise of online platforms, independent filmmakers have more opportunities than ever to share their work with global audiences. Knowing how to leverage these platforms to distribute your film can help you reach your target viewers, build a fanbase, and even generate revenue.

This chapter explores the most effective online platforms for distributing your film, from streaming services to social media, and offers strategies to help you connect with the right audience. By understanding how to navigate the digital distribution landscape, you can maximize the reach and impact of your film.

Why Finding Your Audience Matters

Distribution isn't just about getting your film seen—it's about getting it seen by the *right* people. Identifying and reaching your target audience ensures that your film resonates with those who are most likely to appreciate it. Whether your film is a niche indie project or a genre-specific feature, connecting with the right viewers increases engagement, word-of-mouth promotion, and the potential for long-term success.

Key Benefits of Targeted Distribution:

Increased Engagement: Targeted audiences are more likely to connect emotionally with your film, leading to greater enthusiasm, recommendations, and social media shares.

Monetization Opportunities: When you reach the right audience, you're more likely to generate revenue from rentals, purchases, or subscriptions on distribution platforms.

Building a Fanbase: Finding your audience is key to building a loyal fanbase that will support future projects and continue following your filmmaking journey.

Online Platforms for Film Distribution

The digital age has opened up a wealth of platforms for filmmakers to distribute their films directly to audiences. Each platform offers different features, and selecting the right one depends on your goals, film genre, and target audience.

YouTube

YouTube is one of the most popular and accessible platforms for filmmakers to distribute their work. With over two billion active users, YouTube provides a global audience for your film. You can upload your film for free, allowing viewers to watch and share it, or you can monetize it through ads or rental/purchase options.

Why Use YouTube: YouTube's vast audience makes it an ideal platform for reaching a wide range of viewers. It's also an excellent place for building a community around your film, as you can interact directly with viewers through comments and live streams.

Monetization Options: Filmmakers can earn revenue through YouTube's AdSense program, which places ads on your video. Additionally, YouTube offers rental and purchase options for filmmakers who want to charge for access to their film.

Tip: Optimize your video's title, description, and tags with relevant keywords to help it appear in search results and recommended videos. This will increase your film's visibility on the platform.

Vimeo On Demand

Vimeo is a platform designed with filmmakers in mind. Vimeo On Demand allows you to sell or rent your film directly to viewers. Unlike YouTube, which is primarily free, Vimeo offers more control over pricing and distribution, making it a great option for filmmakers looking to monetize their work.

Why Use Vimeo: Vimeo is known for its high-quality video playback and clean, professional presentation, making it a popular choice for filmmakers who want to showcase their work in the best light.

Monetization Options: Vimeo On Demand lets you set your own prices for rentals and purchases, and you keep 90% of the revenue after transaction fees. You also have the option to create subscription-based content, where viewers pay a recurring fee to access your entire catalog.

Tip: Take advantage of Vimeo's filmmaker-friendly tools, such as customizable portfolios, private links for festival submissions, and embeddable video players for sharing your film on other platforms.

Amazon Prime Video Direct

Amazon Prime Video Direct offers filmmakers the opportunity to distribute their films to millions of Amazon users. Your film can be made available for rental, purchase, or included in Prime subscriptions, providing multiple ways to monetize your work.

Why Use Amazon Prime: Amazon's vast customer base and trusted platform make it an attractive option for filmmakers seeking wide exposure. Prime members can stream your film as part of their subscription, and you can earn royalties based on the number of hours watched.

Monetization Options: You can earn revenue through rentals, purchases, and Prime royalties. While royalties may not be high, the sheer size of Amazon's audience provides significant potential for earnings if your film gains traction.

Tip: To stand out on Amazon, invest in creating a compelling cover image and write an engaging description that captures the essence of your film. These elements are key to attracting viewers browsing the platform.

Film Festivals with Online Components

Many film festivals now offer online components or virtual screenings, allowing you to showcase your film to audiences around the world without the need for physical attendance. This hybrid approach can be a great way to gain recognition, especially if in-person festivals are difficult to attend.

Why Use Online Film Festivals: Online festivals give you access to film enthusiasts, critics, and industry professionals who may not have been able to attend in person. Some festivals also offer prizes or distribution deals to winning films.

Monetization Options: While film festivals themselves don't typically generate direct revenue, they can lead to distribution deals or increased visibility, which can drive traffic to your other monetized platforms.

Tip: Research festivals carefully to ensure they align with your film's style, genre, and goals. Festivals that cater to niche genres or independent films are often more receptive to smartphone or indie productions.

Streaming Platforms (Netflix, Hulu, etc.)

Getting your film on a major streaming platform like Netflix, Hulu, or HBO Max is the dream of many filmmakers. While these platforms have large audiences and can offer lucrative licensing deals, they are also highly competitive and typically require you to go through a distributor or aggregator.

Why Use Streaming Platforms: Major streaming platforms offer huge exposure and can bring in significant revenue through licensing deals. They also provide instant credibility and a large viewership, which can boost your profile as a filmmaker.

Monetization Options: Filmmakers typically earn money through licensing deals, which vary depending on the platform and the film's popularity. Streaming platforms may pay a flat fee or offer royalties based on the number of views.

Tip: Before approaching a streaming platform, try to build buzz for your film through festivals, awards, or media coverage. Having a proven track record can increase your chances of getting picked up.

Niche Streaming Services

If your film appeals to a specific genre or audience, consider distributing it on a niche streaming platform that caters to that market. Platforms like Shudder (for horror), Mubi (for art films), and Gaia (for spiritual and consciousness films) offer targeted audiences who are more likely to appreciate your work.

Why Use Niche Streaming Services: These platforms cater to highly engaged audiences who are passionate about specific genres or themes, increasing the likelihood that your film will be well-received and promoted within that community.

Monetization Options: Like major streaming platforms, niche services typically offer licensing deals, allowing you to earn money based on views or a flat fee for distribution.

Tip: Research niche platforms to find the best fit for your film. Tailor your pitch to show how your work aligns with the platform's audience and mission.

Building a Multi-Platform Distribution Strategy

To maximize the reach of your film, consider using a multi-platform distribution strategy. By releasing your film on multiple platforms, you can reach different audiences, generate more revenue, and build a stronger fanbase. Here's how to approach multi-platform distribution:

Start with Festivals

If possible, begin by submitting your film to festivals that offer both physical and virtual screenings. Festivals give your film credibility and can help build buzz before you release it on other platforms. Winning awards or receiving positive reviews at festivals increases your chances of securing distribution deals.

Release on VOD Platforms

After the festival run, consider releasing your film on VOD (video-on-demand) platforms like Vimeo On Demand, Amazon Prime, or YouTube. These platforms give you control over pricing and allow you to monetize your film through rentals, purchases, or ad revenue.

Promote with Social Media

Use social media to build excitement and drive traffic to your film on VOD platforms. Create engaging content, such as behind-the-scenes videos, trailers, and Q&A sessions with your cast and crew. Social media can help amplify your reach and encourage viewers to watch and share your film.

Leverage Free Platforms for Exposure

Consider releasing your film for free on platforms like YouTube after an initial paid window on other platforms. This approach allows you to reach a wider audience while still giving early viewers the option to pay for the film during its initial release.

Approach Streaming Services for Licensing

Once your film has gained some momentum, approach larger streaming services or niche platforms for licensing deals. Having a proven track record, festival awards, or strong online viewership makes your film more appealing to streaming services.

Engaging with Your Audience

Engagement doesn't stop once your film is available online. Actively interacting with your audience helps build a dedicated fanbase and encourages word-of-mouth promotion. Here's how to engage effectively:

Host Virtual Events: Use platforms like Instagram Live, YouTube Live, or Facebook Live to host virtual screenings, Q&A sessions, or discussions with your audience.

Encourage Reviews and Feedback: Ask viewers to leave reviews or comments on platforms where your film is available. Positive reviews can increase your film's visibility and credibility.

Offer Bonus Content: Share exclusive behind-the-scenes content, interviews with the cast and crew, or deleted scenes to keep your audience engaged after watching the film.

Tip: Respond to comments, engage with fan discussions, and thank your audience for their support. Building a personal connection with your viewers can lead to long-term loyalty and support for future projects.

Finding your audience and distributing your film online has never been more accessible. By leveraging platforms like YouTube, Vimeo, Amazon Prime, and niche streaming services, you can reach your target viewers, build a fanbase, and even generate revenue. A multi-platform strategy ensures that your film is available to different audiences, while engagement through social media and virtual events keeps your viewers connected and invested in your work. With the right approach, you can successfully distribute your film, grow your audience, and turn your filmmaking passion into a sustainable career.

Handling Limited Storage: Managing Your Phone's Capacity

One of the challenges of using a smartphone for filmmaking is the limited storage capacity. High-resolution video files, especially those shot in 4K or with high frame rates, can quickly eat up your phone's available space. Managing your phone's storage effectively is essential to ensure that you have enough room for filming, editing, and other important tasks without running into storage issues in the middle of production.

This chapter will explore strategies for managing your phone's storage capacity, including how to optimize your settings, utilize cloud storage, and offload files efficiently. By adopting these techniques, you'll be able to maximize your phone's available space and keep your film production running smoothly.

Why Managing Storage is Important

As a filmmaker, storage is critical to your workflow. Running out of space in the middle of a shoot can disrupt your project, and scrambling to free up space can lead to lost files or compromised quality. Proper storage management ensures that you can capture everything you need without interruptions, maintain high-quality footage, and avoid technical issues during post-production.

Key Challenges of Limited Storage:

Large Video Files: High-definition (HD) and 4K video files are data-intensive, requiring significant amounts of storage space. A few minutes of 4K footage can take up several gigabytes, leaving little room for other files or additional shots.

App Data: Editing apps, camera software, and other filmmaking tools also consume storage, especially when you're working on multiple projects or using advanced features like color grading or special effects.

Other Media: Beyond your film files, your phone likely stores personal photos, videos, music, and apps, all of which can take up valuable space.

Tips for Managing Your Phone's Storage Capacity

By following these practical steps, you can ensure that your phone's storage remains sufficient throughout the filmmaking process. These strategies will help you optimize your space, avoid unnecessary storage use, and streamline your workflow.

Optimize Your Camera Settings

Before you start shooting, it's essential to review and adjust your camera settings to manage storage use effectively. While filming in 4K or high frame rates provides impressive quality, these settings also require significantly more storage space than standard HD footage.

Consider Lower Resolutions: While 4K footage is ideal for many projects, if you're tight on storage, filming in 1080p (Full HD) can save considerable space without sacrificing too much quality. Full HD is still widely accepted and sufficient for most online platforms.

Reduce Frame Rates: Higher frame rates (60fps or 120fps) are great for slow-motion shots, but for regular scenes, 24fps or 30fps is typically sufficient and saves storage space. Only use high frame rates when absolutely necessary for your artistic vision.

Adjust Bitrate Settings: Some camera apps, like *FiLMiC Pro*, allow you to adjust the bitrate of your recordings. Lowering the bitrate reduces file sizes but can slightly impact video quality. Balance quality and storage based on your project's needs.

Tip: If you're filming scenes that don't require high resolutions or slow-motion effects, switch to lower settings to save space and optimize storage.

Utilize Cloud Storage for Backup

One of the best ways to manage limited storage on your phone is to offload files to cloud storage. Cloud storage services like Google Drive, Dropbox, and iCloud allow you to store large video files without taking up space on your device.

Regular Backups: After each shoot, back up your footage to a cloud service. This not only frees up space on your phone but also ensures your files are safe in case of accidental deletion or phone damage.

Automatic Uploads: Many cloud storage apps offer automatic upload features that back up your media files as soon as you connect to Wi-Fi. This can be a convenient way to ensure that your footage is saved regularly without manually transferring files.

Access from Multiple Devices: Cloud storage allows you to access your footage from any device, which is particularly helpful if you plan to edit on a computer or share files with collaborators.

Tip: Keep in mind that large video files can take time to upload and download, especially in 4K. If you have a large amount of footage, consider uploading overnight or during downtime to avoid delays.

Invest in External Storage Solutions

If you frequently run into storage limits, external storage solutions can significantly expand your phone's capacity. External drives and memory cards can act as a convenient way to store and transfer large files.

Portable Hard Drives: Devices like the SanDisk iXpand for iPhones or USB-C flash drives for Android phones allow you to transfer video files directly from your phone to an external drive. These devices are compact, portable, and easy to use during production.

MicroSD Cards (for Android): If your phone supports expandable storage via microSD cards, use high-capacity cards to store additional footage. Many high-end microSD cards offer fast read/write speeds, making them ideal for 4K video recording.

Tip: Ensure your external storage device is compatible with your phone and can handle the data speeds required for large video files. High-quality external drives are essential for ensuring fast and reliable file transfers.

Offload Files to Your Computer

If cloud storage isn't an option or you need immediate space, transfer your files to a computer for safekeeping. Offloading footage to your computer frees up phone storage while allowing you to organize and back up your files for editing later.

Regular Transfers: Make it a habit to transfer your footage to your computer at the end of each shoot day. This prevents storage from becoming a bottleneck and ensures your files are safely backed up.

File Organization: Create a clear file structure on your computer to organize your footage by scenes, takes, or shooting days. This will make it easier to find specific files during editing and avoid data loss.

Tip: Use file transfer apps like *AirDrop* (for iPhone) or *Google Files* (for Android) to move files wirelessly from your phone to your computer, or use a USB cable for faster transfers.

Use Compression Tools

If you need to conserve space without losing essential footage, use compression tools to reduce the size of your video files. Compression reduces file size while retaining acceptable levels of quality for later editing.

Compression Apps: Tools like *HandBrake* (on a computer) or mobile apps like *Video Compressor* (for iOS and Android) can compress your videos to make them more storage-friendly without sacrificing too much quality.

Selectively Compress Files: Only compress footage that you don't need in full quality for immediate editing or sharing. Keep the original high-quality versions for the final edit if possible, but work with compressed files during production to save space.

Tip: Compression can sometimes lead to quality loss, so only use it when necessary and always test the results before relying on it for important scenes.

Clear Unnecessary Files and Apps

One of the easiest ways to manage your phone's storage is to regularly clear out unnecessary files, apps, and data. By decluttering your phone, you can free up valuable space for your film footage and apps.

Delete Old Files: Review your phone's gallery and delete old videos, photos, or unused files that are taking up space. Offload personal media to your cloud storage or computer to keep your phone focused on your film project.

Remove Unused Apps: Uninstall apps that you no longer use, especially ones that consume large amounts of storage or data. You can always reinstall them later if needed.

Clear Cache: Many apps store temporary files (cache) that can take up storage without you realizing it. Go to your phone's settings and clear the cache for specific apps, especially those related to video editing, social media, or streaming.

Tip: Regularly check your phone's storage settings to see which apps and files are taking up the most space, and clean them out as needed.

Plan Your Shooting Schedule

If you know you have limited storage, plan your shooting schedule to avoid running out of space at critical moments. Shoot essential scenes first, so you don't risk losing footage if storage becomes an issue later.

Prioritize Key Scenes: Start by filming the most important or complex scenes to ensure you have enough space for them. Once those are complete, you can film secondary or filler scenes with any remaining storage.

Plan for Downtime: Schedule time between shoots to back up and offload files. This ensures that you can free up storage before the next round of filming.

Tip: If possible, bring a portable storage solution to your shoot so you can offload files on-site and continue filming without interruption.

Managing your phone's limited storage is essential for a smooth and efficient filmmaking process. By optimizing your camera settings, utilizing cloud and external storage, offloading files regularly, and keeping your device organized, you can ensure that your phone has enough space to capture all the footage you need. With proper planning and the right tools, you can overcome the challenge of limited storage and keep your film production on track without losing any valuable content.

Battery Life Solutions: Filming with Limited Power

One of the biggest challenges of filming with a smartphone is managing battery life. Shooting video, especially in high resolution or for extended periods, can drain your phone's battery quickly. If you're working on a long shoot, filming on location, or using apps that consume a lot of power, you'll need to find ways to extend your phone's battery life and avoid interruptions during key moments.

In this chapter, we'll explore practical solutions for managing your smartphone's battery while filming, including optimizing settings, using external power sources, and employing energy-efficient filming techniques. By taking proactive steps, you can ensure that your battery lasts throughout your shoot, allowing you to focus on your creative work without worrying about power running out.

Why Battery Life Management is Crucial

Your phone's battery powers not only your camera but also any apps you use for video recording, editing, and file management. Running out of battery in the middle of a shoot can delay production, cause missed shots, or even result in lost footage if your phone shuts down unexpectedly. Effective battery management is essential for maintaining a steady workflow, especially when filming in remote locations or on extended shoots where access to power may be limited.

Key Challenges of Limited Battery Life:

High Energy Consumption: Filming in high resolutions (like 4K), using external microphones, or utilizing advanced editing apps can rapidly drain your phone's battery.

Long Shoots: Extended shoots require a significant amount of battery power, particularly if you're capturing multiple takes or long scenes.

On-the-Go Filming: Filming on location or in areas without access to electrical outlets means you need to rely solely on your phone's battery, making efficient power management even more important.

Tips for Maximizing Battery Life While Filming

By following these tips, you can extend your smartphone's battery life and ensure that it lasts through your entire filming session. From adjusting your phone's settings to using external battery packs, these strategies will help you get the most out of your device's power.

Optimize Your Phone's Settings

One of the simplest ways to extend battery life is by optimizing your phone's settings before you start filming. Certain features and apps that run in the background can drain your battery even when you're not actively using them, so it's important to turn off unnecessary functions to conserve power.

Enable Airplane Mode: Filming with your phone in airplane mode can save a significant amount of battery. Airplane mode disables cellular, Wi-Fi, and Bluetooth signals, which reduces the energy spent on searching for networks or maintaining connections. However, make sure you don't need any internet access or Bluetooth for external devices (like wireless microphones) before enabling this mode.

Lower Screen Brightness: The display is one of the biggest power consumers on a smartphone. Lowering your screen brightness to a level that's comfortable but not excessive can help conserve energy while still allowing you to monitor your shots.

Turn Off Background Apps: Before you start filming, close any apps running in the background that aren't essential to your shoot. This prevents unnecessary power consumption and ensures your phone's resources are focused on filming.

Disable Notifications: Notifications not only interrupt your shoot but can also drain your battery. Put your phone in "Do Not Disturb" mode to prevent alerts, vibrations, and pop-ups from using up valuable energy.

Tip: If you're using your phone's camera exclusively for filming and don't need access to other features, consider using "Battery Saver" mode to extend battery life further.

Use External Power Sources

External power sources can be lifesavers during long filming sessions, allowing you to recharge your phone while on the go or extend your filming time without needing to stop for a recharge.

Portable Power Banks: A portable power bank is one of the most effective ways to ensure you don't run out of battery mid-shoot. Power banks come in a variety of capacities (measured in mAh), so choose one that matches your needs based on how long your filming sessions typically last. A higher capacity power bank (10,000mAh or more) can charge your phone multiple times, making it perfect for all-day shoots.

Battery Cases: A battery case combines a protective case with an extra battery to provide additional power while keeping your phone safe. These cases are convenient for filmmakers who want a more compact solution, as they eliminate the need to carry separate power banks.

Car Chargers: If you're filming in or around a vehicle, a car charger can provide a quick and easy way to recharge between takes or while traveling to different locations.

Tip: Always carry multiple power sources, especially on location shoots, to ensure you have enough backup power. Label and charge your power banks in advance so they're ready when you need them.

Choose Energy-Efficient Filming Techniques

Filming in 4K or using high frame rates can drain your battery quickly. While high-quality footage is often essential for specific scenes, there are times when you can opt for more energy-efficient settings without compromising too much on quality.

Film in Lower Resolutions: Consider filming in 1080p (Full HD) instead of 4K if you don't need ultra-high resolution. Filming in lower resolutions uses less processing power and saves battery life, which can be especially helpful for extended shoots.

Reduce Frame Rate: Filming at 24fps or 30fps instead of 60fps or higher can conserve power, as lower frame rates require less processing. Use higher frame rates only when necessary, such as for slow-motion shots.

Limit App Usage: If possible, avoid using power-hungry apps (like advanced editing software or multi-tasking apps) while filming. Editing on your phone during filming sessions can drain your battery faster. Instead, reserve editing for after the shoot or when you have access to a charger.

Tip: Test different camera settings to find the best balance between image quality and battery consumption for your project. Use the highest settings only for key scenes that truly require them.

Turn Off Non-Essential Features

Certain phone features may be useful during everyday use but can drain battery life during filming. Turning off these features when you don't need them can help conserve power.

Disable GPS and Location Services: If you don't need GPS tracking or location-based features while filming, turning off location services can save battery. Location services consume power by constantly communicating with satellites and cell towers.

Turn Off Vibration: Vibration alerts can drain battery power, especially if they're triggered frequently. Switch to silent mode or disable vibration altogether during filming.

Disable Automatic Updates: Some phones perform automatic software updates in the background, which can use up battery life. Disable these updates while you're filming to prevent them from consuming power at inopportune times.

Tip: Review your phone's settings and turn off any features that aren't necessary for your filming session. The more functions you disable, the longer your battery will last.

Manage Charging Breaks Effectively

If you're working on a longer shoot and have the opportunity to recharge your phone, it's important to manage your charging breaks effectively to maximize the power you gain.

Use Fast Chargers: If your phone supports fast charging, use a fast charger to quickly boost your battery during breaks. Fast chargers can recharge your phone up to 50% or more in just 30 minutes, allowing you to get back to filming quickly.

Schedule Charging Breaks: Plan your shoot in a way that allows for regular charging breaks. Use these breaks to review your footage, reset equipment, or take a breather while your phone charges. Even 15-20 minute breaks can give your battery a significant boost if you're using a fast charger or power bank.

Turn Off Your Phone While Charging: If possible, turn off your phone during charging breaks to speed up the process. Charging with the phone off allows it to charge more quickly and prevents background apps from using power while you're trying to recharge.

Tip: Always bring extra charging cables and adapters with you to avoid any issues. It's also helpful to have longer cables so you can keep your phone plugged in while filming in certain static setups.

Carry a Backup Phone

If you have access to an extra smartphone, consider using it as a backup during filming. Having a second phone allows you to switch devices if your primary phone's battery runs out or if you encounter technical issues.

Alternate Between Phones: Use one phone for filming while the other charges. This allows you to keep shooting without interruption and ensures you always have a fully charged device ready when needed.

Divide Responsibilities: Use one phone for filming and the other for tasks like social media updates, behind-the-scenes footage, or taking notes. This reduces the load on your primary filming device and helps conserve its battery.

Tip: If using a backup phone, ensure it has comparable camera capabilities so the footage remains consistent between devices.

Managing your phone's battery life is crucial for successful smartphone filmmaking, especially during long shoots or when filming on location. By optimizing your settings, using external power sources, and employing energy-efficient filming techniques, you can extend your phone's battery life and avoid power-related interruptions. With a little preparation and the right tools, you can keep your phone powered throughout your shoot and focus on capturing the best footage possible.

Mobile Phone Filmmaking Competitions: Finding Your Place

Mobile phone filmmaking has become a dynamic and accessible way for creators to tell stories, and it's no surprise that competitions dedicated to mobile films have emerged, providing a platform for filmmakers to showcase their work, gain recognition, and even win awards. These competitions are not only a great way to share your work with a wider audience, but they also offer valuable exposure and opportunities for networking with industry professionals.

This chapter explores the world of mobile phone filmmaking competitions, including how to find the right competition for your film, what to expect during the submission process, and how to make your project stand out. Whether you're a seasoned filmmaker or just starting out, mobile filmmaking competitions can help you find your place in the growing world of indie cinema.

Why Enter Mobile Filmmaking Competitions?

Filmmaking competitions, particularly those focused on mobile films, offer several key benefits. They provide an opportunity to validate your work, expand your audience, and even gain funding or equipment for future projects. Competing in these festivals can help build your credibility and give you the chance to be seen by influential members of the film industry.

Key Benefits of Competitions:

Recognition and Awards: Winning or being selected in a competition provides credibility and visibility, which can open doors to future projects or collaborations.

Networking: Competitions often include screenings, Q&A sessions, and industry panels that allow you to connect with other filmmakers, industry professionals, and potential collaborators.

Feedback and Growth: Even if you don't win, participating in a competition often comes with feedback from judges or audiences, helping you improve your craft and understand how your work resonates with viewers.

Prizes and Funding: Many competitions offer prizes such as cash, equipment, or production resources, which can be used to fund future projects or enhance your current film.

How to Find the Right Competition for Your Film

With a variety of mobile filmmaking competitions available globally, it's important to choose the one that aligns with your goals, style, and genre. Some competitions are specifically focused on mobile filmmaking, while others accept all formats but have a special category for mobile films. Here's how to find the right competition for your work:

Research Mobile-Specific Competitions

Look for competitions that are dedicated solely to mobile filmmaking. These festivals understand the challenges and unique qualities of shooting on a phone, and the judges are more likely to appreciate your film's creative use of mobile technology. Some well-known mobile film competitions include:

International Mobile Film Festival (IMFF): Based in San Diego, this festival is one of the pioneers in mobile filmmaking competitions. It features categories like short films, feature-length films, and documentary, with a focus on celebrating the art of smartphone filmmaking.

Mobile Motion Film Festival (MoMo): Held in Switzerland, MoMo is another popular competition dedicated to films shot entirely on smartphones. It includes awards for best film, best documentary, and special categories like best cinematography or best editing.

SmartFone Flick Fest (SF3): SF3 is Australia's international smartphone film festival, accepting short films shot on mobile devices from filmmakers around the world. It emphasizes creativity and innovation in smartphone filmmaking.

Consider Genre-Specific Festivals

If your film falls into a specific genre (horror, sci-fi, documentary, etc.), you may want to submit to a festival that specializes in that genre and also accepts mobile films. For example, horror film festivals may have a category for mobile films, giving you a chance to stand out in your niche.

Niche Opportunities: Festivals like the "48 Hour Mobile Film Project" encourage filmmakers to create a short film on their phone within a limited timeframe. These events test your creativity and ability to work under pressure, often leading to surprising results.

Tip: Research festivals that align with your film's themes or genre. Winning in a niche competition can be just as valuable as a larger festival and may even offer a more targeted audience for your work.

Look for Local or Regional Competitions

Local or regional film competitions are often less competitive than major international festivals, but they can be excellent for building connections and gaining recognition within your community. These festivals often celebrate local talent and may offer cash prizes, mentorship, or screening opportunities.

Community Exposure: Winning or being selected in a regional competition helps you establish a local fanbase and attract attention from media and community influencers who may help promote your work.

Tip: Search for local film festivals with mobile categories through platforms like FilmFreeway or Festhome, which list hundreds of festivals worldwide.

Submit to Online Competitions

Many competitions have shifted to virtual platforms, allowing filmmakers from anywhere in the world to submit their work. These online competitions are often more accessible, with lower entry fees and no need to attend in person. They also provide an opportunity for your film to be viewed by a global audience.

Filmaka: Filmaka is an online competition that offers a variety of challenges and themes for filmmakers to create short films using their mobile devices. It offers cash prizes, funding, and mentorship for future projects.

Mobile Film Festival: This annual international festival asks filmmakers to create one-minute films using only mobile devices. The festival awards substantial cash prizes and production grants to help filmmakers take their projects to the next level.

Tip: Take advantage of online competitions to reach a global audience and gain recognition, even if you can't attend a physical festival.

How to Submit Your Film to Competitions

Once you've identified the competitions that are a good fit for your film, it's time to prepare your submission. Each competition has its own submission guidelines and criteria, so it's important to read the requirements carefully. Here's a step-by-step guide to ensure your submission stands out.

Check Eligibility Requirements

Before submitting, make sure your film meets all the eligibility requirements for the competition. Common criteria include the length of the film (many mobile film festivals focus on short films), the device used for filming, and the film's completion date.

Length Requirements: Most mobile film festivals accept short films between 1 to 15 minutes in length, but some have separate categories for feature-length films.

Filming on Mobile: Ensure your film was shot entirely on a mobile device, as some festivals have strict guidelines about the use of professional equipment. However, many festivals allow post-production editing and sound design to be done on other devices.

Prepare High-Quality Video Files

Make sure your film is formatted according to the festival's specifications, typically in an MP4 or MOV format. Submit the highest quality version of your film within the file size limits set by the festival.

Resolution: While mobile films are often shot in 4K or HD, ensure your file is compressed correctly without losing quality. Use editing software to export your video in the correct format.

Subtitles: If your film includes dialogue in a language other than the festival's primary language, you'll need to include subtitles. Even for English-language films, it's often recommended to provide subtitles to increase accessibility.

Create a Strong Synopsis and Logline

Your film's synopsis and logline (a brief, catchy description of the film) are essential for attracting the attention of festival organizers and judges. Write a concise but engaging summary that highlights the unique aspects of your film.

Logline: Keep it short—one or two sentences that capture the essence of your story. For example, "A teenager discovers a time-traveling smartphone and must decide whether to change her past or face her future."

Synopsis: Expand on your logline with a brief summary (around 100–200 words) that introduces the characters, plot, and themes. Focus on what makes your film stand out, such as its creative use of mobile technology or a unique narrative twist.

Submit a Director's Statement

Many festivals ask for a director's statement, where you can explain your creative process, inspiration, and why you chose to shoot the film on a mobile device. This gives judges insight into your filmmaking journey and can help them connect with your work on a deeper level.

Tip: Be authentic and personal in your statement. Judges appreciate hearing about your challenges and the reasons behind your creative choices.

Promote Your Film

After submitting, use your social media platforms to promote your entry. Share updates with your followers, post behind-the-scenes content, and encourage your audience to support your film. Many festivals have audience awards, where public votes contribute to a film's success, so building buzz around your submission can increase your chances.

Hashtags: Use relevant hashtags to increase visibility, such as #mobilefilmmaking, #filmfest, or the specific festival's hashtag.

Trailer or Teaser: Post a short trailer or teaser to generate interest in your film. This gives your audience a preview of what to expect and helps you gain momentum in the lead-up to the competition.

Making Your Film Stand Out

With so many entries in mobile filmmaking competitions, it's important to make your film stand out. Here are a few tips to ensure your submission captures attention:

Emphasize Creativity over Budget

Mobile filmmaking festivals celebrate creativity, innovation, and resourcefulness. Since these festivals focus on films shot with accessible technology, they're less concerned with big-budget production values and more interested in unique storytelling and creative use of the medium.

Focus on Storytelling: A strong, original story will always capture attention. Focus on crafting compelling characters, engaging plots, and emotional depth.

Use Mobile Features to Your Advantage: Showcase the versatility of mobile filmmaking. Use the portability of your phone for dynamic shots, creative angles, or immersive first-person perspectives that would be difficult with traditional cameras.

Experiment with Visual Style

Mobile films don't have to mimic traditional film styles. Take advantage of the unique qualities of mobile cameras to experiment with visual aesthetics, color grading, or non-traditional camera movements.

Innovative Cinematography: Play with how you frame scenes, use natural lighting, or explore different shooting environments. A creative visual style can make your film stand out in a field of more conventional entries.

Pay Attention to Sound

Even though mobile filmmaking emphasizes visual storytelling, sound design is crucial. Use external microphones, high-quality sound effects, and an effective score to enhance the immersive quality of your film. Poor audio quality is a common issue in mobile films, so prioritizing sound will give you an edge.

Mobile filmmaking competitions offer an exciting opportunity for filmmakers to showcase their creativity, gain recognition, and connect with audiences worldwide. By carefully selecting the right competitions, preparing a strong submission, and promoting your film effectively, you can find your place in the growing world of mobile cinema. With dedication and innovative use of mobile technology, your film can stand out and leave a lasting impact on judges and audiences alike.

Mobile App Tools: Enhancing Your Filmmaking Process

Smartphones are powerful filmmaking tools, and mobile apps can further enhance your production process by offering a wide range of features, from camera controls and editing software to sound design and special effects. These apps allow you to achieve professional-level results with minimal equipment, empowering you to create high-quality films on a budget.

In this chapter, we'll explore some of the best mobile apps for filmmakers, focusing on apps that help with shooting, editing, sound, and visual effects. Whether you're just starting out or are looking to streamline your workflow, these tools will help you elevate your filmmaking process.

Why Mobile Apps Matter in Filmmaking

Mobile apps have revolutionized the way filmmakers approach production by putting essential tools directly into the palm of your hand. With these apps, you can control every aspect of your film, from pre-production planning to final editing, all from your smartphone. They offer flexibility, portability, and professional-grade features that were once only accessible with expensive equipment or software.

Key Benefits of Mobile Filmmaking Apps:

Cost Efficiency: Most filmmaking apps are inexpensive or even free, offering budget-friendly solutions to challenges that would otherwise require costly equipment or software.

Portability: You can carry everything you need for filmmaking right in your pocket. This makes mobile apps ideal for shooting on location, during travel, or in spontaneous moments of creativity.

Professional Features: Many apps offer advanced features like manual camera controls, multi-track editing, color grading, and sound design, allowing filmmakers to create polished, cinematic projects.

Streamlined Workflow: Mobile apps enable filmmakers to shoot, edit, and distribute their films seamlessly from a single device, reducing the time spent transferring files or using multiple programs.

Essential Mobile Apps for Filmmaking

Below is a selection of mobile apps that can enhance different stages of your filmmaking process, from pre-production planning to post-production editing. These tools will help you create a more efficient, professional workflow as you shoot, edit, and refine your films on the go.

Filmic Pro (Camera Control and Filming)

Filmic Pro is widely regarded as the go-to app for professional-level camera control on a smartphone. It allows you to take full manual control over your phone's camera settings, giving you access to features like exposure, focus, white balance, and frame rate adjustments that are critical for high-quality filmmaking.

Key Features:

Manual control over exposure, ISO, shutter speed, and focus.

Support for shooting in multiple frame rates, including 24fps (cinematic standard).

Ability to shoot in 4K, 1080p, or lower resolutions, depending on your needs.

Log profiles for better color grading during post-production.

Tip: Use Filmic Pro's focus peaking and zebra stripes features to ensure your shots are sharp and properly exposed, even in challenging lighting conditions.

Adobe Premiere Rush (Editing)

Adobe Premiere Rush is a simplified version of Adobe's professional editing software, Premiere Pro, designed specifically for mobile devices. This app allows you to perform high-quality video editing on your smartphone, with access to multiple tracks, transitions, color correction, and more.

Key Features:

Multi-track editing with support for video, audio, and text overlays.

Simple drag-and-drop interface for easy video trimming and arranging.

Color grading and adjustment tools to enhance your footage.

Integration with Adobe's Creative Cloud, allowing you to start editing on your phone and finish on your desktop if needed.

Tip: Take advantage of Premiere Rush's built-in motion graphics templates to quickly add professional-looking titles and transitions to your film.

LumaFusion (Advanced Editing)

For filmmakers who need more advanced editing tools on their mobile devices, LumaFusion is a powerful video editing app that offers a professional-grade editing experience on your phone or tablet. It's perfect for more complex editing tasks like multi-track timelines, advanced color grading, and audio editing.

Key Features:

Multi-layered timelines for video, audio, and effects.

Advanced color grading tools, including LUT support.

Audio mixing features that allow for precise control over sound design.

Integration with cloud storage services like Dropbox, Google Drive, and iCloud.

Tip: Use LumaFusion's keyframing feature to create smooth transitions and animations, giving your film a polished, cinematic look.

FiLMiC DoubleTake (Multi-Camera Shooting)

FiLMiC DoubleTake is a companion app to FiLMiC Pro that allows you to shoot with multiple cameras simultaneously on your smartphone. This is particularly useful for interview setups, documentary-style filmmaking, or any scenario where you want to capture multiple angles without the need for additional cameras.

Key Features:

Shoot with two cameras at once (front and back or dual rear cameras) to capture multiple angles in real-time.

Use PiP (Picture-in-Picture) mode to monitor both cameras while recording.

Choose from split-screen or discrete capture, allowing you to edit each camera angle separately.

Tip: Use DoubleTake to shoot reaction shots and close-ups simultaneously during dialogue scenes, saving time in post-production.

Shot Lister (Production Planning)

Shot Lister is a professional-grade shot-listing and production planning app that helps you organize and track your shots throughout the filmmaking process. It's an essential tool for filmmakers looking to stay organized on set, ensuring that every shot is accounted for and nothing is missed.

Key Features:

Create and manage shot lists with detailed breakdowns, including camera angles, lenses, and setups.

Set custom time estimates for each shot to keep your production on schedule.

Track progress by marking completed shots in real-time during production.

Export shot lists to PDF or share them with your team for collaboration.

Tip: Use Shot Lister to create a daily shooting schedule, helping you stay efficient and avoid missing crucial shots due to time constraints.

Sun Seeker (Location Scouting and Lighting)

Lighting is one of the most important aspects of filmmaking, and understanding natural light is key to getting the best shots on location. Sun Seeker is an app that helps you track the sun's path at any location, making it easier to plan your shoots based on optimal lighting conditions.

Key Features:

3D augmented reality view showing the sun's path in real-time.

Sun trajectory map with detailed sunrise, sunset, and solar noon times.

Time-lapse feature to visualize how the sun will move across your shooting location throughout the day.

Tip: Use Sun Seeker to plan your outdoor shoots during the golden hour (just after sunrise or before sunset) when natural light is soft and flattering for cinematic shots.

Protake (Filmmaker's Camera App)

Protake is another highly-rated camera app that offers professional-level controls for filmmakers. It's designed to make mobile filmmaking as streamlined as possible by combining intuitive manual controls with a user-friendly interface.

Key Features:

Full manual control over ISO, focus, white balance, and shutter speed.

Auto-focus and exposure-locking tools to maintain consistency between shots.

Real-time color grading with built-in LUTs to preview your final look on set.

Tip: Use Protake's real-time histograms and waveforms to ensure your shots are well-exposed and balanced, even in tricky lighting conditions.

KineMaster (Mobile Editing for Beginners)

KineMaster is a mobile video editing app with a simple interface that's ideal for filmmakers who are new to editing. Despite its ease of use, it offers many powerful features, including multi-layer editing, transitions, and audio mixing, making it a great starting point for filmmakers who want to edit on their phones.

Key Features:

Simple, intuitive interface designed for quick video editing.

Built-in effects, filters, and transitions to enhance your film.

Support for multiple layers of video, text, and images.

Audio mixing tools for balancing sound effects, dialogue, and music.

Tip: Use KineMaster's built-in tutorials to quickly learn how to apply transitions, effects, and cuts, allowing you to produce polished films without prior editing experience.

Ferrite Recording Studio (Audio Editing)

Audio is just as important as visuals in filmmaking, and Ferrite Recording Studio offers a powerful mobile solution for editing and mixing sound. Whether you're editing voiceovers, dialogue, or sound effects, Ferrite gives you the tools to fine-tune your audio for professional results.

Key Features:

Multi-track audio editing with support for fade-ins, fade-outs, and volume control.

Advanced noise reduction and equalization tools to clean up dialogue.

Ability to record directly into the app, perfect for voiceovers or ADR.

Export high-quality audio files or mixdowns to use in your film.

Tip: Record ambient sounds or Foley effects with Ferrite and layer them into your film's soundscape for a richer, more immersive experience.

VSCO (Color Grading and Filters)

VSCO is a popular app for mobile photography and video, offering a wide range of filters and color grading tools that can help you achieve a professional look for your film. The app's powerful editing tools allow you to fine-tune exposure, contrast, saturation, and color balance to give your footage a cinematic feel.

Key Features:

Dozens of professional-grade filters to instantly enhance your footage.

Advanced editing tools for adjusting exposure, contrast, sharpness, and more.

Preset options inspired by film stocks, making it easier to achieve a specific aesthetic.

Tip: Use VSCO's color grading tools to match the tone of different shots, ensuring visual consistency across your film.

Mobile apps have transformed the filmmaking process, providing filmmakers with powerful tools that fit right in their pockets. From camera control to editing, sound design, and color grading, these apps allow you to create professional-quality films without the need for expensive equipment or software. By integrating these mobile tools into your workflow, you can streamline your production process, enhance your creativity, and take full advantage of the flexibility and portability that smartphone filmmaking offers.

Online Resources: Apps and Sites

The digital world offers a wealth of online resources to help filmmakers at every stage of the production process. From apps that streamline your workflow to websites that provide inspiration, tutorials, and even distribution platforms, the right tools can enhance your filmmaking journey. Whether you need help planning your shoot, editing your film, or finding the right audience, there's an app or site that can make the process easier and more efficient.

In this chapter, we'll explore some of the best online resources available for filmmakers, focusing on apps and websites that can help with pre-production, filming, editing, sound design, marketing, and distribution. These tools will give you the support you need to create professional-quality films on your smartphone and share them with the world.

Why Online Resources Are Vital for Filmmakers

In today's fast-paced digital environment, filmmakers have access to a variety of apps and online platforms that simplify complex tasks, allowing them to focus on the creative aspects of filmmaking. Whether you're a beginner or a seasoned filmmaker, these resources can help you:

Streamline your workflow: Online tools help you manage everything from scheduling shoots to editing footage, making your production process more efficient.

Gain new skills: Tutorial websites and apps offer step-by-step guidance on every aspect of filmmaking, from camera techniques to post-production.

Reach your audience: Online platforms make it easier to distribute your film, promote it, and connect with a global audience.

Collaborate remotely: Many resources allow for collaboration across distances, enabling teams to work together on scripts, editing, and production without being in the same location.

Essential Apps for Filmmakers

The following apps offer a range of tools that can assist with filming, editing, sound design, and even marketing your work.

Trello (Project Management)

Trello is a project management app that's ideal for keeping your filmmaking process organized. It allows you to create boards for different stages of production, break down tasks, and assign them to your team members, ensuring that everything stays on track.

Key Features:

Customizable boards, lists, and cards for project management.

Task assignment and deadline tracking.

Collaboration features, allowing multiple team members to work on the same project.

Tip: Use Trello to create a shot list, track production tasks, and manage your film's post-production schedule.

Celtx (Scriptwriting and Pre-Production)

Celtx is a comprehensive tool for screenwriting and pre-production planning. It allows you to write scripts, create storyboards, develop production schedules, and manage every aspect of your film's pre-production process.

Key Features:

Collaborative scriptwriting tools.

Storyboarding and shot planning.

Budgeting, scheduling, and production tracking tools.

Tip: Use Celtx's scheduling feature to map out your entire production timeline, keeping everyone on the same page throughout the shoot.

Storyboarder (Storyboarding)

Storyboarder is a free app that helps filmmakers create detailed storyboards for their films. Storyboarding is an essential part of pre-production, allowing you to visualize your scenes, plan camera angles, and communicate your vision to your team.

Key Features:

Easy-to-use interface for drawing or adding pre-made images to storyboards.

Time and dialogue integration to match your storyboard with your script.

Ability to export storyboards into various file formats for easy sharing.

Tip: Storyboarder syncs with other production software, so you can seamlessly integrate your storyboard into the rest of your pre-production workflow.

FiLMiC Pro (Filming)

As mentioned in earlier chapters, FiLMiC Pro is a leading mobile camera app that gives you professional control over your smartphone's camera. It's ideal for filmmakers who want to maximize the quality of their footage with manual settings for exposure, focus, and white balance.

Key Features:

Advanced camera controls, including manual focus and exposure.

Support for shooting in various resolutions, including 4K.

High dynamic range (HDR) video capture for enhanced image quality.

Tip: Combine FiLMiC Pro with other editing apps like LumaFusion to create a seamless workflow from filming to post-production.

LumaFusion (Editing)

LumaFusion is a professional-grade video editing app for iOS that offers multi-track editing, color correction, audio mixing, and more, all from your smartphone or tablet. It's one of the most powerful mobile editing apps available, making it a top choice for filmmakers.

Key Features:

Multiple layers for video, audio, and effects.

Color grading tools and LUT support.

High-quality export options, including 4K resolution.

Tip: Use LumaFusion's multi-track editing to layer video and audio seamlessly, giving your film a polished, professional look.

Splice (Simple Editing)

For filmmakers looking for a simpler editing solution, Splice is an easy-to-use mobile app that offers basic editing features like trimming, transitions, and adding music. It's perfect for beginners or for quick edits on the go.

Key Features:

Easy drag-and-drop interface for trimming and arranging clips.

Built-in music and sound effects library.

Direct export to social media platforms like Instagram and YouTube.

Tip: Use Splice for quick edits or to create short teasers and trailers for your film, ideal for sharing on social media.

Ferrite Recording Studio (Sound Editing)

Ferrite Recording Studio is a powerful mobile app for editing audio, making it ideal for filmmakers working on sound design, voiceovers, or podcasts. It offers multi-track audio editing with advanced features like noise reduction and equalization.

Key Features:

Multi-track audio editing with support for fade-ins, fade-outs, and layering.

Advanced noise reduction and equalization tools to improve audio quality.

Export options for high-quality audio files suitable for professional projects.

Tip: Use Ferrite to record and edit voiceovers or clean up dialogue captured on set, ensuring your audio is crisp and clear.

Procreate (Storyboarding and Visual Design)

Procreate is a digital illustration app that can be used for creating storyboards, concept art, and visual designs for your film. It's an excellent tool for filmmakers who want to sketch out their ideas visually or collaborate with designers on set pieces or character designs.

Key Features:

Powerful drawing tools for creating detailed illustrations or storyboards.

Layering, brushes, and color tools for creating polished visual designs.

Export options that allow you to share your work easily with collaborators.

Tip: Use Procreate to create detailed concept art for your film's locations, costumes, or character designs, helping you visualize your project before shooting.

Essential Websites for Filmmakers

Beyond apps, there are numerous websites that provide resources, tutorials, and platforms for sharing and distributing your film. Here are some of the most useful sites for filmmakers:

FilmFreeway (Film Festival Submissions)

FilmFreeway is the leading platform for submitting your film to festivals around the world. It's an essential resource for filmmakers looking to get their work in front of audiences and industry professionals.

Key Features:

Easy submission process for thousands of film festivals worldwide.

Searchable database to find festivals by genre, location, or submission fees.

Tracking and notifications to keep you updated on your submission status.

Tip: Use FilmFreeway to research and submit your film to festivals that align with your film's genre and goals.

MasterClass (Filmmaking Courses)

MasterClass offers online courses taught by industry professionals, including filmmakers like Martin Scorsese, Jodie Foster, and Werner Herzog. It's a valuable resource for learning the craft of filmmaking from some of the best in the business.

Key Features:

In-depth video lessons on various aspects of filmmaking, from directing to editing.

Downloadable workbooks and assignments to help you apply what you learn.

Access to a community of filmmakers and students to share feedback and insights.

Tip: MasterClass is a great way to gain insights from industry veterans and improve your skills in key areas like directing, cinematography, and storytelling.

No Film School (Tutorials and News)

No Film School is one of the most popular websites for filmmakers, offering tutorials, news, and discussions about everything from filmmaking techniques to industry trends. It's a great place to learn new skills, find gear recommendations, and stay updated on the latest in film technology.

Key Features:

Tutorials and guides for every stage of filmmaking, from pre-production to distribution.

Forums and discussions where filmmakers share tips, experiences, and advice.

Gear reviews and recommendations for budget-conscious filmmakers.

Tip: Regularly visit No Film School to stay informed about new gear, techniques, and film industry trends that can enhance your projects.

ArtGrid (Stock Footage)

ArtGrid is a stock footage platform that offers high-quality clips for filmmakers. Whether you need B-roll, establishing shots, or specific visual elements to complete your project, ArtGrid provides a variety of footage to suit your needs.

Key Features:

A vast library of professional-grade stock footage in 4K, 6K, and 8K resolutions.

Footage categorized by themes, moods, and formats for easy browsing.

Simple licensing options that give you full rights to use the footage in your films.

Tip: Use ArtGrid to enhance your film with high-quality stock footage, saving time and money on filming additional scenes.

Online resources, including apps and websites, have become indispensable tools for modern filmmakers. Whether you're managing your production schedule, shooting on location, or distributing your film to a global audience, these digital tools offer solutions for every stage of the filmmaking process. By integrating these resources into your workflow, you can streamline your production, improve the quality of your work, and connect with audiences more effectively. The right tools can transform your smartphone into a complete filmmaking studio, empowering you to create and share your stories with the world.